THE 10
LAWS OF
CAREER
ESSENTIAL SURVIVAL SKILLS FOR ANY ECONOMY
RE INVENTION

THE 10
LAWS OF
CAREER
RE ESSENTIAL SURVIVAL SKILLS FOR ANY ECONOMY
INVENTION

PAMELA MITCHELL

RENEW
WASHINGTON

The Renew Washington grant project is made possible by the Washington State Library (Office of the Secretary of State), Library Services & Technology Act, Institute of Museum & Library Services, and the Bill & Melinda Gates Foundation.

DUTTON

PUBLISHER'S NOTE

This publication is designed to provide accurate and authoritative information in regard to the subject matter covered. It is sold with the understanding that the publisher is not engaged in rendering legal, accounting or other professional services. If you require legal advice or other expert assistance, you should seek the services of a competent professional.

DUTTON
Published by Penguin Group (USA) Inc.
375 Hudson Street, New York, New York 10014, U.S.A.
Penguin Group (Canada), 90 Eglinton Avenue East, Suite 700, Toronto, Ontario M4P 2Y3, Canada (a division of Pearson Penguin Canada Inc.); Penguin Books Ltd, 80 Strand, London WC2R 0RL, England; Penguin Ireland, 25 St Stephen's Green, Dublin 2, Ireland (a division of Penguin Books Ltd); Penguin Group (Australia), 250 Camberwell Road, Camberwell, Victoria 3124, Australia (a division of Pearson Australia Group Pty Ltd); Penguin Books India Pvt Ltd, 11 Community Centre, Panchsheel Park, New Delhi – 110 017, India; Penguin Group (NZ), 67 Apollo Drive, Rosedale, North Shore 0632, New Zealand (a division of Pearson New Zealand Ltd); Penguin Books (South Africa) (Pty) Ltd, 24 Sturdee Avenue, Rosebank, Johannesburg 2196, South Africa

Penguin Books Ltd, Registered Offices: 80 Strand, London WC2R 0RL, England

Published by Dutton, a member of Penguin Group (USA) Inc.

First printing, January 2010
10 9 8 7 6 5 4 3 2 1

REGISTERED TRADEMARK—MARCA REGISTRADA

LIBRARY OF CONGRESS CATALOGING-IN-PUBLICATION DATA
Mitchell, Pamela, 1964-
    The 10 laws of career reinvention : essential survival skills for any economy / by Pamela Mitchell.
    p. cm.
    ISBN 978-0-525-95146-9 (hbk.)
    1. Career changes. 2. Vocational guidance. I. Title. II. Title: Ten laws of career reinvention.
    HF5384.M58 2010
    650.14—dc22   2009036177

Printed in the United States of America
Set in Bell MT Std
Designed by Sabrina Bowers

While the author has made every effort to provide accurate telephone numbers and Internet addresses at the time of publication, neither the publisher nor the author assumes any responsibility for errors, or for changes that occur after publication. Further, the publisher does not have any control over and does not assume any responsibility for author or third-party Web sites or their content.

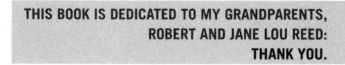

THIS BOOK IS DEDICATED TO MY GRANDPARENTS,
ROBERT AND JANE LOU REED:
THANK YOU.

Every new beginning comes from
some other beginning's end.
Lucius Annaeus Seneca

CONTENTS

INTRODUCTION: IT IS TIME TO LEAVE 1

THE REINVENTION MINDSET 7

THE 10 LAWS OF CAREER REINVENTION 15

LAW 1 IT STARTS WITH A VISION FOR YOUR LIFE 17

LAW 2 YOUR BODY IS YOUR BEST GUIDE 37

LAW 3 PROGRESS BEGINS WHEN YOU STOP MAKING EXCUSES 53

LAW 4 WHAT YOU SEEK IS ON THE ROAD LESS TRAVELED 69

LAW 5 YOU'VE GOT THE TOOLS IN YOUR TOOLBOX 87

LAW 6 YOUR REINVENTION BOARD IS YOUR LIFELINE 107

LAW 7 ONLY A NATIVE CAN GIVE YOU THE INSIDE SCOOP 129

LAW 8 THEY WON'T "GET" YOU UNTIL YOU SPEAK
THEIR LANGUAGE 147

LAW 9 IT TAKES THE TIME THAT IT TAKES 165

LAW 10 THE WORLD BUYS INTO AN AURA OF SUCCESS 187

EPILOGUE: THE LAST TAKEAWAY 211

WORKBOOK 215

ACKNOWLEDGMENTS 251

WORKS CITED 255

INDEX 257

ABOUT THE AUTHOR 267

ABOUT THE REINVENTION INSTITUTE 267

AUTHOR'S NOTE

With the exception of the ten profile stories, most of the names and some personal details in this book have been changed to protect the identities of the people involved. The inspirational quotes used throughout are not meant to suggest an endorsement of this book by those artists and authors.

Special thanks to Alton Brown for graciously agreeing to be interviewed for this book.

Jeffery Rudell story: © 2009 Jeffery Rudell

10% of the author's net royalties from sales of this book will be donated to charity.

THE 10
LAWS OF
CAREER
RE INVENTION

ESSENTIAL SURVIVAL
SKILLS FOR
ANY ECONOMY

IT IS TIME TO LEAVE

here are no more "safe" industries. The ability to reinvent your career at any moment is the new—*and only*—form of job security. Even when you desire change, the familiar always exerts a powerful magnetic pull. But when the world is changing and you are seeking refuge, career reinvention is your safest—and often your only—choice.

In *The Prisoner*, a 1960s British TV series, a spy wakes up one morning and finds himself in an outwardly pleasant, picture-perfect seaside village where each day is like the last and nothing unexpected ever happens. A person could happily live there forever. The villagers are all content—except for Patrick McGoohan, who plays the spy. He senses menace beneath the placid, homey exterior. There is no free will, no opportunity for change or possibility for growth, and no way to leave. Whenever he tries to escape—say, by swimming out to sea—a big white balloon bobs up and nudges him back to shore. This isn't paradise. It's a prison. Yet the balloon could have hauled those villagers *into* the water and pushed them out to sea, and most of them would have swum back to the comfortable jail of their seemingly perfect lives.

But you can't stay in your comfortable old career if there are no jobs available. Whether you are among the legions of the downsized and the sidelined, or a victim of industry consolidation, job scarcity, ageism—or just plain job dissatisfaction; whether you are a corporate job hunter responding to the realities of business or ready to stake your claim in a small business, or among the artistically inclined and wondering whether it's possible to put your "hobby" center stage; whether you're a baby boomer hedging against a shrinking portfolio, an employee beefing up your experience to stay competitive in a digital world, a freelancer who wants the benefits of a staff job, or a staffer who wants the freedom of going it alone: You have no idea what step to take first.

Whether you are willing to leave the familiar trappings of your seaside village by choice or the white balloon is in the process of evicting you: Either way, it is time to leave.

GETTING THERE SAFELY

The 10 Laws of Career Reinvention is the first book to give you all the necessary tools for navigating the full arc of career change between different fields. It will help you take that first step and the next nine—all the way to a successful new career. But know one thing: This book is about using vision and creative thinking to repurpose your skills and find new outlets for your abilities without having to depend solely on the job listings du jour. This book is *not* for you if you are merely looking for a promotion to the next level in your career, or if you are hoping to replace your old job with its counterpart at the competition across the street. Those goals belong to a traditional job hunt, and there are plenty of "old-school" books to help you polish your résumé and dress correctly for an interview.

The book is divided into ten lessons that combine my hard-won expertise with real-life success stories. Changing careers can be quite a culture shock, but you can ensure a smoother transition by mastering the techniques outlined in these laws. They have been successfully applied thousands of times by my clients in the real world. I will help you explode the myths you've been harboring and choose a destination, and I will teach you how to translate your background and skills so that you are understood—and valued—by potential clients or hiring managers there.

Each law begins with an in-depth profile of a dramatic—and successful—career reinvention that illustrates the principle. You'll meet people such as the popular Food Network personality Alton Brown, who began his career on the other side of the camera as a videographer; public relations pro-turned-mental health advocate Terrie Williams, who used the starry client list she built through her eponymous firm to bring attention to the problem of depression in the African-American community; Reggie Mebane, the former COO of Federal Express Trade Networks Transport & Brokerage (a $2 billion subsidiary of Federal Express), who parlayed his expertise in the logistics of handling packages into the logistics of saving lives when he went to the U.S. Centers for Disease Control; and Felina Rakowski-Gallagher, a cop who left the force to open New York City's first breast-feeding boutique. I will break down the steps they took (and the mistakes they made) to reinvent their careers, so you can see up close how it's done.

It's a myth that all you have to do is land one perfect job and you'll be set for life; in fact, the Bureau of Labor Statistics reports that among jobs started by late-stage baby boomers in their late thirties to early forties, 31 percent ended in less than a year, and 65 percent ended in fewer than five years. With industries imploding seemingly daily, this trend is on track to accelerate. Whether you are a baby boomer, Generation Xer, or Millennial, throughout your working life you will find continual uses for these 10 Laws.

Career reinvention is a life skill. When you have the ability to reinvent yourself, you'll possess an aptitude for adapting that will help you evolve with life's phases (just ask Madonna) or cope with its surprises. When you integrate the 10 Laws into how you live your life, the next time the ground shifts beneath you—*for whatever reason*—you will know exactly what to do to regain your footing.

WHY I DO WHAT I DO

What qualifies me to lay down the 10 Laws of Career Reinvention? How does a girl from the Midwest whose family preached the sermon of "find a safe job" take anyone on this roller-coaster ride?

The answer begins on Wall Street—at least the Wall Street that existed just before the big market tumble of 1987. It was the place to be, the ultimate sign that you'd arrived, and like many others in those days, I was desperate to work there. Everyone spoke of working "on The Street" as if it were a cosmic destination. For me, it actually *was* cosmic. Let me explain.

The idea struck like lightning on an appropriately rainy day in 1983. I was sitting in a cramped college lecture hall, a wet-wool-and-rubber dampness rising from my fellow students as they took their seats. The professor stepped up to the lectern, and when he spoke, an electric surge coursed through my body. Dr. Joseph Nye was lecturing that day on Latin-American politics and political systems. I began to see a clearly illuminated path unfurl before me. At the end of it was my dream career: *I want to travel the world and have someone else pay for it.*

At nineteen, this seemed to me like a reasonable, if ambitious, request. I felt a rush of emotion and clarity I had never known. The topic may have been dry, but to me the dream was alive with promise.

I set my sights on getting a job in international banking with Citibank. Why Citibank? Because the glossy photos in the recruiting brochures showed polished, multicultural men and women in suits against the backdrop of glamorous foreign locales. They were smiling. They seemed prosperous. It looked like fun.

With breathtaking singleness of purpose, I worked worked worked my way from Harvard to an MBA at the Thunderbird School of Global Management, then to Knight-Ridder Financial, a company that sold online financial information to brokers and traders. Citibank was one of their clients, and I thought that was a good first step.

All those years of study and strategy paid off. I made it to Wall Street, literally (Knight-Ridder's offices were at 75 Wall Street), and was ready to take the world by storm. And within one year of living my dream career, I realized that . . . *I hated it.*

My heart told me to quit, but I felt I had invested too much at that point. And I had a great boss who threw more money and responsibility my way every time I made noises about being unhappy. Before I quite knew what had happened, one year had turned into nearly five.

You might think that money can paper over the less stellar parts of a job. The truth is that there is not enough money in the world to soothe an unhappy soul. I dragged myself to work, my stomach in knots. Each morning when I got off the train, the anxiety in my chest began to climb, crablike, higher and higher until—in the short walk from subway to office—it had lodged in my throat. I could barely breathe.

This was my life.

One night, I was entertaining some clients at Delmonico's. If Wall Street was the center of the universe, Delmonico's was the center of the center—one of those posh, mahogany-paneled downtown clubs that Wall Streeters frequent after a satisfying day of multimillion-dollar death matches. The banquettes were lined in red leather and there was that familiar Wall Street-y smell of expensive scotch and illegal Cuban cigars.

I looked around at the starched white shirts of my male colleagues (there were few women on Wall Street, then as now), each shirt bracketed by what Wall Street calls "braces" and the rest of us call suspenders. They droned on about T-bills and basis points and bragged about how much money they had made that day.

The white shirts were blinding me, the cigar smoke was choking me, and the conversation was boring me. Enough with basis points. I wanted to talk about something *else* for a change.

By then, the office politics had gotten poisonous and my wonderful boss had departed—but I had been in such pain and denial for so long that I'd never had the time or space to figure out what I wanted next. I had dreamed of and worked toward that job for years. I quit anyway.

Walking out like that—without a Plan B—is a drastic move, one I don't normally recommend. There are healthier, safer ways to make a transition. If I had known then what I know now . . . but that's the point. I *didn't* know, and there were no road maps to follow or laws to guide me. There might have been a supportive community for me somewhere, but I couldn't find it. I desperately needed help to figure out what to do next, create a strategy for getting there, and translate my experience into terms that would show hiring managers in other fields what I had to offer. I didn't know how to fill the gaps in my experience or build a network of contacts in a new industry. (In an ideal world, workers in every field would know the basics of career reinvention long before they were forced out, quit in pain, or hit a dead end.)

I finally targeted—and landed—a great job in the entertainment field. For the next nine years, I lived that dream and I loved it. I traveled the world negotiating deals and informally mentoring others who were making career switches.

By 2003, my priorities had shifted. I was done with the planes-trains-automobiles lifestyle. I decided to create the kind of company that would have helped me back when I left Wall Street. That's when I became a certified coach and launched The Reinvention Institute, where we teach career reinvention as an essential life-management skill. Since then, in seminars and speeches around the country to individuals, corporations, and industry groups, I and my company have helped thousands of people—some of whom you'll meet here—transform their careers. Our most popular classes are our Career Reinvention BootCamps, an intensive course designed to jump-start a reinvention, and our Reinvention Team coaching groups, weekly calls where clients mastermind their plans.

What I learned on my journey, and while helping thousands of others through theirs, is that true career reinvention is not really a leap into the abyss, even if it sometimes feels that way. It proceeds according to codified laws. You may not get to where you want to go overnight. But if you learn and practice the techniques in this book and follow the 10 Laws of Career Reinvention, you *will* get there, and safely.

— Pamela Mitchell,
Miami, January, 2010

THE REINVENTION MINDSET

Career reinvention skills are a survival response that will give you the strongest advantage in adapting to a new world order. You don't have to read the newspapers to know that what's happening in your work life is being affected by larger societal trends. Eighteenth-century British statesman Edmund Burke famously said: "Those who don't know history are destined to repeat it." If he were working in today's world, he'd say that those who don't know history are destined to get left behind, career-wise.

In order to navigate where you need to go, you must examine the road—the modern history of jobs, employment, and career opportunity—that led you to this spot. It may be difficult to believe, but the type of corporate career that employs so much of our society in the United States is a recent development, historically speaking.

Alfred Dupont Chandler, Jr., author of the Pulitzer Prize–winning book *The Visible Hand*, points out that the multiunit business corporation that is so common in this era did not even exist in 1840 because the volume of economic activity in the country wasn't enough to justify layers of administrative management. The advent of the railroads and the availability of cheap coal to power them brought fast and reliable transportation for moving goods around the country, which meant merchants could more easily sell beyond their local markets. This created the multiunit enterprises that needed an administrative infrastructure to manage the flow. By the 1920s, the modern corporate structure had become prevalent in the U.S. business landscape.

The Company Man, 1950s: The end of World War II ushered in the era of the "Company Man," when companies took a very paternalistic attitude toward their employees. William H. Whyte, Jr., in his seminal book *The Organization Man* (his term for "Company Man"), summarized the prevailing philosophy of companies at that time: "Be loyal to the company and the company will be loyal to you." In practice, this meant that you did what the company told you to do and went where the company sent you. You didn't complain. You didn't say no. Although today the phrase "Company Man" carries negative connotations of "spineless" and "bland," back then showing independence or following your own path was often equated, in the company's eyes, to being a rogue employee. The goals of the organization and the goals of the individual were supposed to be one and the same. Refusing a company's request often meant the death knell for your career.

In that era, companies prized loyalty because business cycles were longer: Firms routinely laid out strategic plans that ran ten years or more, and they needed employees to stay on and see them through. In return, businesses offered a number of enticements: cushy benefits, regular raises, opportunities for career development and advancement. But the biggest carrot of all offered to Depression-era babies who'd just been through a war? Job security.

During this same period, labor unions were on the rise. They made sure that the rank and file—the hourly-wage workers—received the same guaranteed salary increases and benefits and the same holy grail: job security.

As a Company Man, your oath of fidelity to the organization

meant you weren't supposed to switch companies, much less industries. In an era when tenure at a firm held the highest value, having multiple career changes on your résumé was an indication that you were damaged goods. Union workers, with their strict tenure-based promotion systems, were heavily penalized for moving by being relegated to the bottom rung at a new employer. Both groups got the message loud and clear: Keep your end of the bargain by staying loyal and you will be rewarded with guaranteed employment, a fat pension, and the proverbial gold watch. It didn't matter whether you *enjoyed* your work. Jobs weren't about "fun." They were there to provide safety and refuge.

The Free Agent, 1980s: By the 1980s, corporate attitudes were shifting. Wall Street was rising in power and using the tool of stock price to reward companies for abandoning their focus on long-term profitability in favor of shorter-term gains. A corporate CEO was presented with a challenge: how best to record a quick profit on the books? Answer: reduce expenses. With redundancies in their organizations due to their latest merger, technology streamlining their operations, and globalization giving them access to cheap overseas labor for a fraction of their current cost, what's the most natural expense to cut? Their people.

With that, companies began breaking their implied contract of lifetime employment. There were mass layoffs in the form of early retirement packages and downsizings. Yet in industry after industry, from the lifers at IBM to the workers at "safe" Ma Bell, people thought that if they waited it out, everything would go back to "normal." But the trend was well under way and would never reverse itself: The world was becoming a more competitive place.

Daniel H. Pink, author of *Free Agent Nation*, calls this era the end of our country's economic adolescence. He traces the rise of the free agent, which he defines as an independent worker who serves multiple clients and customers instead of a single boss—think temps, consultants, and other 1099ers—to four key factors: the death of the social contract whereby employees traded allegiance for lifetime security, a long run of relative economic stability that dulled the collective memory of the Depression and allowed workers to think of work as a vehicle that should deliver meaning in life and not just a paycheck, the tools of wealth creation becoming accessible to individuals, and the rapid life cycles of companies and industries (remember Web 1.0?), assuring that most people would outlive the businesses for which they worked.

Nevertheless, many employees still worked for companies, but the free agent philosophy pervaded the workforce at large. In this dog-eat-dog period, with employment guarantees dead, the prevailing attitude became: Screw the company; it's every individual for himself (or herself, as women had entered the workforce in large numbers by then). As free-market forces began to rule, companies made their employees shoulder more responsibility for their careers. The yardstick that measured a company's most valuable players changed: Tenure was still important, but stars were more often the ones who delivered tangible results to the bottom line. This brought increased flexibility to workers who produced along these lines; company stars could negotiate for bonuses, assignments, and transfers. It was suddenly okay to switch among companies—gotta go where the best opportunities are—but frequent job-hopping was still frowned upon. There was less incentive to change fields, as superstars were often raided by competitors and rewarded handsomely for their in-depth knowledge of and contacts within a particular industry. Job security—the brass ring of generations past—was now delivered by the field you went into, rather than the employer you worked for.

The Reinventor, 2007 to the present: Economists point to December 2007 as the official start of a recession in the United States, and with it we formally entered the age of the Reinventor. Technology, along with ever more rapid business cycles (three years is now considered long-term planning, as opposed to five to seven years in the 1980s), has reduced not only the half-life of companies but the half-life of entire industries. Former safe-haven fields such as automotive, newspapers, and finance are all going through huge shocks and decline. Off-shoring gobbles up pink-collar and white-collar jobs, and with economies such as China and India ascendant, there is huge competitive pressure on U.S. companies. Unions have had to face the new reality; as their power base erodes, they can no longer offer their members protection from market forces. Businesses are coming to realize that the only way to survive these turbulent times is to continually reinvent themselves, and anyone working in today's world must follow suit.

In this era, lengthy job tenure has lost its value. It's not how long you last somewhere that counts; it's what you bring to the table. Companies have grasped that with a three-year business cycle, the addictive habit of layoffs/rehiring is no longer a viable strategy for realigning the skill set of their workforce. They know that since it takes a minimum of eighteen months for an employee to become fully integrated into the organization, they're at a competitive and financial disadvantage if they can't quickly redeploy their staffers to pursue new opportunities. And with changing business models forcing entire industries to build completely different channels of revenue, those new opportunities most likely require cross-pollination with other fields.

We have reached a perfect storm in how employers need to think about talent and how individuals need to think about what they have to offer. Smart companies have changed tactics; they've relegated the almighty industry and functional experience to the bench and moved toward skills-based job-matching for internal and external hiring. In this new game, transferable skill sets are a more valuable commodity than industry experience, and tangible accomplishments that demonstrate those skills are its currency.

The people who will thrive in this new world order are those who can repeatedly and successfully transform themselves: *Reinventors*. Reinventors know that in order to survive and thrive in this challenging era, they must take themselves out of the industry box and be prepared to make a change at a moment's notice.

What are the hallmarks of Reinventors? They're adaptable and resolutely flexible. They think strategically about their portfolio of skills, matching them to the trends. They treat moving between fields like moving between countries, learning to speak new languages and honing their cross-cultural abilities. They continually cross borders, speaking to natives and building connections across industries. *They've stopped looking outside themselves for job security, relying on only their ability to reinvent themselves.*

Reinventors know that companies—like life—can offer no guarantees. They stand as equals, adult-to-adult, with whoever hires them.

Employees or 1099 workers, they are now collaborators who are determined to experience a richer, more varied career. With the ability to change and adapt to whatever life throws at them, they wield power and true control over their work lives. They have the ability to shape their careers as they evolve and weave their passions into their work. To deliver results, they're willing to put in the time at an organization— and they do—but, knowing that market forces can upset the best-laid plans, they reject the stigma of job-hopping dilettante. With their eye on the horizon, Reinventors know that it's wisest not to offer their loyalty to a company or to themselves, but to those opportunities that expand and develop their skills.

To attract and retain talented Reinventors, corporations have changed their practices. They're apt to offer interesting assignments, latitude for creativity and adjustments in schedule, the autonomy to control the details of their work, and sometimes even a stake in the results through profit sharing. With lifetime employment dead and pensions vanishing like mirages in a desert, these are the new "gold watches" on offer to reward effort. And you don't have to wait thirty years to earn one.

YOU: REINVENTED

What's past is past. Resistance to the tides of change is futile; as the old saying goes, you can't push the river upstream. Whether you started off as a Company Man or a Free Agent, you are now, by dint of a shifting landscape, a Reinventor.

It is important not to get stuck emotionally in things that are already history. Getting angry about broken promises won't revive lifetime employment. Feeling resentful about disappearing pensions won't bring them back. Being nostalgic for the old models of the workforce won't help you find your way through the new ones.

Step up to the challenge. In many ways, the rewards for work in today's world are much greater than ever. You have the power to shift and change, to craft your career according to your passions and abilities. You can sculpt your work to adapt to the changes in your life.

This book gives you the tools—pick them up and use them. As you build your pathway to a new career, keep your eyes on the prize: a sense of freedom and fun that Depression-era workers could only dream of, the knowledge that you've got the skills to adapt to whatever life throws at you, and the *real* security that comes from knowing that the only person who controls your destiny is you.

THE 10 LAWS OF CAREER REINVENTION

areer reinvention is simple. But it's not easy.

You might be coming to reinvention with the notion that those who succeed at it already had the skills and know-how, leaving you to spend your time battling lifelong fears and scrambling to catch up. It should come as a relief, then, that the main ingredients of successful reinvention are not IQ, nerves of steel, or membership in an exclusive club—but attitude, commitment, and the willingness to follow the principles laid out in these 10 Laws.

Each of the 10 Laws includes a reinvention story; an in-depth examination of the lesson behind it; a Hidden Conflict analysis that will help you anticipate the challenges of that particular Law; and it wraps up with a Living the Law section that gives you concise, practical techniques for putting that Law into practice.

A bonus section at the end of the book contains workbook exercises to help you implement each step of the reinvention process and give you the experience of living each Law. When you see ▯ along with a footnote, check the workbook for an exercise related to that point. Some exercises can be completed as you read along with the book; others will take more time. Some will be applicable to your situation immediately; others won't be helpful until you reach a later stage in your reinvention. Don't feel compelled to complete each exercise in lockstep; it is perfectly okay to go back to them at a later time. *Follow the process that works best for you.*

▮ ▮ ▮ ▮

Ready to begin? Let's get started . . .

LAW 1

IT STARTS WITH A VISION FOR YOUR LIFE

*"There is no use in trying," said Alice; "one can't believe
impossible things."*

*"I dare say you haven't had much practice," said the
Queen. "When I was your age, I always did it for half an
hour a day. Why, sometimes I've believed as many as six
impossible things before breakfast."*

—Lewis Carroll

Bruce Irving has his reasons, even if they don't always make sense to others.

You want examples? When Bruce was accepted both at Harvard and Williams, he chose the smaller liberal arts college in the Berkshires because they welcomed him with a handwritten note. Harvard sent a form letter. "That didn't seem to bode well on the humanity front," Bruce recalls. His impulse, then and now, though it would take time to fully flower: to shape what he did to match what mattered to him in life, rather than the other way around.

When he lost his job as executive producer of the venerable PBS series *This Old House* in 2006, everyone expected Bruce to get another TV gig. But when a certain home-design guru approached Bruce about producing her new show, he said, "Yuck."

Bruce has always had an inner pilot guiding him through the firmament of life, even before he was aware of it. He began to recognize how much he owed to this inner pilot's great steering when he was forty-four. That's when he came face to face with his true self "in a near-swoon of recognition, love, and gratitude."

Although Bruce had spent seventeen years producing, researching, writing, editing, shooting, and designing new offices for *This Old House*, his inner pilot banked the plane and headed in a different direction. Since then, he's carved an unexpected niche for himself as a renovation consultant. By saying "yuck" to the obvious choice and matching his career to the life he wanted to live, Bruce is now truly happy for the first time.

I I I I

Bruce was born and raised in the leafy, bucolic suburb of Darien, Connecticut, where all was serene—except for the basement explosions and windows breaking.

"Good" Bruce was the boy with the paper route who mowed people's lawns, had the best grades, and became high school valedictorian. "Bad" Bruce ran with an unsavory crowd and built bombs in the basement from firecrackers and model-kit rockets. "I never had a burning career ambition in my life," says Bruce. "I wasn't focused on the future. I never hit upon any activity that struck me as the thing I must do."

For want of a better idea, Bruce majored in English at Williams, graduated in 1983, and applied to ad agencies in New York "because it seemed like a fun thing to do." The ad agencies didn't feel quite as festive; none of them responded.

Bruce did some writing and editing for a start-up photography magazine in New York—not because of any particular love of photography, but because he couldn't get a job at any other magazine. Then he temped. Then a career counselor from Williams called and asked if he'd be interested in a job in investment banking. He wasn't, really, but he applied anyway. He was, however, very interested in the young woman who interviewed him, and he followed her to Japan.

Two years later, the same woman enrolled at the Kennedy School of Government in Cambridge, and he followed her to Boston. He didn't know anyone there, but the wheels were turning even before he arrived. "I think I'd like to be a filmmaker or maybe something in TV," he thought. But he had no money to go to film school. So he ran through his mental Rolodex, looking for someone he knew who did that kind of work.

Five years earlier, during summer breaks from college, Bruce had worked at the Straight Wharf restaurant on Nantucket. The restaurant was like a second home to Bruce; the chef, Marian Morash, was his surrogate mother.

"Dear Marian," wrote Bruce. "Do you remember me?"

She did.

Marian Morash was quite a chef. She was the star of *The Victory Garden*, a highly successful cooking show on Boston's public television station. Marian's husband, Russ Morash, was the first producer to see the potential in Julia Child and in cooking shows in general. He was known as the father of the "how-to" genre, and his latest hit was *This Old House*, "the granddaddy of home-improvement shows."

Bruce became the producer—and, when Russ retired, the executive producer—of *This Old House*. He wrote the occasional column for *This Old House* magazine.

Perfect, no? Bruce had finally found a situation he enjoyed and in which he could stay for a while. Right?

I I I I

"I'd been there for about a year or two, and I thought, this sucks," says Bruce. He wasn't passionate about the subject, he was having issues with a couple of his supervisors, and he was still working part-time in restaurants because his job on the show paid so poorly.

He briefly considered law school, but chose Debby instead. They married in 1993 and had two daughters, Emily and Jane. Bruce settled down at home and on the show, which he grew to love. "The next thing I knew, I'd been there for seventeen years."

In 1997, Time Warner licensed the name of the show and broadened the concept, then bought it outright from WGBH in 2001. The pressure was on. "We had to make money. We had to start a new show. We had to do this, that, and the other thing. We had *This Old House*. We started a new show, called *Ask This Old House*. We made specials. We started a line of house paint. There was an intense amount of pressure to turn the franchise into a profitable business."

By now, Bruce was a walking compendium of home-renovation expertise. Who else was announcing that LED fixtures were "weak light for a silly price," or that bamboo flooring wasn't eco-friendly because it's held together with glue and formaldehyde? Who knew more about microbeveling in manufactured flooring?

Despite this knowledge—plus an Emmy—Bruce was axed from the show just before Christmas 2005, a victim of his big executive producer salary and the weakened state of the parent company. He breathed a sigh of relief and said, "Thank you, Universe!" It was an involuntary opportunity to reshape his life. Luckily, he had a newly acquired vision ready to go.

I I I I

A couple of months before Bruce's career was forced to undergo a gut renovation, Debby had laid down the law. "You have to do something for yourself," she'd told her husband. "I've tried to make you a happier person, but we've run out of tricks in the Irving house. I'm tired of walking around on eggshells. You're a grumpy asshole."

To transform himself, Bruce signed up for The Hoffman Process. Originated during the sixties, Hoffman is a weeklong program that uses psychoanalytic theory to help adults change their responses to their childhood dramas and family dynamics. Bruce heard about Hoffman "from an artist who I dismissed in my cynical way as 'flaky,'" and then from a very cool, hip, and accomplished TV producer. "If it worked for these two guys," he thought, "maybe there's something to it."

"It's not a cult," Bruce is quick to point out. "It's a deep dive into yourself, how you behave, and who you really are."

Hoffman was the subject of a three-year study by the University of California at Davis, which found statistically significant benefits of the program that went way beyond the temporary "halo" effect of fads. "It's the most profound thing I've ever done in my life, without question," says Bruce. "I came out completely blown open. I basically look at my life as Before Hoffman and After Hoffman."

The Hoffman Process put Bruce in tune with his inner pilot: "A 'real me' who was helping me make choices that were good for me. I just didn't know it, because I didn't believe in him. He'd been inside me all along."

Being downsized from Time Warner gave Bruce a chance to manifest his brand-new vision. "I knew more clearly than I've known anything that I had to do something else with my life. Time was a-wasting."

ı ı ı ı

"When you're a proctologist," Bruce says with characteristic bluntness, "people are always asking about the sore on their ass. People were always asking me, 'I have this thing in my house.' Once they knew I was the *This Old House* guy, I was constantly giving advice about products, design, who to work with, and how to approach the project."

What he loved most, he realized, about working on the show was "putting together the teams and then carrying out the rescue of houses. There's the architect, the builder, subcontractors, town officials, material suppliers, and homeowners. Everyone has a different agenda, and they don't always align perfectly with the homeowner's. What if I was the guy who made everybody play nicely together and had the homeowner's back?"

Bruce knew the players and the products. He was in touch with his new vision for himself. So he turned his back on the obvious choice— the lucrative offer from the TV diva—and hung out his own shingle.

"Renovation Consultant," it said.

Bruce is neither a contractor nor an architect. He's coach, facilitator, hand-holder, and advocate. One client likened him to a wedding planner. *Newsweek* called him "The House Whisperer." Bruce has pretty much invented the field, the same way he reinvented his life.

All that Hoffman training—recognizing both his vision for himself and the importance of sticking to it—came in handy when the housing market crashed. Wanting to remain light on his feet yet gain steady cash flow, Bruce took a temporary gig as a series producer on a new show, *This New House*. He still does consulting. He still writes a column, now for *Design New England* magazine. He's free and clear of the corporate politics he always despised.

Bruce describes this latest twist as "the never-ending mix of fun and games I'm up to." Sounds like a great vision for a life.

THE LESSON BEHIND THE LAW: WHAT YOU WANT IN LIFE COMES FIRST

Career reinvention starts with a vision for your life because careers and jobs are delivery devices for the kind of life you hope to lead. They are a conduit for becoming the kind of person you want to be, experiencing the things you want to experience, having the things you want to have. Happiness in your career is directly tied to how much your work brings richness to your world.

In order to be truly happy, *your career must serve your life*, not vice versa. We often forget that the whole point of working is to help create a life we love living. If you have young children at home who you want to spend time with and yet choose a science research career that requires being sealed off in the Antarctic for six months of the year, you have cooked up a recipe for discontent. Most of the misery felt by clients who come to The Reinvention Institute can be traced back to the conflict between the life they desire to live and the life their job actually delivers.

The first question most people ask themselves as they embark on a career reinvention is: *What do I want to do?* But in order to answer that question, you must start with the *why*.

"Because I've been laid off," "Because I could lose my job at any moment," "Because I hate my work"—any of these could well be true. But reasons that have their root in external sources do not illuminate what you hope to achieve in your life. They do not tell you what it is you *seek*.

You must think about the things you value in your life—apart from work. *Why am I doing this? What more do I want in my life? What do I hope to gain?* If you do not take time to ponder these questions at the beginning, in the end you will get a new job but you will not get what you *want*.

This requires being precise: The answer to the question "Why?"

can't just be "I want something better" or "I'm looking for something more interesting." It has to include the specific details of the lifestyle you hope to build. It must encompass all facets of your world: where you live, who surrounds you, what you enjoy. Work is a part of that vision, but it is *how* you work—the flow of your day, what you spend your time doing, the kind of environment you work in—that is your focus at this stage. Your goal is to have a clear image in mind of your desired life. *What* you do comes later; you can calculate backward from your image to discover the career options that will deliver it.

Crafting this picture of the life you dream of living is the first step to charting a path to your new career. Imagining its details, rhythms, and essence will inspire the passion that will fuel you throughout your reinvention. But before you rush off to put a down payment on that villa in Bora Bora you've always fantasized about, let me first explode a few myths.

Myths

The Greek gods were said to have created thunder to express their bad moods—but that's another myth for another day. The kind of myth we're talking about in terms of career reinvention is a belief system, a rule book drawn from old wives' tales, fears, overheard conversations, worst-case scenarios, and the mothballs and tumbleweed that occasionally float through your brain, such as: "When I get a new job, I'll be happy at last."

Myths are fundamental beliefs about the world around you that you develop or nurture lovingly or accept without question. They can be positive or negative ("When I have that, life will be great" or "People like me can't have that") and usually appear in the guise of self-evident truths ("After forty, it's all downhill"). Here are some of the most typical career reinvention myths I hear:

Without a degree, I don't stand a chance.

I'm over fifty—I'm too old.

I've been doing my job for so long, I'm stuck in this industry.

My life will be better when I change careers.

The things I hate about my current career don't exist in the new one.

You have to "know somebody" in order to get in.

All my problems will be solved when I switch careers.

Myths always come with a downside. Negative myths turn into self-fulfilling prophecies ("I'll never make it, so I might as well not try"). Positive myths add the weight of heavy expectations to your dreams ("I'll know I'll have arrived when I make a million dollars"). Even if you keep plugging away and reach your goal, myths can set you up for disappointment ("I thought I'd be happy. When will that kick in?").

Myths are blindfolds that keep you from being able to sort fact from fiction. If you expect a job to deliver all that you seek, you may not recognize patterns of thought and behavior within you that need to change. The result is that the same problem crops up, job after job, even though you thought a new career would be just the tonic for what ailed you.

I once had a consultation with a woman named Theresa who came to me because she felt unappreciated at work. She was a business development executive at a Web design firm; earlier in her career she'd worked in printing services.

"Why do you want to make a career switch?" I asked.

"I think vice presidents in other industries earn more money," she said.

Theresa had a nice salary but felt resentful because she thought she should be earning well over "six figures." There was just one catch: She refused to work more than forty hours per week. She arrived at 9 A.M. on the dot, and clocked out promptly at 4:59 P.M. each day. Weekends? Don't go there. Theresa's company was fine with this arrangement; still, she felt she wasn't being adequately compensated given her title.

"Would you be willing to work more hours at another firm?" I asked.

"I shouldn't have to," she replied. "I'm a vice president."

Theresa was under the illusion that salary rewards were tied to title, not effort. She also believed the fallacy that the higher your position in the company, the less you had to work. Theresa was unwilling to accept the truth behind the myth: If she wanted to earn the bigger paycheck, she'd have to be willing to trade off the evenings and weekends she so cherished. I checked in with her a year later and she was still feeling unappreciated at her company and seeking a new position. When myths cloud your vision, it's hard to see that what needs to change isn't always the job. Sometimes it's you.

By holding on to myths you can also get stuck in a holding pattern and miss seeing what you could be doing right now that would make your life better (the "I'll be happy when . . ." syndrome). If you find yourself saying "I'll be happy when . . ." ask yourself: What can I do to be happy *now*?

Fantasies

Fantasies are a close relative of myths; in fact, they're practically kissing cousins. What's wrong with a little fantasy, you ask? Isn't it all about hope and thinking big? Didn't you just tell me to picture my villa in Bora Bora?

Yes, I did. There are many practical and constructive uses for fantasy. Positive thinking and visualization, for example, are techniques you will use in career reinvention to help you stay the course. But the definition of "fantasy" includes both "visionary idea" and "a supposition based on no solid foundation." Visionary ideas have made the world a better place, and we admire the people who come up with them. Thank you, Thomas Edison. Thank you, Jonas Salk. But when you choose your career destiny from "a supposition based on no solid foundation," your dream lifestyle is built on quicksand.

When I worked in entertainment, a woman named Stacey cold-called me one day. She'd read an article in a magazine about the international deals I'd done for my company and was eager to have a job like mine "because it sounds good."

I asked her how much travel she had done for work. Well, she hadn't done any. How much experience did she have negotiating complicated joint venture deals? None. Did she speak any foreign languages? *Nada.*

Stacey's vision of a life on the go was carved entirely from imagination. In other words, when she said my job "sounded good," she really had no idea what I did for a living. "You get to fly business class to Tokyo!" she said. True. But if Stacey wanted to clear up her fantasies, she should have followed up with specific questions: How long was I usually away? How much of that time was spent working? Did I enjoy reading through hundreds of pages of contracts? When was the last time I had seen my friends? How were my houseplants doing?

Basing important career decisions on fantasy interferes with your chances of making a reinvention stick. You may find yourself chasing the wrong rainbow, just as I did when I diligently worked ten years toward a Wall Street career that was not, ultimately, a good fit for me. Only late in the game did I realize that I had filled the gaps in my knowledge of Wall Street with my fantasy of "Wall Street." My daydream of free international travel was true, but that fantasy hadn't taken into account the grinding hours or the fact that I didn't have a deep interest in arcane financial data. These turned out to be big negatives of the job that, for me, would outweigh the positives.

To Get You Have to Give

Career reinvention, by its very nature, offers the possibility of a more rewarding and fulfilling life. But as the saying goes, to whom much is given, much is also required. Put more simply: You don't get without giving.

To craft a pathway to your envisioned lifestyle, reinvention requires that you:

Be flexible. There will be times when you'll have to change your tactics, thinking, even your goal. Sticking to one plan—especially when you can see it's not working—defeats the whole purpose of reinvention. You have to evolve in response to the circumstances you encounter. When the bottom fell out of the housing market and his client pipeline slowed to a trickle, Bruce was willing to take a temporary contract position producing another television show. You must be willing to shift your ideas, plans, and strategies along the way.

Be honest with yourself. There's always the possibility that you're getting in your own way, and you have to be willing to face it. Maybe it's an ingrained attitude that's self-defeating, or a basic limitation that needs to be acknowledged: "Am I *really* a great multitasker?" "Do I truly prefer to run things? Or am I better at doing the job itself?"

One of my clients, Patty, was tired of her eight years in financial services marketing. "I hate that my job is all about servicing the sales department," she said. So she applied for a marketing job with Google.

"But Google is nothing if not an ad sales–driven company," I pointed out.

"It will be different there," she said.

Patty was not being honest with herself. If she hated helping sales where she worked at that point, she'd hate helping sales at the next company because she hates helping sales *period*. It's better to know the difficult truths about yourself, your likes and dislikes, before signing on for more of the same misery at a different firm. Have the courage to look within so that you can head toward what you want, not run from what you can't face.

Be willing to live outside your comfort zone. The reinvention process is not as bad as being thrust into a culture where they make you walk across hot coals before they feed you, but still, whenever there's change, there's going to be a certain level of discomfort. The more you practice tolerating it, the easier it gets.

You know this intuitively, but there's actually a scientific basis for it. When new information floods in—as it will on a daily basis as you reinvent yourself—it is stored in the prefrontal cortex, the brain's home for working memory. This is the brain's "holding area," where it stores new input to be compared with other information. This part of the brain is an energy hog; it can hold only so much data before it begins to get overwhelmed (think how you'd feel if someone sat you at the controls of the space shuttle and told you they'd give you all the instructions on how to get liftoff—and, oh yeah, you're going to be handling it yourself in an hour). The trick is to make these "new" things familiar—to get comfortable outside your comfort zone—so that they move from the prefrontal cortex to the basal ganglia, a less energy-intensive part of the brain where the neural circuits of long-standing habits and routines are stored.

Be okay with your dream. The most important thing the first law of reinvention requires you to do is to give yourself permission to pursue what you want. Although you might think this happens automatically—"Of *course* it's okay to go for what I want!"—the minute you start envisioning a new lifestyle, your subconscious will start throwing up a whole host of roadblocks.

HIDDEN CONFLICT THAT COULD STOP YOU: NEEDING A PERMISSION SLIP

When you were in grade school, you needed to ask permission for everything. "Can I have another cookie?" "Can I have my coloring book now?" "Can I go to the bathroom?" It was drilled into your head that the minute you had a desire, you needed to get authorization before you fulfilled it.

Even though you are now an adult, those childhood habits are stored so deeply in your basal ganglia, you don't even realize they're still there. But the minute you start crafting your imagined lifestyle, from the depths a question will arise: *Is it okay?*

You run the risk of sabotaging yourself until you sign a consent form that allows you to:

Want it: Reaching for a reinvention goal that far outstrips the accomplishments of your friends and family could make you feel guilty or disloyal, or as if you are leaving them behind. You'll find yourself saying: "I can't have all that." "I'm asking for too much." "I don't need to have everything." Not giving yourself permission to "want it" can cause you to lessen the scope of your goals and undermine your success before you even get started.

Have it: If your anxiety mounts the closer you get to turning your vision into actuality, you're probably not giving yourself permission to "have it." You'll find yourself saying: "That seems like a lot." "I'm not certain I can handle this." "Am I sure this is the right thing?" You pull back just when you're on the cusp of success because secretly you don't think you deserve it.

I had one client, Rachel, who almost torpedoed her reinvention over this issue. Rachel was a psychotherapist who dreamed of becoming the next Dr. Laura. She offered popular seminars on mother-daughter communication and was compiling her advice into a book. She diligently sent out informational packets to the press about her work. One day she got a call from a local TV morning show looking for an expert on the topic and asking her to make an appearance.

Rachel immediately left me a panicked voice mail, but I happened to be coaching other clients so it took me several hours to return her call. When I reached her, I asked if she'd called the show producers back.

"No, of course not! They want me to come on the show in three days."

I couldn't believe my ears . . . except, of course, I could. I knew Rachel was anxious in the face of finally having her dream. But morning-show producers are a time-sensitive bunch; they've got airtime that must be filled. If you don't get back to them right away, they'll find somebody else to take your spot.

My coaching call with Rachel had to set a record for speed because I had one thing to say: "Call them back immediately and say *yes*."

Be it: You've become ruler of the realm, but the crown on your head feels too heavy or big . . . as if it were meant for someone else. There is only one thing you say: "Me?" Not giving yourself permission to "be it" can cause you to undermine your efforts subconsciously so you won't have to choose between two dreaded options: feeling unworthy of the royal title, or embarking on a major overhaul of your fundamental beliefs about money and success.

Here are some permission slips that have just crossed your desk, and you need to sign them before you get to go on the reinvention field trip:

I, ___, give myself permission to change. The reinvention process is a road with occasional potholes and dead ends. Give yourself permission to take full control of the steering wheel and detour from your original plans.

I, ___, give myself permission NOT to be perfect. An insistence on getting it "right"—whether it means the "right" answer or doing it the "right" way—can bog you down in details and make you lose sight of the big picture.

I, ___, give myself permission to please—or not please—others. Your loved ones will not necessarily meet your reinvention plans with a ticker-tape parade. Your spouse may not be happy when you quit your astrophysicist position at NASA to fulfill your life's ambition of becoming a tango instructor. It's just as bad if your spouse has been telling you for years to pursue tango and you refuse to quit NASA—despite having just won the World Tango championship—because you don't want to give him or her the satisfaction of being right. One important thing to remember when signing this particular permission slip: It's not a Get Out of Jail Free card on the Monopoly board of life. You still have to honor your commitments to those who depend on you or who are affected by your decisions.

When you sign these self-consent forms, be prepared for fallout. There are consequences to deciding to pursue your reinvention. You will need to stand strong in the face of disagreement from friends and family. You will have less time on your hands. You will face fear. But like Charlie's golden ticket in the Wonka Bar, your permission slip will swing open the door to a glorious new world.

LIVING THE LAW: THE LIFESTYLE YOU WANT—AND THE CAREER TO DELIVER IT

At this juncture in the reinvention process, your only task is to come up with ideas. Let me say at the outset that reinvention doesn't promise that you'll reach an idyllic state of being. Instead, it's about having a genuinely fulfilling life, with all the ups and downs, messiness, and trade-offs that being human entails. It means putting up with things you don't like—like wild dogs and sand flies—to have the things you do like: a villa in Bora Bora. To have a life you love—for real—you must make choices.

Crafting a dream lifestyle is a matter of weighing personal priorities against tough decisions. Is your dream compatible with your life? How can you balance your important obligations with your passions? The trick is to find a workable intersection of career interests and lifestyle; getting most of what you want in both arenas is a recipe for satisfaction.

To do that, follow this three-step process:

Uncover Your Myths and Fantasies

To clear up any illusions that you might be harboring, it's time to do a little myth-busting and fantasy cleanup. [📖]¹

Ask yourself the following questions:

1. What problems do I think will be solved by my reinvention?

2. What things will I finally get that I've been waiting for?

3. What are the barriers I think will stop me from getting there?

4. What are the cool things I'm looking forward to in my new career?

5. What won't I have to deal with once I make this switch?

Make a list of your responses and keep them at hand. As you move through your reinvention, you will test your assumptions. Sometimes they may be based in fact (grounded in independently verifiable data; e.g., vice presidents often work evenings and weekends); if that's the case, then you know your expectations are on target for your goal. When they're not based in fact, check to see if there are some emotion-based "truths" (e.g., "I am not appreciated at work") that might be clouding your vision and giving rise to a few myths and fantasies that might be holding you back.

Visualize Your Ideal Life

You may have heard the saying: "If you can see it, you can be it." This is the principle to employ when taking this next step. You want to create a detailed picture in your mind of the kind of life you're shooting for.

---

¹Exercise on Page 217: Myth Busting and Fantasy Cleanup

The best way to start creating a life vision is by imagining a picture of your ideal day. 📖² You wake up in the morning—where are you? What does the room look like? Who's with you? Visualize all these details and make them real. You get up and get started with your day—what do you do? Do you have a leisurely breakfast with your family on a sunny patio, or go for a long run, or roll down to your home office to check out the latest headlines online? It's your day—start it the way that makes you happiest.

After that, you begin work. Don't panic here—you don't have to know exactly what you're doing! Just know that you begin work and decide what that looks like for you. Do you leave to go to an office filled with people, or head off to a quiet writing studio in your backyard, or go to a sunny loft and greet your small team? Is the environment intense and invigorating, relaxed and laid back, or creative and a bit crazy? What do you do for lunch—go to a new restaurant with your coworkers, read a book in the park, go for a quick bike ride?

Your ideal day should speak to your heart, excite you, make you thrilled and a little bit scared, and bring you a sense of fulfillment. If it doesn't, then dream bigger! Don't be afraid to stretch yourself and create a picture that seems almost scary in its possibility to make you happy. This is what the priorities and passions of your life look like.

Brainstorm Career Ideas

Now that you have designed your ideal lifestyle, it's time to come up with a list of careers that have the potential to deliver it. Get your creative juices flowing by asking yourself these six questions: 📖³

1. **When am I in flow?** Flow, as defined by psychologist and author Mihaly Csikszentmihalyi, is an optimal state of mind that happens when you are totally absorbed in an activity, when time seems suspended and you feel a deep sense of satisfaction. What do you normally do that is so effortless and joyful that you could happily do it for hours? When Bruce sat down and thought

²Exercise on Page 219: Visualize Your Ideal Day
³Exercise on Page 222: Brainstorm Career Ideas

about what he loved about working on *This Old House*, he realized it had nothing to do with it being a TV show. The moments that were the most fun for him were in putting together the teams and rescuing the houses.

2. **What feels "easy"?** This is the talent you have that feels as natural as breathing. People probably call you all the time for . . . something. What is it? What problem do people always come to you to solve? When and why are you the "go-to" resource for family and friends? What do your friends always tell you you're so good at? Once people found out that Bruce was the *This Old House* guy, they started asking him for recommendations on home improvement products, design, contractor resources, etc. He realized there might be something in that, even if it wasn't the path people would have expected of him and even though he'd been offered another producing job on the design diva's show.

3. **What seems "obvious"?** This is something that seems so abundantly clear to you that you wonder why others don't see it or do it. It's so obvious! Bruce wondered why no one acted as an advocate for the homeowner during a renovation. He thought, "There's a constellation of people involved in renovation—the architect, the builder, subcontractors, town officials, material suppliers, and homeowners. Chances are that the homeowner has never done anything like this before. Also, everyone speaks a slightly different language with a slightly different accent. Frankly, they all have different agendas, and they don't always align perfectly with the homeowner's."

4. **What are my inexhaustible interests?** These are the things that spark an unending sense of curiosity, or that you can never get enough of. In my first reinvention, after I left Wall Street, I didn't know where on earth to look for my next career. I had been so bored with all that financial talk about basis points and derivatives. If only they would talk about what I was devouring in magazines! I love magazines. I had subscriptions to everything, and I could happily sit and leaf through them for hours.

I pored over magazines and newspapers because I had an endless fascination for pop culture. *That's when I realized I was a media junkie.* Here was a topic that would never bore me. Once I had identified this feeling within me, this love of pop culture, I could bring in my reasoning to help flesh out my choices.

5. **What do I gravitate toward in my current career?** You can be so desperate to leave a job that you forget how much of it does work for you. If you leave all that behind, you could be setting yourself up for more unhappiness—only instead of yearning for what you don't have, you'll miss what you left behind. Even if you hate your job, there are always a few parts to like. What are they? Bruce realized that he enjoys talking to people and working with them. He enjoys the psychology behind matching people's desires to their budgets and finding the right resources for making those desires come to fruition.

6. **What should exist in the world but doesn't—perhaps to buy or eat or do or read?** This is a great question for entrepreneurs in search of a market niche. Think of the Post-it. The bra. Those sun visors that hold two cans of beer, straws dangling, to wear to football games. These are examples of where there was a *need,* and someone came along and met it. That's how Bruce did it: He knew that when people renovated their homes, there were a thousand decisions to make that required the juggling of architects, contractors, and suppliers. He knew that in other industries, consultants were the "neutral party" brought in to assess the overall situation and make recommendations tied to the client's goals. Bruce combined the two.

Gather the data from your answers to these questions and compare them to the lifestyle you want to lead. Come up with a list of three or four possible careers that both match your interests and can provide the lifestyle you envision.

At this stage in your reinvention, your goal is to keep your options open. Don't be afraid to throw a few blue-sky ideas on your career list; as you move through the rest of the book, you'll learn how to evaluate them. You've got a lot of work ahead of you to make reinvention happen, so right now pause for a moment and relish your dream.

The Takeaway: Careers and jobs are delivery devices for the kind of life you hope to lead. You begin by creating a picture of your desired lifestyle and making sure your reinvention plans are not infected with myths and fantasies.

Watch Out for . . . Forgetting to give yourself a permission slip to pursue a different and bigger life.

Putting the Law into Action: Make a list of three or four ideas that could deliver your desired lifestyle.

Something to Think About: What are the things I love most about my life right now?

LAW 2

YOUR BODY IS YOUR BEST GUIDE

*A trembling in the bones may carry a more convincing
testimony than the dry documented deductions of the brain.*
—Llewellyn Powers

Cristina Garza was fifteen when The Viper roared into town.

The Viper was a roller coaster, a spaghetti tangle of forest green steel track that soared over eighty feet in the air and could move 1,700 riders per hour. And it was *loud*. The passengers were louder. They screamed themselves hoarse when the ride pitched them upside down.

The Viper debuted at Houston's AstroWorld amusement park in 1989, and fifteen-year-old Christina was on the spot—not to ride it, but to work it. She sold mugs with candid photos of the screaming riders. The noise didn't faze her, because Christina grew up in a "bright, vivid, colorful, and noisy" Houston barrio known as Magnolia, where kids played in the street and neighbors souped up their cars on the lawn. "There was always something going on," recalls Christina. "People were playing loud music and arguing. I'll never forget my godmother's husband; he had this sneeze that would shake the whole neighborhood."

The house shook as well from the train whose tracks ran alongside the wooden house where Christina lived with her Mexican-born mother, Juanita. Early on, Christina developed the skill of tuning out the noise so she could hear the messages her body was sending. "If there is something that I love to do, I'm energized and happy, I'm excited, and my heart is racing," she says. "I've got this adrenaline thing going."

It was this ability to read her body's signals that gave Christina safe passage through the adrenaline-rush of her reinvention.

I I I I

Juanita married relatively late in life and was forty-four when Christina was born in 1973. Two years later, she lost both her much-older husband and her mother. "My mom was working wherever she could work," says Christina. "For a long time she babysat from home. She did a lot of odd jobs."

There was an unspoken promise in the household that Christina would grow up to honor her mother by taking care of her and making her proud. "My culture has a lot to do with it, too, because you don't dare leave your home in the Latino culture," says Christina. "There came a point where I really just needed to start looking out for my wants and needs instead of being the caretaker."

Juanita had never finished grade school, and was adamant that her only child would do better. "She made sure I had perfect attendance at school," says Christina. "As a matter of fact, she would walk me to school every day and pick me up. She would always tell me, 'I don't want you to have the kind of life that I did.'"

Christina started out wanting to be "everything." Teacher, doctor, cop . . . you name it. She ended up at a magnet high school for math and science—the sensible choice in Houston, a city built on chemical engineering and home to most of the country's oil conglomerates—and spent her senior year getting on-the-job training at Shell Oil. With a scholarship to the University of Houston, it looked like everything was in place—except that the normally buoyant Christina was lethargic. She never lit up over chemical engineering the way a friend of hers did when talking about his journalism major.

"I procrastinated on everything. I would cram for exams. I was up all night, studying. I would hit the snooze button three times. It's literally a dragging feeling, like something is weighing you down."

Her body had a message for her: If Christina were going to enjoy life instead of plodding through it out of a weary sense of obligation, things would have to change.

For the first time in her life, Christina decided to follow her gut instinct. The minute she switched her studies to journalism, just like her friend, "My attitude changed. My grades dramatically improved. It seemed to be the perfect fit for me."

In 1995, Christina had a two-week internship at the Spanish TV station Telemundo, which turned into a part-time job there as a writer. They hired her full-time after she graduated in 1996, and then came the day all broadcast journalists wait for, the day that the news director turns to you and says, "You're on, kid!" Christina did her first live, on-camera, on-deadline reporting, and the initial jitters gave way to a crazy euphoria. She was hooked. She went on to do something that few Spanish-TV reporters ever manage—she broke into the English-speaking market and went mainstream as a senior reporter and week-end anchor for the local FOX affiliate.

In all, it was a career that required working nights, weekends, and holidays, in the rain and cold or oppressive heat. But Christina was able to tune out the noise and listen to her body's message: *Bring on the adrenaline.*

I I I I

During a visit to a friend in Geneva in September 2006, Christina stopped off in Paris for three days. "When I came back to Houston, all I could think of was Paris and how could I get back there," she says.

Paris. The word alone sent a tingle down her spine. "It was like walking on clouds. It was such a light feeling." She agonized over whether to leave TV journalism to follow this new passion. Her employers helped her out of that bind by offering her a chance to renew her contract, but to start whenever she felt like returning from Paris. The job would be waiting.

Intellectually, this deal was a winner. It was a guaranteed escape hatch in case things didn't work out in Paris. But when Christina went in to sign the new contract, a strange thing happened. "Something else came out of my mouth. It was, 'No, thank you.' When I uttered those words, my head said, 'What did you just say?!' It was just the craziest feeling and episode. It was like you see on TV, when your brain is thinking to say one thing, but your mouth sputters something else. It was such a liberating thing."

Christina's body knew that she did not want to feel obligated to return, or locked into any particular future. "Somehow it didn't sit well in my stomach. It just didn't feel right," she says. "They always say that your gut feeling is the right feeling."

Christina was thirty-three when she arrived in Paris in the spring of 2006 with two big, wheeled suitcases and a small handbag. One suitcase held her clothing. The other was packed with tortillas, peanut butter, and picante sauce. "I can't live without my peanut butter," she explains. "And there are no tortillas in France."

In a foreign land, sometimes you need a little piece of home.

I I I I

When Christina returned to Houston in 2006 after three months in Paris studying French and soaking up the culture, she was renewed in spirit and ready for a quieter, saner life. She opened her own business teaching Spanish, funded at first by some freelance work from her former job. Then she heard about a media-relations job at the Greater Houston Partnership that called for all the skills Christina had amassed over the years. "They wanted someone who was connected and who understood the workings of media. They wanted somebody who would be able to help with story ideas, creation, and development. They wanted somebody who was knowledgeable about the Houston region. Of course being bilingual was a plus."

The new job at the Greater Houston Partnership gave Christina a slice of "normal" life she'd never experienced: a regular nine-to-five job, with evenings and weekends off. Holidays, too.

Today, there are still moments when Christina is "flying at a thousand miles an hour," but not every day, not every hour. She no longer lives with her mother; instead, Juanita lives with *her*. It's not just a difference in semantics. To Christina, it's the difference between living on autopilot and . . . living.

"I hear people say, 'Someday I'm going to take a trip to Europe. Someday I'm going to buy my dream house. Someday I'm going to get that car I want,'" says Christina. She knows it well, that sensation when your body aches for something that feels just beyond reach.

"Why can't that someday be today?"

THE LESSON BEHIND THE LAW: INSTINCT VS. INTELLECT

All good decision-making requires an ever-shifting balance of intellectual and instinctual input. But some decisions are better left to the first clear signal your body sends—assuming that you're paying close attention and can pick up on it. If, by chance, you miss that sign, your intellect has the ability to step in and play spin-doctor with the facts, but as the great choreographer Martha Graham once said, "The body never lies."

Yes, I know what they told you about the intellect representing your higher self, blah blah. You've no doubt bought into the vision of your intellect being off at Oxford on a Rhodes Scholarship while your instinct sprawls with a beer on the couch, flipping channels. But that's not the full picture. Your intellect is smart and clever—which means it is also capable of lying to you ("You do NOT look fat in that outfit!"). The intellect's motivation may be altruistic, as in a meager attempt to make you feel classier or better about yourself, or to rewrite history a little in your favor, but when you're using your intellect to make life-changing decisions during a reinvention, you want to be sure you're getting solid advice, not a whitewash that boosts your ego. For that, you must turn to your gut.

Your Instinct Is Wise

I was driving north on the FDR highway in Manhattan in a rental car with a GPS system. The machine's soothing female voice gave me my first instruction:

"Turn right."

If you know anything about Manhattan, you can see the problem. When you are headed north on the FDR, you have Manhattan in all its glory on your left, and on your right is . . . the East River. Not: a couple of blocks and a gas station and *then* the East River. Just a river.

I ignored the instructions and continued north. *"Recalculating route,"* said the GPS voice, betraying a touch of annoyance. After some clicks and whirrs, the voice was ready with an all-new instruction:

"Turn right."

Look, lady, I can't make a right. To the right is a large body of water.

The intellect often functions like that faulty GPS as it tries to steer you toward a route that you know in your heart-of-hearts is unwise. The reinvention process will often present you with turning points at which you must decide which signal to follow—your personal, internal GPS, or the mass-market system that everyone else is using. At a crucial moment in Christina's reinvention, when she ended up turning down a TV gig even though it had sounded like a good offer when she first considered it, her body took over from her mind and made the decision that "felt" right instead of "sounded" right. Instead of feeling panic over her choice, she felt liberated. The right choice doesn't have to make sense intellectually. If it results in an overwhelming feeling of relief, it's a sign that you're on the path that's right for *you*, the path that ultimately will make you happiest.

Let's examine the alternative. When you override a strong gut instinct and instead follow your intellect's directions, you can end up with the reinvention equivalent of being dunked in the river. This was what happened to Lila, a student in one of my coaching groups. Lila, a former insurance claims adjuster, had changed careers. She prized job security, but what made her heart sing was holistic health counseling, so she decided to . . . *take the safer route and become an occupational therapist,* a career that did *not* make her heart sing. By the time she came to me, she had been an occupational therapist for five years and was suffering constantly from indigestion, headaches, and exhaustion. It's interesting that when Lila ignored the signals from her gut, other parts of her body staged a rebellion. Although she had made the "smart" choice in terms of job security, she followed a path that dunked her in the river: She was miserable and bored. She came to The Reinvention Institute to ensure that her second reinvention delivered the happiness and fulfillment that she hadn't gotten from her first one, the "smart" choice.

When Something Feels Right

It's easy to disparage instinctual decision-making as "knee-jerk" (or the slightly less loaded "intuition"), except we all do it in certain circumstances, and then excuse it as an aberration, or refuse to see it as that method we disapprove of:

1. Within the first few minutes of meeting a candidate for a job, you decide to make that hire (or not) based on how that person "feels" to you.

2. You hear about a new project at work and volunteer because it sounds "interesting," even though you don't know all the details.

3. You scan the room at a networking breakfast and decide to sit next to someone who has "good energy." You come away with a great new business contact.

4. It's a busy day, but you get a "flash" that you ought to call a customer you haven't spoken to for a while. You end up getting a new order.

Snap decisions—psychology calls it "rapid cognition" or "thin slicing"—are made quickly and unconsciously. There are numerous situations where this method makes more sense and is more accurate than the decisions we turn over and over in our minds. The reason "snap decisions" get such a bad rap is that we never know how to explain ourselves after we make them. *There's* the problem—not that we sometimes depend on our body's signals for guidance, but that we're embarrassed we can't defend those choices intellectually. Malcolm Gladwell advises in *Blink* to "respect the fact that it is possible to know without knowing why we know and accept that—sometimes—we're better off that way."

Most of my clients come to The Reinvention Institute with the idea that they'll need to sift through mounds of information to isolate the best reinvention path. It sounds smart and responsible to say they're going to meticulously gather data and study it to the *n*th degree. But short-term memory can only juggle an average of seven items at a time (such as a seven-digit telephone number); after you hit the magic seven, your brain is full. How many times have you thrown up your hands after hours of tortured cogitation about a choice and just picked from a hat to put an end to the agony?

It sounds somewhat counterintuitive, but the more choices you have, the less likely you are to choose well. Car dealerships count on that when they offer you a slew of add-ons that overload your circuits and weaken your resolve. When your brain is too busy, you're more likely to make an inappropriate decision—say, chocolate cake over a healthy fruit snack. (One study actually offered subjects that very choice, and the ones who were preoccupied carelessly chose the cake.)

When it comes to deciding what you really want to do or be, your body is the ultimate guide. Gladwell describes it as "the ability of our unconscious to find patterns in situations and behavior based on very narrow slices of experience." Instinct helps you winnow your choices down to a manageable level. Your mind may insist that you evaluate ten or twelve different career options, but your body can tell you without a pause that only three of them feel right. While the brain is busy cataloguing and processing a nonstop stream of information, the body simply tunes all that out and focuses on the essentials it is concerned with—not how well the numbers crunch but whether something *feels* right. It isn't concerned with amassing data to support its conclusion. It wants what it wants.

How will your body let you know its conclusion? It's often through physical signals and symptoms, such as elation or discomfort, or feelings of lightness or heaviness. You might feel doubt, guilt, a sudden shadow of something being "off." Or you might experience a satisfied feeling, a sense of relaxation that tells you something is "right." Your body's alarm signals explain why some situations look good on paper but don't work out in practice: Just because the brain gives the all-clear doesn't mean the body is ready to sign off on it.

I'm not suggesting that *every* decision be made on the spot, or that you should push aside intellectual doubts, or neglect your homework. That's why there is the "buyer's remorse" clause that lets you cancel certain contracts a day or two later for big-ticket items such as gym memberships and life insurance. It's well known that people sometimes act impulsively, but also that what seems thrilling in the moment (buying something because it's 40-percent off) is not necessarily in your best long-term interests (it's cheap, but you don't need the item in the first place). It may take a cooling-off period for this truth to sink in.

Feeling good about something is not the same as jumping on it after hearing a forceful sales pitch—the first bubbles up from within, the second is a knee-jerk response to outside pressure. But in career reinvention, ignoring the ongoing messages of your body is folly. The intellect—the practical part of your brain that likes to chew things over—should be used primarily for nudging you closer toward what feels right instinctively.

After I left the entertainment field, I stayed for a while at a friend's place in the south of France to clear my head and contemplate the next phase of my life. I was ready for another reinvention, although I wasn't sure what it would be. While I was there, my mother called from Wisconsin for advice about her own career; after working for nearly forty years, she was ready to find a job with a more flexible schedule.

"You can certainly get flexibility if that's what you want," I said. "But if you don't go in with a plan, you're going to end up with the same thing you've always had." My mother dreamed of a more fluid lifestyle, but was still mired in a nine-to-five mentality.

"I'm not saying you can't have what you want," I went on. "I'm only saying that you need a plan. I can help you with that."

As I said those words, I felt an intense physical rush. It was a feeling through my whole body that said: *This is what I am supposed to do.* I'm supposed to help people figure out how to have the career that delivers the life they want.

It was one of those burning-bush flashes, and I immediately did what most people do after an operatic moment like that: I fled.

I fled because I got scared. My intellect started in right away, with "I can't do that" and "I don't think so." I spent an entire year ignoring my body's message about my calling. As so often happens when you're avoiding those signals, things in my life stopped working. Everything got hard. Even things I was normally good at became difficult.

It was a full year of tug-of-war between my intellect and my body. Since you're reading this book, you know which one ultimately prevailed.

HIDDEN CONFLICT THAT COULD STOP YOU: YOUR MIND TRIES TO TALK YOUR BODY OUT OF ITS TRUTH

Many careers appeal directly to the intellect, and our minds will sometimes try to control the decision-making instead of helping us figure out what feels right in our bodies. At such times, your brain is like a huckster trying to sell you something you don't really want. For example, some career aspirations sound more impressive than others, and knowing that people will widen their eyes with awe at the mention of them makes those goals seem, intellectually, like a good deal. Being head of a team at Doctors Without Borders, for example, sounds impressive, even noble. But just because a career sounds awesome doesn't mean it's a good fit for you. If you can't stand the sight of blood, "doctor" is probably a poor career choice for you.

Your brain is easily swayed by what sounds good. This is not because you are shallow. We are social beings, hardwired to crave the respect and support of the community so that we won't be abandoned (metaphorically or otherwise) on a hilltop. As long as we live in a society where "doctor" sounds impressive, it will be hard to break with the pack and start a business selling cupcakes.

Perhaps in the future we'll all have portable MRI machines that we can take with us to restaurants and other places where we need to make hard decisions. The noninvasive snapshot of brain activity from the scan would be a real time-saver, because it would show that it takes only a second (or less) to arrive at certain decisions. You could capture the first pinpoint of your desire—a single cell lighting up—

and from there print out a report, attach a cover sheet, and fax it to yourself . . . all before your conscious mind had an inkling that it was about to order the veal parmigiana. But until that time, we have to rely on our own instincts.

There are many times where you're feeling stuck about what to buy or wear or eat, when in reality your body has already registered your decision with quiet certainty and is waiting for you to tune in. This happens with career choices, too. Are you catching the signals your body is sending? And will you act on those messages, even if they're contrary to the outcome you anticipated? *To resolve this conflict, listen to your body's signals and be willing to use the data to adjust the details of your reinvention plan.*

Sometimes you get lucky, like Christina. Your body takes the wheel and saves you from making a wrong turn into the river. Other times you struggle, like I did, until your body finally wins out. But if you are inclined to completely ignore your body's unmistakable signals, you could end up like Max, a participant in one of my Reinvention BootCamps. Max was a successful pharmaceutical sales rep who had taken top awards for several years running. But he was burnt out from nearly twenty years of this, and his body was sending clear signals: He had so much less energy at work that his sales were slipping. He had headaches that abated only on weekends. As the end of the month approached, when his quota reports were due, his heartburn would flare up.

By contrast, Max exhibited no such physical symptoms of distress when he volunteered at the local soccer league, as he had done for years. Whenever he spent time with the league, he bubbled over with ideas for how they could increase ticket sales and attract community sponsors. The thought of spending even more time helping them boosted his energy. Secretly, what he was really hankering for was to start a youth soccer camp, but every time he considered making a move, his brain was flooded with such intellectual rationalizations as "Pharma is prestigious, I can't leave it"; "I know I'm unhappy, but I can make this work"; "I've been in pharma for so many years I might as well stick it out." These messages shouting in his brain drowned out the ones from his body.

By the time Max left BootCamp, he was determined to stay in

touch with his body's signals so he could venture out on the path he knew was right for him. But when I checked in on him a few months later, his intellect was once again firmly in control. Max had decided to "wait and see" how things would go with his career in pharma, thinking that maybe the situation would turn around and he'd find ways to love his job again.

Two years later, I heard from one of Max's fellow BootCampers that he'd been laid off and regretted having endured additional years of stress and misery when, in the end, his intellectual gamble didn't pay off.

LIVING THE LAW: LISTENING TO YOUR BODY

As you reinvent your career, you will be choosing among a number of options and opportunities. How will you be able to tell which ones have the potential to be "the one"? You start by tuning in to your "inner voice," the one that always tells the truth about how you feel. Look for signals such as:

1. **A Feeling of Relaxation.** Are your shoulders dropped? Is your jaw unclenched, your stomach calm?

2. **Having More Energy.** Is your adrenaline flowing? Does it make you want to hop up and get started right away?

3. **Smiling.** Does the mere thought of one particular option bring a smile to your lips?

4. **A Feeling of Openness.** Does your chest feel more open? Do you find it easier to breathe?

5. **A Sense of Peace.** Does your body quiet down? Can you feel it deeply within?

Another unmistakable signal your body will send is a feeling of passion. Christina's love for the City of Lights was ardent, ranging from feverish desire to a feeling of walking on air. If she hadn't been in the habit of listening to her body, she might have mistaken this fever of passion for a head cold.

In the era of the Reinventor, you must be willing to listen to the signals your gut gives you and *take action on them.* Your body's signals will try to get your attention, but you have to be honest with yourself. Don't brush off your instincts as minor irritants. Pay attention to the little red flags that pop up in the form of uneasiness and discomfort. Be willing to abandon the path you are on if it just doesn't feel right, no matter what your mind tries to argue.

Intellectually, Christina's new contract at the TV station made sense. Signing it would have been financially prudent. But Christina's body was sending a drumbeat of distress at the thought of being pigeonholed or feeling obligated ("I owe it to them to hurry back to work"). Her Paris sojourn led her to realize that she wanted a calmer lifestyle, causing her to take a different career path upon her return. Instead of automatically going back to television, she ended up at the Houston Partnership with a public relations position that was better suited for an ex–adrenaline junkie like Christina who desired a quieter life. What she learned—and what you as a Reinventor also must learn—is that what sounds sensible and prudent in the moment can still get in the way of future change. Understanding this, and acting on it, is what reinvention is all about.

What happens when your intellect insists on overriding your body's signals and you start down the wrong path? Don't worry. Your body won't leave you stranded there. Instead, it will send increasingly unpleasant signals in an effort to grab your attention. When you think about a particular reinvention path, watch out if you find yourself barraged by the following symptoms:

- Headaches

- Upset stomach

- Tightness in the throat or chest

- Clenched jaw or gritted teeth; jaw pain in the morning from grinding at night

- Tensed shoulders

- Lack of energy

- Interrupted sleep

- Furrowed brow

In the interests of medical safety, I have to insist that if you are indeed experiencing any of these symptoms, you visit a doctor to rule out an underlying medical condition. You need to be sure whether that stomachache is a rare tropical disease or a cry for TLC. If you're in good health but you chug Pepto-Bismol every time you think about becoming a late-in-life astronaut, your body is probably trying to offer you a piece of advice.

Here's an experiment: Turn your mind for a moment to Brussels sprouts, a vegetable that seems to divide people as no other food can. Some people hate them; some love them. No one is neutral on Brussels sprouts. Now, when you think about a nice, big bowl of steamed Brussels sprouts, do your eyes shine in anticipation? Does your mouth water? Or are you filled with a sense of dread and a pro-testing rumble in your stomach?

Your body won't lie to you. It simply cannot pretend to like something it hates, whereas your brain can do that with ease. "Yum, my favorite!" your brain instructs you to say so that you don't offend your host.

At this early point in your reinvention, you are still gathering data by tuning in to your body. You will use this skill at every step in your reinvention, from choosing a target (Law 4) to deciding how to launch your strategy (Law 6) to adjusting your plans to keep the momentum flowing (Law 9). Start by recording five simple decisions you made today, such as what to eat for breakfast, when to read your e-mail, or what to do after work. Recall what your intellectual side had to say about each of these decisions, and compare that with what your "gut instinct" told you. Notice which "side" you tend to gravitate toward. [4] As patterns emerge, you will be able to see what turns you on or off, as well as how much input you allow your body to have in your daily decision-making.

[4]Exercise on Page 225: Body Tune in Practice

Once you are able to listen to your body's signals, they will point you unerringly toward where you want to go—and away from where you *don't* want to go. You will see that your authentic voice is there, inside, whenever you are ready to hear it.

The Takeaway: Your body is a more reliable indicator than your intellect of what you truly want or don't want.

Watch Out for . . . Your intellect shouting down or drowning out your body's messages.

Putting the Law into Action: Pick an area of your life—work, nutrition, friendships—and practice tuning in to your body's signals when making decisions in those realms.

Something to Think About: What is my body telling me that I'm afraid to hear?

LAW 3

PROGRESS BEGINS WHEN YOU STOP MAKING EXCUSES

And the day came when the risk to remain tight in a bud was more painful than the risk it took to blossom.

—Anaïs Nin

Jeffery Rudell was born in 1963 into a flat world. The whole state of Michigan never rises more than 1,060 feet above sea level—and certainly not in Lawrence, a flat little town known mostly for its annual ox roast. "It was poor, rural, economically depressed, undereducated, and conservative," says Jeffery. You don't know how flat life can feel until you've gotten up at 4 A.M. to milk cows on a farm off Red Arrow Highway, a road pointing nowhere.

At age fourteen, Jeffery was already six feet tall, still six inches shy of his adult height. Everyone assumed he'd go out for basketball, but Jeffery was unusually clumsy, the result of childhood amblyopia, which can happen when there is not enough stimulation from the visual part of the brain. "I'm essentially blind in one eye," says Jeffery. "I was miserable at basketball, hurdles, and all those things that require distance judging. Everything is flat. I live in a flat world."

Jeffery added dimension to his life by telling stories and making things. One of his earliest memories is of wanting a typewriter from the Sears Wishbook so badly that he made one for himself out of an egg carton and put it under the Christmas tree. It was one of the rare times that Jeffery knew exactly what he wanted and didn't let any excuse stand in the way of getting it.

I I I I

Jeffery's first career ambition, at age five, was to be Santa Claus. He and the elves could hang out in the workshop making stuff all day. At worst, he could be a journalist. But his dad had other plans. "My father pulled me aside and said that he had talked to Joe Blow at the local CITGO station and arranged for me to be taken on as a part-time night manager," says Jeffery.

"If you work hard," his dad told him, "in ten years or so you can work up to full night manager."

"I remember thinking that I would have to kill myself," says Jeffery. "I would have to find a way to step in front of traffic or hang myself."

The idea of college didn't occur to him until an aunt brought it up. With financial aid and part-time work waiting tables, he went to Michigan State, but two things happened in quick succession that would change the course of Jeffery's life: He failed math, which infuriated his parents, and he fell in love.

With a guy.

Jeffery had suspected for years that he was gay. Now that he was in love, he was so uncharacteristically buoyant that his mother was suspicious.

"Nothing is wrong," he said. "I'm happy!"

"You're not a happy person," she said.

"Yes, I am."

"No, you're not. You're not happy. You don't have any friends."

Jeffery drove home to straighten everything out. Despite their failings, his parents had raised him with strong values—love, forgiveness, the whole nine yards—so he thought if he leveled with them and told them he was gay, this too would pass.

It didn't.

His mother pronounced him dead and cleaned out the joint account that held Jeffery's tuition money. His parents wouldn't speak to him again for ten years, and very few times thereafter until they died. His mother went around the house collecting everything Jeffery had owned, made, written, read, or loved, and gathered it into a bonfire that burned for more than seven hours. A spark escaped and took down a majestic sugar maple, too.

❘ ❘ ❘ ❘

School was off the table; of this, Jeffery was certain. "I failed one class. I come from an economically and academically poor part of the state. There's no chance. I'm not good enough." He bought into those excuses too well to explore the subject further.

"Now that I look back, there might have been a way," concedes Jeffery. "Coming from an impoverished part of the state, I probably could have gone to a four-year college on full scholarship."

While waiting tables at a restaurant known for lively exchanges between staff and patrons, he dumped a bowl of soup in the lap of an obnoxious diner. The man turned out to be a state legislator in need of someone with moxie to manage his upcoming campaign.

"I've done a lot of campaigns," said Jeffery smoothly. The next day, he went to the library and checked out a book on how to run political campaigns. Two days later, he had the job.

As a legislative aide, Jeffery became so well known as a "fixer"— give him a problem and he'll solve it—that he was either recommended for jobs or seemed to fall into them. At twenty-eight, the former farm boy who had been allergic to the hay he baled moved into a world of mansions and chauffeured Bentleys as chief of staff for a mercurial billionaire Kuwaiti diplomat in New York City. After that, he worked for a cantankerous fixture of Manhattan's society and fund-raising circles. His next job was with the New York office of the American Academy in Rome, which awards prizes to artists and scholars. After six years with the Academy, its president, Adele Chatfield-Taylor, sat him down and asked what he wanted to do with his life.

"I see myself in five years really taking more of a leadership role here at the Academy," said Jeffery.

"This place doesn't offer that," said Adele. "I think that you need to make some decisions in your life."

Jeffery had never taken the reins of his career because he assumed that he lacked all the things he needed to get anywhere. Spurred on (and somewhat hurt) by Adele's words, he interviewed with an investment-banking firm in Lower Manhattan.

"Where do you see yourself in five years?" one of the partners asked over a dinner at which Jeffery assumed he'd be offered the job.

"I see myself as an integral part of your organization by then, having been through the orientation and gotten up to speed," said Jeffery.

There was an awkward pause. "That's not going to happen," said the partner. "We like you, but you're not corporate material. You're too independent-minded. Have you thought about working for yourself? Do you have a business plan?"

Jeffrey trotted out his fallback excuse. "I don't have two nickels to rub together," he said indignantly.

"Well," said the partner, "you'll never get anywhere without a plan."

After the meal, Jeffery went over to Barnes & Noble and picked up a copy of *Business Plans for Dummies*.

▌ ▎ ▍ ▊

Jeffery needed $74,000. He took his new business plan back to the banker who had shot him down and offered the guy first crack at investing in Jeffery's proposed design firm.

"Do you have a degree in design?" asked the partner.

"No," said Jeffery.

"Are you good at it?"

"We'll see."

"How will you pay me back?"

Jeffery suggested that the partners give his new company as a "donation" to their favorite charities. The charities would get free graphic design. The investors would get tangible results and a tax write-off. Jeffery would get his start-up capital. As it turned out, he got more than that—the charities liked his work and hired him independently. It was 1999, and business was good.

Then it was 9/11, and business was not so good. "I was depressed and felt worthless," recalls Jeffery. "I didn't know what had changed. I assumed it was the world around me because I was still the same, doing the same thing."

It was time to give up the excuses and start stepping up his game.

▮ ▮ ▮ ▮

Jeffery wasn't the easiest client The Reinvention Institute has ever had. He stubbornly refused to see how the creativity and problem solving he had used as a "fixer"—along with the wealth of experience and connections he had amassed—was just as valuable as the college degree whose absence he bemoaned. He was thoroughly invested in the idea that his lack of money, education, and loving parents made him unworthy enough that no one would ever pay him well for his "collection of random skills" or his art. Jeffery needed to learn to value himself. This was the real impediment to his success and happiness, and it wasn't going to change until he gave up his litany of excuses.

It takes a lot for a client to get under my skin, but Jeffery managed. I remember saying something uncharacteristically curt on the phone to him. He remembers it, too.

"What was the turning point for you?" I asked him recently.

"Some nasty thing you said. You got very short with me once after I'd been very short with you for the course of an hour. You said, 'How's that working for you? Good luck with that.' It was like you were saying the time for talking has passed," says Jeffery. "Then I hung up and cried. I was very angry at me, you, and the world."

Gradually, Jeffery weaned himself off the excuses, and that's when everything began to turn around. After a lifetime saying he was going to write, he sat down and wrote. He performs frequently at The Moth, a nonprofit storytelling organization, where he turns tales of his boyhood—like the one about the newborn calf loose in the house—into funny, poignant theater. After so many years of wandering in the world without a home, he now owns a house on the beach where he can see the ocean while he creates the most extraordinary things.

Today, Jeffery Rudell is a paper artist. The typewriter he once made from an egg carton was an early clue to his talent. From paper, he can make a snowstorm. A dodecahedron. A Baroque headdress. He makes a "valentine" so heartbreaking you could weep—and not just because it is made from the skin of an onion. Jeffery gets fan mail from other crafters and paper artists who follow him religiously on his blog; one post reads in its entirety: "Will you marry me?"

He is also a designer and business consultant. But for someone whose vision failed him because of a childhood condition and who claims to live in a flat world, Jeffery creates reams of beauty in three dimensions from the plainest and flattest of objects.

"My skills didn't change between last year and this year," he says. "I just started doing it instead of talking about it, wanting it, and wishing for it."

No more excuses.

THE LESSON BEHIND THE LAW: EXCUSES BLOCK YOUR REINVENTION

People come up with all sorts of excuses to avoid the effort and risk of reinvention. They're only acting in their best interests—or what they *think* are their best interests—because reinvention is all about change, and excuses give you an out so you can avoid or delay the pain of change. Your conscious, rational mind understands that reinvention is merely a strategy for managing your career, but your subconscious experiences it as a leap off a cliff without a bungee cord.

Excuses can get so elaborate and creative that it may seem there are a million of them. But psychologist Barry Schlenker's "triangle model" boils them down to three types: denying personal obligation, denying personal control, and denying "prescription clarity" (you didn't understand the instructions so you assumed they didn't apply to you). Here is how these three categories of excuse play out in career reinvention:

"It's not my job." Like the classic joke about the one waiter in a small restaurant who insists, "It's not my table," this is where you construct excuses that deny your responsibility in the situation. I speak frequently to groups in industries that are going through rapid change, and the version I often hear is: "My company hasn't created any new opportunities for me." Or "My company won't reimburse me for training in the new technology." When you fall prey to this excuse, you put the obligation for your reinvention onto someone else.

"It's out of my hands." This is where you lay all the blame on your circumstances, just as Jeffery did; e.g., lack of funds, not having the right connections or a college degree. But the truth is that career reinvention *is* in your hands—you can always find a way to overcome a situation. Even Jeffery later had to admit that he probably could have gotten a scholarship if he had thought to look into that possibility at the time. Instead, he had told himself that college was off the table because he'd failed one class and came from an economically disadvantaged background. He didn't bother to think of ways to continue his schooling because he believed he had no control.

"I don't know enough." Here you blame your inertia on a lack of sufficient knowledge. Perhaps you think others have not given you all the information you need, and you can't do a thing until they come through: "I waited for them to call me back. I didn't know I was supposed to call them." In this case, you use not understanding as an excuse for not moving forward.

All three types of excuses imply that you'd be perfectly willing to take action *if only these things weren't stopping you.* However, if you look closely, you'll see that nothing is stopping you but your assumption that you cannot proceed.

If there's one industry that's rapidly being forced into a reinvention, it's media—particularly newspapers and publishing. The Internet has upended their circulation and advertising models, and the industry is scrambling to adapt. And if the industry is scrambling, so are the people in it.

I was in Chicago recently to give a talk to a group of media executives at Northwestern University. It was a room full of shell-shocked people who had given from ten to twenty-five years of their lives to an industry that was collapsing before their eyes. On the whole, journalists are a tough, smart bunch. They are used to finding a way to get the story even when obstacles seem insurmountable. But when it came to their own reinvention, all of a sudden they were blocked, with no hope of progress. They came up with one reason after another—some of them quite persuasive—for why they simply could not do this or that thing, or why their lives could not possibly change.

I decided to ask each one to name the number-one reason why their reinvention was impossible. Out came the litany of excuses:

> *"I started working at the paper right out of high school so I never got a college degree."*

> *"My schedule is jam-packed so I can't carve out the time to investigate a new path."*

> *"I don't have any mentors who can guide me."*

> *"I've always wanted to do [insert long-held dream here], but I don't know how."*

> *"I don't have enough money to [insert action step that would take them closer to their dream]."*

On it went, until all sixty had spoken. When finally the room was quiet, I asked them another question:

"Of all the excuses you have heard this morning, was there *one* that could not be overcome?"

I had to squint as I looked around the room. The flash of sixty lightbulbs going off at once was blinding.

Excuses = Fear

It's simple, really. *Excuses are a manifestation of fear.* There are few guarantees in your reinvention journey, but this I promise you: You will come face-to-face on a regular basis with fear. In fact, of all the emotions you'll likely experience throughout reinvention—excitement, sadness, annoyance—fear will be your steady companion.

Fear is a healthy sign that you are venturing beyond your comfort zone, which you must do repeatedly if you want to move closer to your goal. You might think that a necessary requirement of reinvention is that you "get over" your fears. *This is not possible.* Fear is a biochemical reaction that is necessary for ensuring the survival of the species. Even if you wanted to get rid of all traces of fear, humans are hardwired for it—and you should be grateful for it. Thanks to fear, your forebears ran for their lives whenever a saber-toothed tiger came around, and the human race did not go extinct before you made it onto the scene.

In modern times, fear does a decent job of keeping us safe and creating boundaries—without which too many people would go around looting and running wild. (This is also known as "a conscience"; those who don't have it are called "sociopaths.") It's also true that fear is a Stone Age instinct that has not kept up well with the times. Fear is not very sophisticated when it comes to distinguishing between a saber-toothed tiger and a job interview. Either situation—one life-threatening, the other life-enhancing—can cause the same sweaty palms and urge to flee.

Fear is necessary. It is here to stay. However, it is prone to setting off false alarms, where you freeze up in the face of the good stuff or for no reason at all. These false alarms create and contribute to unnecessary panic during reinvention. That's why you have to learn to *manage* your fears, not *master* them. The key is to be able to tell the difference between functional fears (the ones that keep you from walking into traffic) and false fears (the ones that keep you from walking into the office of a hiring manager).

Here are a few examples:

FUNCTIONAL FEAR	FALSE FEAR
I have $5 in my bank account, so I have to focus on earning money today so I won't run out.	I have twelve months' expenses in my bank account, so I have to focus on earning money today so I won't run out.
They're reporting heavy traffic today, so I'd better start out early for my interview.	What if I'm late for my interview next week?
This job description says there's a lot of heavy spreadsheet work, and I hate working with numbers.	If I get another job I might have to work with numbers, and I hate working with numbers.
I got a pink slip today and I don't have my reinvention plan in place.	I don't have my reinvention plan in place because I am worried it won't work out.

Functional fears are a response to a situation that exists today and that requires you to take action in the moment to forestall a negative outcome. False fears are when your mind goes to potential negative outcomes that may or may not happen in the distant future. Many of your fears can be put into perspective simply by asking yourself whether you are in actual danger this very moment. (Hint: If you have time to ponder this, then the answer is usually no.)

Most reinvention fears break down to a number of anxious what-ifs. *What if everything fails? What if I'm making the worst decision of my life?* Go ahead and imagine the worst that could happen. If "everything fails," will you be able to deal with it? Are there really no alternatives? Will your life come to an end? Reinvention is a process of change, but it won't kill you. Maybe someone will say no to you. Maybe a meeting will end in discouragement instead of elation. Maybe you'll find a particular path isn't for you and you'll have to switch course and try another one. So far, you're still breathing.

Moving Through Fear

Reinvention does not require you to get over your fears, only that you be willing to take action *in spite of them.* We all know someone who has been complaining since forever that he coulda, woulda, shoulda been the next Bill Gates. But Bill Gates is the one who actually sat down in front of a computer and began learning to program it. If you're waiting to get started on your reinvention until you're finished slaying all your dragons, forget it. You won't make progress on your career reinvention unless you are willing to give up the excuses and take action in spite of fear. As the Chinese proverb says: *Talk doesn't cook rice.*

To reduce your fears enough to get moving, here are some of the techniques we teach at The Reinvention Institute:

Find a shoulder to lean on: Share your fears with supportive people in your life (friends, therapists, coaches) who can serve as a sounding board.

Distract yourself: If you've ever engaged a child in a sing-along to divert attention from the doctor with the needle, you know this technique works: Redirect your focus to another absorbing activity.

Your brain cannot handle major competing claims for its attention, so the more you distract yourself, the more the fear subsides.

Take a walk down Memory Lane: Survey your past and make a list of the times you managed to succeed in the face of fear and doubt. This will reassure you and remind you that even when taking action seems daunting, survival is all but guaranteed.

Identify the real culprit: Go deeper into your fear and identify the core value you feel is being threatened. Is it your sense of safety? Is it your sense of identity? Once you've gotten beneath the superficial layers, you can objectively analyze how to address the situation. For example, if your sense of security feels threatened because you fear you will run out of cash during your reinvention process, review your budget and contingency plans to see whether this fear has a solid foundation.

Look for role models: Doubtless you are very special, one of a kind. But you are not unique in your fears. Other people have faced and overcome the very same ones. Seek out such people; they can serve as inspirational role models and provide tactical information on how they managed.

Talk back to your fear: Politely acknowledging your fear while insisting that it step aside is a way of asserting yourself over it: "Thanks, but no thanks."

Feel the fear and do it anyway: Like the slogan says.

HIDDEN CONFLICT THAT COULD STOP YOU: ALLOWING YOUR EXCUSES TO BECOME SELF-FULFILLING PROPHECIES

Being mired in fear to the extent that you continually make excuses carries a penalty far worse than simply falling behind in your reinvention timetable. Excuse making is actually habit-forming. Studies show that excuses become a crutch that you teach yourself to reach for until it's second nature—in *all* aspects of your life, not just reinvention.

Excuses feel as comfortable as an old blanket. And like a blanket, they can smother the life out of your life. This is what happened to my friend Samantha. We first met years ago when we were both students at the local high school, dreaming of leaving Milwaukee to make our mark in the world. Sam was a talented artist who planned to show her work internationally. She received school-wide accolades and won several local art competitions.

Deep in her heart, Sam didn't believe she was worthy of making it in the big leagues. She occasionally confided that she was scared, but more often she made excuses. When it came time for us to graduate, she said she didn't have the money to go to art school. I loaned her a book I had on how to get scholarships, but she was always too busy to read it. After I moved away, Sam and I lost touch.

At our ten-year high school reunion, I ran into Sam. She'd held a series of jobs, mostly in factories, but told me she was still doing her art on the side. I encouraged her to send samples of her work to a gallery in our hometown, and I put her in touch with a contact I had there.

Several weeks later, Sam called, excited. They wanted to see more of her work! There was just one problem: They wanted slides. Naturally, I told her to go have some made.

"I don't have the money," she said.

"Well, how much does it cost?" I asked.

She didn't know, but she was sure it was "a lot." I asked her how few slides she could get away with; she didn't know, but she probably didn't have "enough" samples of her art to make the cut.

On it went, in an endless loop. By the time I hung up the phone, I was exhausted.

Some years later, I ran into a mutual friend who told me that Sam was still working at a factory and talking about how she had just as much talent as the big-name artists, but she just couldn't get a break.

Like Sam, you can let your excuse-making habit become so ingrained that it's your fallback response to every fear. It's who you are. Over time, you'll feel less empowered to create a different outcome, which in turn diminishes the likelihood of success in future life endeavors. It's a self-fulfilling prophecy.

To overcome this conflict, you must give up your cycle of excuses. You can always find ways to change your situation, get more information, or take the initiative. You have the power to transform circumstances once you take responsibility for doing so—just as Jeffery realized when he finally set aside his excuses and made it his job to learn how to write a business plan and seek funding for it.

LIVING THE LAW: LETTING GO OF EXCUSES

What are *your* reasons for why you're stuck or unhappy, or unable to change or make progress in your reinvention?☐[5] Certainly there are times when an excuse is legitimate—"The hurricane prevented me from hanging out the wash"—but for the most part, excuses aren't the rational explanations you think they are. To be a Reinventor and thrive in this challenging new world, you have to want to reach your reinvention goal more than you want to hold on to your excuses.

In addition to working through your fears using the tactics mentioned earlier—such as sharing them with a supportive person or reminding yourself of previous fears you've successfully overcome—you must do the following:

1. **Give up complaining.** Complaining is excuse-making in an angry mode. It is victim behavior, another way of avoiding responsibility—"denying personal control," according to Schlenker's triangle model. Complaining creates a downward spiral that draws energy and attention away from the options at hand. When you give up complaining, you admit that you always have a choice—even though some choices involve difficult decisions and significant effort. The moment you give up complaining, your future is transformed. Jeffery's childhood was devoid of rich educational opportunities and financial abundance, and that could not be changed. But when he embarked on his reinvention, he realized that, as an adult, he could choose to stop complaining about things that were long past and to take responsibility for creating financial abundance and educational opportunities in his life right now.

---

[5]Exercise on Page 229: Make a List of Your Excuses

2. **Make a commitment.** At The Reinvention Institute, we define "commitment" as taking action, even when you don't want to. It's not enough to say you're committed to reinventing your career. It's all in the *doing*. A client of mine—Sylvia—had been a marketer at a major consumer packaged-goods company but wanted to position herself as an independent branding expert. On the form I have every new client fill out, she ranked herself a "10," on a scale of 1 to 10, in terms of her level of commitment to reinvention, but I subsequently discovered that she hadn't followed up on my coaching request that she set up a meeting with a well-known speaking agent who had expressed interest in her. Not only that, she said she often didn't follow up on opportunities. Some of her excuses: *I'm swamped. I have nothing prepared. I need to finish this other project first. I'm not feeling confident. I don't have enough information. If I take the meeting before I'm ready, I'll blow it, and I'll never find another agent of that caliber. I won't have the time or resources to follow up on the meeting. I'm scared.* I've heard it all, and more. I told Sylvia that if she wouldn't put in the effort to stretch beyond her comfort zone, then coaching would be a waste of her money and my time. Shocked by my response, Sylvia began to take meetings, even when she hated them. "I was scared straight," she told me. She realized that if she wanted a successful business, she would have to follow through on her commitment to make it happen.

3. **Match your actions to your words.** In the previous example, Sylvia learned that her actions didn't match the "10" she gave herself for commitment. To give up your excuses, you have to realize you're making them! The way to do that is to examine your actions in light of what you claim you want. Ask yourself the following: What does my mouth say I want? And when I shut my mouth, what do my actions say I want? █[6] You may be surprised by the disconnect between what you say and what you do.

4. **Step up your game.** You've got to want better results. Jeffery finally buckled down to creating a business plan, but that wasn't

[6]Exercise on Page 230: Match Your Actions to Your Words

enough. His initial vision for his company didn't include a strategy for using his artistic talent with paper creations—and this was the real problem behind Jeffery's feeling of being stuck. He wasn't using enough of his many talents. When Jeffery came to The Reinvention Institute, he was working at things he was good at, but he wasn't working at the things he most loved. Only when he learned to value himself could he appreciate what was unique about him, and that meant his art had value, too. Now he was willing to step up his game and seek ways to monetize his creative output. Today Jeffery is a high-priced consultant. Craft and paper manufacturers seek him out to help with product development, and he has a multi-book deal with Sterling Publishing for do-it-yourself craft and paper constructions books.

Many people never muster the courage to begin a career reinvention, so deep is their terror. They continually reach for the bottle of excuses to dull the pain of their fear. But until you master this Law and break yourself of the excuse habit, progress will be intermittent, and lasting change will be elusive. The moment you move past your fear and give up your excuses, you leave the shallows of your life and swim into an ocean of opportunity.

The Takeaway: Making excuses is a habit motivated by fear, allowing you to avoid or delay the pain of change. To manage your fears and take action in spite of them, you must give up your excuses.

Watch Out for . . . Believing your excuses so deeply that they become a stumbling block to your progress.

Putting the Law into Action: Pursue three options for getting around your biggest excuse.

Something to Think About: What would your life look like if you gave up all your excuses?

LAW 4

WHAT YOU SEEK IS ON THE ROAD LESS TRAVELED

People cannot discover new lands until they have the courage to lose sight of the shore.

—André Gide

During a break in a "sustainable seafood" event he was hosting at the Smithsonian, Alton Brown decided to take his wife and daughter to see a certain exhibit. In 2001 Julia Child, the former "French Chef" whose groundbreaking cooking show paved the way for everything you see on The Food Network today, had donated her entire kitchen to the museum. It was trucked down to Washington, D.C., piece by piece from Massachusetts, and meticulously reconstructed down to the smallest chestnut cutter, lamb bone holder, oyster opener, and butter curler. It was all just as it looked in 1961.

You would think that for Alton this would be a religious pilgrimage, a chance to worship at the shrine of tele-cuisine. Alton is the star of the innovative Food Network show *Good Eats*. He has written five books about food. He has ridden cross-country on a motorcycle to search out the best meals. But instead of a spiritual epiphany, Alton experienced something akin to eating a bad clam.

"Oh my God, look at all the junk!" Alton said. "This lady owned everything! Every unitasker in the joint! See those fifteen things? I would use one screwdriver for all of those jobs!"

Alton is the human equivalent of the kitchen multitasker. He wears so many hats on his show, no wonder his shocks of blond hair often stick out at weird angles like a crazy professor in the midst of an electricity experiment gone wrong. He is so hands-on with the scripts, the props, even the colors of paint on the walls of his vast Atlanta TV studio set, you wonder how he has time to actually cook any food. His hero is TV secret agent MacGyver, who solved a multitude of problems by working miracles with his ever-present Swiss Army Knife.

To reach this hectic place in his life, though, Alton had to slow to a dead stop. "If you have done any sailing or spent any time out on the water, sometimes at night you have to close your eyes and listen to where the foghorn is coming from." Sometimes you have to get very still to see the beam of the beacon in the distance, guiding you through uncharted waters.

I I I I

Alton's parents were from rural Georgia, and their families couldn't have been less alike. On his father's side, the message was clear: The road less traveled was strictly off-limits. Unless you were a white-collar professional, you weren't even on their radar. "That's why my dad, up until the day he died, didn't feel he was successful," says Alton. "Even though he ran a newspaper, a radio station, and several printing operations, since he wasn't a doctor or lawyer and didn't run a bank, his family didn't feel that he was a success."

His mother's side had a different perspective. Over in the town of Cornelia, Alton's grandparents were "merchant-class, self-made people from families that were dirt-poor, Appalachian itinerant farmer types." His grandmother had worked in a clothing mill and went on to own a dress shop, Flair for Fashions. His grandfather had a stroke of genius after World War II when he predicted, "One day there'll be Volkswagens in America." He ran a car repair shop where, for years, he was the only mechanic in Georgia who could service a Volkswagen.

"On that side of the family, I came from a long line of innovators," says Alton, shedding some light on the origins of his maverick gene. His great-grandfather on his mom's side had been a farmer in north Georgia, who got it in his head to build a power plant. He built one of north Georgia's first dammed power plants on his property.

Alton was born in Los Angeles in 1962. He was named for his father, Alton Crawford Brown, an account executive for NBC who was a mix of dreamer and tech geek. When Alton was seven, his father bought radio station WRWH in White County, Georgia, and packed up the family in a Chrysler Sedan to move back east. In 1970, he sold the station and bought the *White County News*. From that bully pulpit he spent the next three years haranguing local politicians, railing against pollution and polluters, publishing photos of roadsides blighted by trash, editorializing against front-yard collections of junked cars and in favor of an actual landfill.

The death of Alton's father, at age thirty-nine, was ruled a suicide. But because of how he stirred things up on environmental issues, not everyone is buying it. Alton, for one, says his father was "murdered."

The next few years were exquisitely painful for Alton. His position in the family changed. His mother remarried, so there were a stepfather and stepsiblings to deal with. For a while he was farmed out to live with his maternal grandparents. He was bullied at school. No one took him seriously. "If anybody recognized anything, it was a general dullness. They would always say, 'Alton's not living up to his capabilities.' I was a classic underachiever."

His mother and stepfather sent him to college to study business. Big mistake. After a brief, miserable stint as a business student at LaGrange College, he transferred to the University of Georgia to study filmmaking, delivering pizzas to pay his expenses and using the cooking skills he'd inherited from his grandmother and his mother to spice up his dating life. After graduation he started working as a cameraman, and spent the next decade working as a cinematographer and video director. He shot and directed commercials. He made a music video for R.E.M. and spent his spare time watching cooking shows on TV.

Alton experienced a lot of frustration and failure in his first career. "I got to a point where I was extremely unhappy," he says. "I wasn't very good at what I did because I wasn't very good at politics. In advertising filmmaking, politics is extremely important, and I don't put up with that kind of crap very easily."

By 1993, he was at a crossroads. Happily married to film production manager DeAnna Collins, Alton nonetheless felt lost. He needed a new career, and he needed the strength to create one for himself. "I was going through a spiritual evolution," he says, "actually believing that God can make anything for good if you shut up, listen, and just do what He says. You have to be still enough to figure out what that is."

For the next six months Alton turned his engines off. He went to work every day but saw no one and talked with no one other than his wife, "trying to keep the radio frequency open for what I might receive." During that time he asked himself hard questions: "What have I learned about myself? What am I good at, and what am I not good at? What can I live with, and what can I not live without?"

For years Alton had been talking to his wife about making what he called "a food show for our generation," but the distance between his experience and his aspiration was daunting. Filmmaking skills? Check. Did he have food-show-producing skills or professional-level culinary skills? Not so much.

Being what Alton calls "good Southern Christians," he and DeAnna consulted a higher power to discover what it was they were meant to do. In the end, it was DeAnna who delivered the message: Go to culinary school and get the education you need to create the food show you've been talking about forever. And then she proposed a deal: If you get accepted, I'll do whatever it takes to make it possible. Alton took DeAnna's offer as a sign from God.

I I I I

Alton applied to three top schools and was accepted by all of them. Despite DeAnna's aversion to cold weather, they decided together that his best choice was the New England Culinary Institute in beyond-chilly Montpelier, Vermont.

As he readied himself to embark on his next quest, siren voices were calling him to turn back to ostensibly safer shores. "My career was never viewed by anyone in my family as a real job," he says. "When I decided to go off to culinary school, they said, 'You're crazy. You're not going to be able to support your family.' They said I'd be on welfare."

"Luckily," he adds, "I had a wife who was also in the film production industry and was supportive of making a significant course alteration."

And so, like his father before him—and despite the warnings from everyone in his life except DeAnna—Alton packed up his wife, his hopes, and his dreams and moved across the country to start a new life.

The reality proved harsher than the fantasy. "Once I got to culinary school and found myself at two A.M. sweeping floors, there were plenty of times when I asked God, 'What have I done? What exactly is this you want me to do? Sweep floors? Are you sure?'"

DeAnna got a job in the Culinary Institute's marketing department, and the couple lived on her modest salary. They never had enough time or enough money, Alton says, but, "in the end, we didn't give up anything that mattered. What would have mattered is giving up a great possibility. The opposite of fear is faith."

I I I I

Alton graduated from the Culinary Institute in 1997, and he and DeAnna returned to Atlanta, ready to get to work on his ultimate dream: a cooking show that he himself would want to watch. Alton wrote two sample scripts, "Steak Your Claim" and "This Spud's for You," for a new food show he called *Good Eats*. Friends in the Atlanta film production community helped them raise the money to shoot the pilots.

Throughout 1998 he and DeAnna tried without success to sell the show. To pay the rent Alton taught cooking classes—most of them poorly attended—and DeAnna took what Alton calls "a soul-stealing job" in marketing at Coca-Cola. Then, the miracle they'd been waiting for: a Food Network executive happened to see the pilots and called Alton in for a meeting. "We'll write a check to cover the first two episodes," he told Alton. "But you have to be the host of the show."

Alton realized that the network was trying to save money on a host, but that didn't change his reaction. He knew what he didn't want. He didn't want to be in front of the camera.

Behind the camera was where the fun was. In his years as a videographer, he loved to write, produce, make decisions.

"I said, 'No. That's insane. I can't do that.' I got halfway down the hall to the elevators and thought, "'Wait. What did I just do? Whoa! I do have a theater degree, after all.'"

He walked back into the office and said he'd host the show. It was time to start down a new road.

I I I I

Today Alton's career path is more like an eight-lane highway. The self-described "underachiever" has evolved from cinematographer to culinary expert to writer, director, and host of *Good Eats*—one of the Food Network's top-ranked shows for the past ten years—and *Feasting on Asphalt*. A lifelong film buff, he incorporates his love of movies, and his love of a good laugh, with episode names like "Pork Fiction" and "Citizen Cane."

In what passes for his spare time, Alton is also the commentator on the zealously dramatic cooking-show competition *Iron Chef America*, and, in partnership with Shun Cutlery, the designer of Alton's Angles, a line of knives with a knuckle-sparing angle to their handles. The naysayers who predicted that Alton's choices would lead him to the welfare rolls still have some waiting to do. Along with the proceeds of his TV work, cookbooks, and his line of knives, Alton commands princely sums for his speaking engagements, corporate events, and endorsements.

Just because Alton's life is in such a great place, the inveterate trailblazer has no plans to stand still. "I never pursue one thing at a time," Alton concludes, stating the way-obvious. "I don't even know what I'm going to do when I grow up. I'm not there yet."

It was Yogi Berra who famously declared, "When you see a fork in the road, take it." This much is clear: Alton Brown will always be searching for the next fork in the road. Whenever, wherever, however he finds it, he'll take it. And if he can't find a fork worth taking, he'll pull a MacGyver and jury-rig one of his own.

THE LESSON BEHIND THE LAW: NEW ROADS LEAD TO MORE OPPORTUNITY

The current economic climate has altered the way we need to view the "same old"—the career paths that once represented security. Before, if you lost your job, the obvious step was to get another just like it at a competing company. In today's climate, that's not necessarily smart—or possible. Automatically grabbing the tried-and-true option, far from being "safe," can leave you dangerously vulnerable to changes in your industry. When it's time to make a career shift, today's Reinventor always explores the road less traveled.

The old thinking was that the well-traveled path had to be "right" and the alternatives were necessarily riskier. This no longer holds true. In practice, what you'll usually find on the road less traveled is simply more opportunity. The less obvious path—in addition to possibly being a better fit—forces you to think outside the box and therefore generate new ideas.

Ambiguity: Why "The Road Less Traveled" Is . . . *Less Traveled*

Taking a different, unexpected path is really about exploring multiple alternatives—in other words, *seeing things as they might be, not as they are*. That's a challenge for the human brain, as it is wired to categorize people, thoughts, impressions, and occasional dust balls into tidy, recognizable bundles. As we saw in Law 2 (Body), the brain can process only so much information at a time. By lumping things together in those bundles, it has to keep track of only a few major items instead of hundreds of jigsaw puzzle pieces. Taking the road less traveled is asking your brain to pry apart those clumps of information so that you can experiment with putting Tab A into Slot D for a change. Your brain won't be happy about this. It may zap you with a headache. But that's nothing compared to how your brain will feel when it finds out what else you're planning to throw its way.

If there's anything people seem to dislike more than Brussels sprouts, it's ambiguity. There's even a phrase for it—"ambiguity aversion," an inability to tolerate fuzziness when what we crave is cold, hard facts. Ambiguity aversion is more common than the common cold. It's part of our internal makeup, and it can throw up a major roadblock when it's time to choose a reinvention path.

I sought out Dr. Gregory S. Berns, author of *Iconoclast* and the director of the Center for Neuropolicy at Emory University School of Medicine, for insight into why Reinventors often shy away from potentially golden opportunities while gravitating toward a path that, while predictable, doesn't head anywhere. Berns explained that when it comes to uncertainty, most people would rather lose their shirt at the craps table than face the slightest ambiguity about their future. "There are different kinds of uncertainty," said Berns, and each kind provokes a different set of reactions. There's the uncertainty of the roulette wheel, which is really about "risk," according to Berns—"because you have all the information in front of you and you know what the odds are." Then there's the ambiguity of trying to divine the future without any information to go on. "In the first case, the uncertainty comes from the fact that you might fail or lose," Berns explained. "In the second case, you have uncertainty because you simply don't know. Dozens of studies on this have shown that people have a strong aversion to the ambiguity. They'll generally prefer a known risky situation to one that's ambiguous."

This is a major reason so many people cross the road less traveled off their itinerary even as their industry falls to pieces—there's just too much uncertainty involved. They'd rather roll the dice on a similar gig in the (dying) field they know than face the not-knowing of a new path.

When faced with ambiguity, people tend to assume it's an either/or situation—triumph or ruination, with no middle ground—and that the odds are heavily weighted toward ruination. There's usually no information to support this conclusion, but people tend to ignore that.

Odds and ambiguity are two different things. One is about knowing where you stand—good or bad. The other is about *not* knowing where you stand—also good or bad. Successfully navigating your reinvention requires being able to tell the difference between a situation where you can reasonably assess your odds, and one where you will have to deal with ambiguity. Here's how to tell the two apart:

EXAMPLES OF RISK	EXAMPLES OF AMBIGUITY
My company is laying off 20 percent of its workforce.	My company might lay people off.
There are two finalists up for that position, and I am one of them.	I have interviewed for the job, but they are still talking to other candidates.
I'm going to leave my company and become a consultant, and 75 percent of the consultants in my specialty make more than $50,000 a year.	I'm going to leave my company and become a consultant.
I have six months' worth of expenses in savings, but my new gig starts in seven months.	I have six months' worth of expenses in savings, but I don't know when I'll land a new gig.

In the scenarios in the first column, you can actually quantify the risk you're taking. In the examples on the right, it is impossible to get a handle on your odds. What's important to realize is that the odds in the second column could, in fact, turn out to be *better* than those in the first. You just don't know. And you *can't* know until you get further down the path.

Although it's difficult to tolerate "not knowing" the outcome of your reinvention, the process of reinvention forces you to get more comfortable around ambiguity. To begin with, focus on how ambiguity is about *not knowing*, not about *poor odds*. In fact, ambiguity is risk-neutral. You can't call the spread when you don't know how many horses are on the field. The wonder of exploring the road less traveled is that by opening yourself to multiple races, you increase your opportunity to place a bet on the winning horse.

Finding Your Own Road Less Traveled

This is the point in your career reinvention when you choose which paths to explore. Because this is about reinvention—and not about maintaining the status quo—it is important to think outside of the box and try something new: your own road less traveled.

"This special path—it just doesn't exist for me," some of my clients say. They feel as if there can only be one clear path, and it's usually the one that's the next logical step from what they were doing before. If you are finding it difficult to see new possibilities, it's usually a sign that you're overly focused on the obvious path. "Inattentional blindness"—the failure to notice something appearing in front of your eyes because you are consumed with a particular task—makes it nearly impossible to notice the on-ramp to the road less traveled. When your vision is thus narrowed, the brain tunes out alternatives and competing bits of information until you literally don't see them. You become blind to any other options.

This is great for athletes. It helps them stay focused on, say, the slalom course, without their minds wandering off to how the competition is doing or whether there's hot cocoa waiting at the lodge. One goal, one mindset, one road. This doesn't work so well when you need to reinvent your career. You will have to let go of your laserlike focus on the path you already know and open yourself to the idea of other possibilities before you can begin to see any.

I've been guilty of inattentional blindness myself on occasion. There was the time I was talking to a jovial seatmate on a plane who turned out to be a successful entrepreneur. "Go ahead, guess what I do," he said.

"Software?" I ventured. "Business services?"

"Name tags," he said and leaned back with a Cheshire-cat grin.

"Really? How interesting," I said politely, even though I didn't think so. I mean, how many name tags can a person sell?

Millions, it turns out. The man had a multimillion-dollar business selling name tags. It blew my mind. "Excuse me, but who on earth would buy that many name tags?" I asked.

He reeled off a list: cruise ships, fast-food restaurants, retail chains. All high-turnover businesses with a continual need for made-to-order name tags.

Now when I see a customized name tag, I smile. There's a guy out there making a fortune off a simple idea that was hiding in plain sight.

HIDDEN CONFLICT THAT COULD STOP YOU: THE SIREN CALL OF OTHER VOICES TRYING TO LURE YOU BACK TO THE "SAFE" PATH

In *The Odyssey*, the sailors of ancient Greece had to be tied to the masts of their ships to make it through a particular stretch of sea without succumbing to the irresistible song of the Sirens. The lovely, plaintive voices lured the sailors back from where they'd just left with promises of something better, but the ships would crash upon the shoals.

When you reinvent your career, you will hear the siren songs of two persuasive forces: the people in your world and the voices in your head. Both types can be highly motivated to make sure you don't stray too far from home.

The people in your world are accustomed to seeing you in a certain light, and they want to keep it that way. Some have an agenda—jealousy, competitiveness, or the fear that you will leave them behind. Some are anxious that you're taking too great a risk. Any of these reactions could stem from a natural aversion to change and, in many cases, they can't help it—they're under the spell of the brain's innate need to categorize people, things, and ideas. When you change up on them and they can no longer file you away under the usual cataloguing system, they can feel puzzled, disoriented, even angry. You're messing with their filing system!

The easiest solution from their point of view is to nudge you back toward the "safe" shores of the known by singing their siren's song. If you haven't lashed yourself securely to the mast, you'll hear such confidence busters as "Are you sure?" and "You don't seem like that kind of person to me" and "That doesn't sound like a good idea."

The voices in your head are even louder and more insistent. They are what we coaches call the "uninvited committee members"—the embodiment of all the negative voices you've heard in your lifetime. If ever a person expressed doubt about your abilities, that person's voice has been preserved in your brain in a recorded loop. Here are some typical uninvited committee members:

- **The Mom:** Sometimes sounding like the voice of your real-life mom, sometimes not, but the one in your head who warns of every disaster that could possibly befall you. A favorite phrase: "But what if . . . ?", followed by every conceivable doomsday scenario.

- **The Dad:** Sometimes sounding like the voice of your real-life dad, sometimes not, this one assures you that you haven't learned enough yet to undertake such a big endeavor. A favorite phrase: "But you haven't done X yet," the implication being that without X, your odds of succeeding are the same as winning the mega-million-dollar Powerball lottery.

- **The Baby:** This will sound oddly like your own voice from some preschool age as it cycles between two fixed pronouncements: "I don't wanna" and "I'm scared." Trying to reason with this committee member is like talking to a two-year-old—the answer you'll get is usually "No."

- **The Underminer:** The voice of every frenemy and hiring manager who ever rejected you, all rolled into one committee member who has made a point of collecting and cataloguing—for handy retrieval—the comments of every unsupportive person you've ever met. These comments are all variations on "You're not good enough" (you don't have sixty-five years of experience plus two Ph.D.s) or "You're overqualified" (No one over the age of thirty gets a job anymore, so who are you kidding?).

Although the uninvited committee members are only voices in your head, they act like real people. They pretend to look out for your best interests, but the real goal of all these doomsayers is to keep you in the box they're most comfortable seeing you in. To break free and move down the road less traveled, you will have to combat their negative talk.

The power of the siren's song is fear. When you feel fearful, you are susceptible to their call, because you are afraid that maybe in some small way, they're right. The first step in combating all these plaintive voices is to manage your fear using the tactics in Law 3 (Excuses)—

finding a supportive shoulder to lean on, distracting yourself, finding a role model—so that your armor is strong. Remind yourself of past successes and of the times you overcame hardships, and that you'll be able to do the same in the future, even when these hardships take a different form.

One of the most powerful tactics for combating "concerned" friends and uninvited committee members is to blend the "talk back to your fear" and the "feel the fear and do it anyway" strategies from Law 3 (Excuses) into the all-powerful "fake it till you make it" strategy. "Fake it till you make it" relies on a stock set of phrases, so that at the first sign of "back in the box" talk, you're prepared with a comeback.

"Are you sure?" asks the siren call.

"*Yes,*" you say.

The key is to stop right there—don't offer any explanation! Don't fill any silences with nervous babbling! Are you sure? *Yes.*

The great thing is that "yes" can be used to deflect a whole line of questioning.

"Have you thought about this?"

"Yes."

"Do you know what you're getting into?"

"Yes."

You do NOT have to add ". . . although I have my doubts." We all have a few, and it's fine to talk them over with someone who is open-minded and helpful. But don't trot them out when someone is singing a siren song.

Here's another great "fake it till you make it" line to keep handy: "I'll be fine." I used this one on my mother when she was freaking out that I was leaving my career in entertainment to become a coach.

"That sounds risky!" said my mom.

"I'll be fine."

"You're leaving New York to move to Miami! What if I have to come rescue you?"

"I'll be fine."

My mom has come to Miami many times—to visit me, not to rescue me.

Sometimes there's an unusually persistent siren in your life or in your head who just won't quit. This siren seems to have a megaphone and a litany of reasons why yours is the worst idea in the world. When this happens, don't engage in any back-and-forth discussion. Don't try to reason or argue. Just pull out the favorite phrase of preschool teachers everywhere:

"Thanks for sharing."

LIVING THE LAW: CHOOSING YOUR ROAD LESS TRAVELED

In selecting his road less traveled, Alton chose a uniquely entrepreneurial route. But that is certainly not the only option. Veering from the expected path simply means thinking harder and more creatively about your next steps. One of my clients, Amelia, has built a career as a Reinventor in the corporate world. She started off as an account exec doing client support for Broadway's hottest ad agency, then moved on to become director of sales at a firm that did online ticketing for Broadway shows. Now she is set to add nonprofit to her roster with a gig as marketing director for a major regional theater group.

By the way, don't assume that this route off the beaten path runs through a gated community reserved for high-level executives or the wealthy and privileged. No matter your financial situation or where you sit on the corporate ladder, it is always possible to strike out in a new direction. My uncle Terry, for example, had twenty-plus years working on the factory floor as a machinist; today, in his fifties, he is a computer hardware specialist. He had a hobbyist's interest in computers that grew out of the same curiosity he'd demonstrated about new technology in the machinist sector, and although it took him six or seven years, sometimes working two extra jobs on the side, he eventually made the switch.

Selecting a Reinvention Target

We have come to an important juncture in your reinvention journey. This is where the true essence of reinvention lies—at a fork in the road where you do NOT head straight for the obvious career choice.

In Law 5 (Tools), you will learn how to take the skills and talents you have—your tools—and pave the road that will get you to a new destination. Before you do that, you still have to identify which of these alternative paths you'd like to explore.

Here you'll be relying on what you learned in Law 2 (Body): *Trust your instincts.*

Remember, they will let you know, analysis-free, *what* you like. But now is the time to invite your intellect to the party to answer the question: *How will you make it happen?*

To understand why you should rely on instinct to choose and reason to assess the choices (instead of the other way around), it's helpful to look at science.

"Researchers are just beginning to understand how the brain makes up its mind," says Jonah Lehrer in his book *How We Decide.* There's almost never a time when you can pretend you are all intellect or all intuition. The general rule of thumb, according to the latest brain research, is that *simple, straightforward problems require reason.* Should you open a pizza parlor, yes or no? That's a simple problem, so you'd rationally digest the relevant data to see if a pizza parlor was feasible and, if so, how you'd go about it, then weigh your options ("I like twirling the dough, but I'm allergic to oregano"), then make your decision.

It may seem counterintuitive, but *complex problems require a primarily instinctual response.* The pizza parlor example is simple because there are only two options: yes or no. The "how" can be answered by straightforward data. But what if the question could be answered dozens of ways? Try this: Of all the ice cream flavors in the world, which is your favorite? (The Japanese have one called "Ox Tongue Ice Cream," and I'll bet that's not it.) In this case it would be a waste of time to assess the merits of each flavor intellectually, when all you really have to do is go up to the Baskin-Robbins counter, tune in to your body, and see which flavor it asks for. When there are too many options, your rational brain will stay up all night and never settle on an answer, while your instinct already knows exactly what you want.

"Which career path do I want to choose?" is more like the ice-cream question—complex, with many possible answers. So put aside your rational brain for a moment, and pose the question in a way that relies on intuition: Of all the things in the world you could choose to do for a living, what would you ask for if you walked up to the six-hundred-flavor career counter this minute? ▯[7] It's almost time to pick a Reinvention Target, so spend a day or two pondering this question; you can jot your ideas in the workbook. It is important to give your body time to weigh in with ideas.

Next you'll pull out the list of possible careers you brainstormed in Law 1 (Vision) when you created your lifestyle vision. See what matches there are between your brainstorm list and what your body came up with and put those on the "explore" list. If there are no obvious matches, use your intellect to begin the analysis by asking yourself a few questions:

The "Explore" List ▯[8]

1. Of the ideas from my Law 1 (Vision) potential careers list and what I came up with by tuning into my body, which one seems like the most interesting path?

2. What have I always wanted to do, but never felt I could?

3. If I didn't have to earn money, what would I do?

4. When I was ten years old, what did I want to be when I grew up?

Force yourself to look at and think about other careers that are far outside the "safe" confines of your current box. Imagine what you might do elsewhere, in other environments or scenarios, just for the fun of it. If you're in finance, visualize yourself running a wellness center; if you're a lawyer, imagine yourself as a chef. The point of this mental exercise is to force you to look at connections in a new way, stimulating your creativity. You can take it a step further by going out and actually experiencing a path you're considering: If you're in bio-tech but have always dreamed of becoming an interior designer, take a class and design a few rooms for a friend. You might not become a designer, but by consistently challenging yourself to do something new, you're training your brain to keep coming up with novel ideas.

Once you have a few options on your "explore list," ask yourself

[7]Exercise on Page 231: Body Brainstorm
[8]Exercise on Page 232: Create an "Explore" List

an important question: *How can I make these work?*▢[9] Asking yourself "how" triggers your intellect and activates creative problem-solving, a necessary talent for Reinventors. Alton did this; when "cooking show" was on his list, the "how" was professional culinary school and teaching cooking classes to earn money. (Note: Stay away from the question *"Can* I make this work?" This question activates fear.) Come up with ideas and strategies for each of the options on your "explore" list; don't be afraid to take a few weeks to do this. Sometimes "how" questions need to percolate for a while before the answers show up.

Once you've got your "how" ideas down for each of the careers on your list, *pick one.*▢[10] This is not *Jeopardy!*, where you press the buzzer too early, your answer is wrong, you lose the money, and everyone in your family is mad at you. There will be plenty of opportunities to tinker with your goal or even change your mind completely. It's more important at this point to choose *something* than to make the "right" choice. If you keep looking for the "right" choice, you'll never get started.

Next, *pick a second idea.* Put this goal in your back pocket; it is your backup should your first choice not work out.

Now get going.

> **The Takeaway:** Exploring the road less traveled forces you to become more creative about your career options.

> **Watch Out for . . .** The uninvited committee members of your mind (or in real life) who insist that you stay inside the box they've always known you in.

> **Putting the Law into Action:** Begin exploring two unobvious career options.

> **Something to Think About:** What other times in my life have I pursued the road less traveled and succeeded?

---

[9]Exercise on Page 232: Brainstorm the "How"
[10]Exercise on Page 233: Pick a Reinvention Target

LAW 5

YOU'VE GOT THE TOOLS IN YOUR TOOLBOX

*Only as you do know yourself can your brain serve you as a
sharp and efficient tool.*

—Bernard M. Baruch

R eggie Mebane is a visual contradiction in terms: an elegantly
dressed man with the four-point pocket square of a dandy and
the presence of a linebacker; a dead-serious, highly placed executive with the rat-a-tat timing of a stand-up comic.

"We grew up in North Memphis, Tennessee, very poor," he says.

How poor were you, Reggie?

"We were so poor we couldn't afford music on our radio. We used
to have to go next door to borrow a comb and brush, that's how poor
we were."

Reggie's kidding, of course. Or is he?

"We lived next door to the projects. We couldn't afford to live in
the projects. That would have been a step up for us."

Definitely not kidding now. Reggie grew up on food stamps and
government cheese. He was the third of four children, and for a long
time they lived across the street from the Dixie Homes Housing Development, a housing project with a particular place in American
history. Built in 1935, Dixie Homes was the first of two separate-and-
probably-not-equal projects of the newly formed Memphis Housing

Authority: Dixie Homes for low-income black citizens, Lauderdale Courts for whites.

Reggie's mother was a cook and waitress. His father, who had a reputation as a hustler, worked odd jobs as a laborer. When Reggie was young his parents separated; the children stayed with their father. He died of a heart attack when Reggie was twelve, at which point Reggie's mother returned to take over the household, and the family was bumped a step up to Section 8 housing (subsidized rentals for low-income families and individuals).

But Reggie's is not a predictable hard-luck story. He's quick to say that life has a way of providing the tools we need to succeed in life, whether we recognize them or not.

Take Reggie's first job, the one he worked after school throughout tenth grade, as a dishwasher at a Memphis Holiday Inn. When Reggie talks about the skills he acquired on that job, he's not talking about producing squeaky-clean plates. He's talking about survival skills developed in his early years, later repurposed to help him navigate the stormy seas of a distinctly unpredictable career.

Growing up with a bird's-eye view of Dixie Homes, making his way through his gang-infested neighborhood to get to school or the corner store, Reggie learned much about the difference between hustling and succeeding, and the difference between how he didn't want to live and how he did. He carries that knowledge with him every day, and says that his current job at an organization whose mission is to save millions of lives and prevent bioterrorist threats utilizes "the same skills it takes to be a successful gang leader and survive on the streets."

I I I I

Mean streets and Dixie Homes 'hood notwithstanding, Reggie did so well in high school that he won a scholarship to a summer program at Exeter, one of the nation's most prestigious prep schools. And he did so well in the summer program that he was offered a full scholarship to attend the school year-round.

Reggie turned Exeter down. There was another black kid at the elite New Hampshire school that summer who insisted on being called

Le*ROY* instead of *LEE*roy. Reggie knew why, and he didn't want that to happen to him. "He was black as night and totally white," Reggie says. "I think I would have lost who I am if I'd gone to Exeter. I would have lost that sense of African-American history and pride."

By refusing Exeter's offer, Reggie didn't intend to disqualify himself from the affluent life that graduating the school promised. But as someone who has since filled five binders with his family history dating back to 1860 when his great-great-grandfather, Tom Mebane, appeared as No. 35 on the 1860 Slave Schedule of Fayette County, Tennessee, he knew that some identities were too important to leave behind.

When he graduated from high school Reggie accepted a $60,000 college scholarship from the U.S. Air Force Academy. Once he'd entered the Academy, he discovered that his high school fantasy of being a pilot was nothing like the day-to-day reality of the job. "It looks exciting from the ground," he says, "but it's very routine and mechanized."

Reggie did some checking and learned that the GI Bill would count the time he'd spent at the Academy as active duty and then pay for college. So he left the Air Force with an honorable discharge and enrolled in the psychology undergraduate program at the University of Memphis, then known as Memphis State.

There was only one fraternity option for an African-American man at Memphis State who wanted to be on the fast track to success. Joining it bestowed upon Reggie the appropriate moniker: "Alpha Man."

Alpha Phi Alpha, founded at Cornell in 1906, was the first intercollegiate fraternity established by and for African Americans. Reggie was well aware of the frat's bona fides—among them an alumni roster that included Martin Luther King, Jr., and Olympian Jesse Owens. But Reggie had another, more practical motive for pledging Alpha Phi Alpha. One of the "Alpha men" worked in the personnel department at FedEx—a company Reggie had targeted as his next employer of choice.

In 1981, then in his junior year, Reggie started part-time at FedEx, loading airplanes and unloading trucks. He finished his undergraduate studies in psychology in 1982, but continued working the night shift, where he met his future wife, LaRhonda, on the package-sorting line. They were married in late 1986, just as Reggie was beginning his graduate studies in psychology, also at Memphis State.

Soon LaRhonda delivered a life-changing surprise. Make that two. Before they'd completed their first year of marriage, LaRhonda and Reggie were the proud and somewhat stunned parents of twin girls, Mallory and Lindsey.

With this overnight doubling of the number of mouths to feed, LaRhonda returned to work (she was now in financial services), and Reggie took on more jobs than there were infants to feed. More jobs, possibly, than any mortal man might be expected to do.

While his fellow students were cramming for exams, FedEx-worker Reggie was on the loading dock beginning his 9 P.M. to 4 A.M. shift. While the other students slept, he was clocking out, then racing home to catch a power nap. As the sun rose, adjunct-professor Reggie would sprint to the University of Memphis to teach his morning psychology or sociology class. He'd hurry home for another quick snooze, then dash off to the Midtown Mental Health Center, where psychiatric-case-manager Reggie would see clients. Three hours later, he'd zip back to FedEx to catch his next shift. There was overtime pay for weekend work at FedEx, which he couldn't afford to turn down, and he picked up the occasional therapy client on the side. He took graduate school courses when and where he could fit them in. And so it went for eight years.

| | | | |

While juggling jobs and school, Reggie was moving up the ladder at FedEx. He had always considered himself a leader, and his coworkers and "superiors" saw him that way, too. Their high regard manifested in an unexpected opportunity: In 1995 Reggie was invited to join the FedEx Leadership Institute, a program designed to groom top FedEx employees for management and executive positions.

Reggie's participation in the Leadership Institute led to a position that was a perfect match for his interests and his skills: working at the Institute itself, teaching leadership and management practices to FedEx employees around the world. A special assignment bestowed by the CEO, only the best of the best were accepted to teach there. Reggie was one of that elite cadre.

Reggie's years at the FedEx Institute left their mark: leadership became his passion, and he realized that his style is personal as well as professional. "It even goes deeper than the job," Reggie says. "It's not just about how you do your job leading people at work, it's about how you live your life."

I I I I

FedEx was growing and so was Reggie. What began as a single flagship company was now a huge conglomerate with five operating companies, including FedEx Trade Networks Transport & Brokerage, Inc., a new division in Buffalo, New York, that specialized in electronic customs clearance. When Reggie was first hired at FedEx, ninety thousand packages were coming through the Memphis hub. When he moved his family to Buffalo in 2001 to serve as chief operating officer of the latest acquisition, there were more than a million packages transported every night. The scale was different, but the organizational, logistical, and political skills Reggie had developed while rising through the ranks of FedEx, including a stint as managing director of FedEx's international customs clearance and freight operations at the Memphis hub, made him well equipped to reorganize the Buffalo unit.

Reggie was at the top of his game—thriving in his role as COO of FedEx Trade Networks Transport & Brokerage, family settled happily in Buffalo—when it all came crashing down. One day in the fall of 2003, his boss called him into his office, closed the door, and told Reggie that due to a company-wide restructuring, his position was being eliminated. Despite Reggie's training in psychology and leadership systems, after twenty-three years, it was a crushing blow. "The rug was jerked out from under me. I felt like they had just castrated me. The bottom line was that I'd been married to this company for all those years, and all of a sudden she wanted a divorce."

I I I I

After the "breakup," he made a few short but painful career missteps. He accepted a COO position in Chicago, moved his family there, and then— days before he was due to start—took a job with Gibson Guitar in Nashville. This left his daughters finishing high school and living in a new house in Chicago, while their dad was commuting home on weekends from Nashville. After six months, the Gibson job went up in smoke.

Now unemployed, Reggie posted his résumé on a Web site for senior executives in search of their next opportunity. One day a recruiter called with a listing at the Centers for Disease Control in Atlanta, Georgia. The position was top-tier: chief management officer. It would make use of the skills Reggie had honed in his years at FedEx. This job, too, involved delivery of packages that absolutely, positively had to be there overnight—but these packages contained life-saving vaccines.

The CDC wanted a candidate with strong corporate management skills; as a COO at FedEx, Reggie headed a $2 billion division. The CDC wanted a candidate with a background in operations and logistics; Reggie's rise through the ranks at FedEx gave him practical experience from the ground up. The CDC wanted a candidate who was gifted at inspiring and motivating people; Reggie, from his days as a psychiatric case manager and years at the FedEx Leadership Institute, was deeply knowledgeable about the psyche of human performance.

Reggie was hired in February 2005 as one of the CDC's seven chief management officers. He's directly responsible for managing the $6.4 billion budget of the CDC's Coordinating Center for Infectious Diseases, which includes business operations, human capital, information technology, grants, facilities and administration services for HIV/AIDS, Viral Hepatitis, STDs, TB, and the H1N1 virus. In his office in the CDC's huge Beltway complex, the awards, certificates, and photos he brought to remind him of his FedEx years are slowly being replaced by equally impressive mementos of his current job.

The position calls on every skill he's ever mastered. But then, Reggie's used to that. His survival—in the tough executive boardroom and the even tougher streets of Memphis—has always depended on his ability to draw on everything he's got.

Especially in today's ever-shifting work environment, as Reggie points out, change is inevitable. "It's not a matter of whether or not you can do it. It's how, when, and where you'll do it." Sometimes you have to leave your old identities behind and find new ones. But you always take your tools with you.

THE LESSON BEHIND THE LAW: YOU'RE NOT STARTING FROM SCRATCH

One of the biggest myths of reinvention is that your previous work life has been a complete waste of time and effort, and that you'll need to start over from zero, hat in hand. Believing this can be a hindrance to any further progress. You're assuming that the effort to build a whole new skill set is too much work, and I agree: It *is* too much work. But the initial premise of this belief is wrong—you don't have to start over from scratch. That's not how things go in reinvention.

The reality is that your current skills and experience are portable. They are the tools you take with you when you leave your old job or career. You couldn't leave them behind if you tried! Whether you realize it or not, you're always drawing on skills you developed in the past. Your knowledge and skills are part of you and come into play each time you enter a different environment or try something new. You learned to read in first grade and now you're a magazine editor. You won awards for debate in high school; now you're a lawyer. You did this unconsciously when you were young; launching a career reinvention requires you to analyze and draw upon your skill set in a more systematic and deliberate way. Repurposing your old skills—identifying the ones you used in your old field and converting them for use in a new career—is part of the definition of reinvention. It sums up the basic strategy that will help you thrive in this era: Reinventors continually use the tools that are already in their toolbox in creative new ways to build and broaden opportunities.

Your toolbox comes with you. But there *is* something you'll have to leave behind . . . and this one is gonna hurt.

Let Go of Your Old Identity

If you are a CIA spy, this next step will be a breeze. As a secret agent, you are accustomed to shedding identities the way the rest of us go through Kleenex.

For the majority of you who do not make a living traveling the world pretending to be someone else, I have a message for you: *You are not your job.*

You've heard this bit of kitchen table wisdom before—that you are more than what you do or what your job title says. You are unique. Not from the assembly line. You are more than the sum of your job responsibilities. I'm sure you have always agreed with this in theory. It's a different matter when you have to live it yourself. And now you must, because when it comes to career reinvention, you must literally *stop identifying yourself by what you used to do.* You have to stop this in your head and in what you tell people about who you are and what you do.

Refraining from this is tough—especially in the U.S., where we use career as shorthand to define who we are and what we are worth in society. When people ask what you do for a living, it's convenient to respond: I am a doctor. I am a lawyer. I'm in finance, health care, software. I'm a shoemaker, I'm a repo man. A horse trader. A Royal Canadian Mountie. Each of these roles comes with what sociologists call a mental "frame," a set of values and behaviors, ways of looking at the world and your place in it. Frames give you a way of defining yourself, both internally and to everyone else. They give people a reassuring shorthand for classifying you and sizing you up. Like saying "I'm American," or "I'm French," or "I'm Brazilian," framing ourselves through our jobs is usually the fastest, most convenient way of telling the world at large just what culture we belong to.

But the frame of your old identity can be a liability when you're trying to get the world to see you in a new light. The label of your former career has grown on you like a second skin, but you'll have to shed it if you expect to grow a new one. When you continually slot yourself into your old frame while talking up your new one, it creates cognitive dissonance on both ends of the conversation. Neither you nor the person you're talking with will truly understand what you want. "I am a Royal Canadian Mountie" is a confusing message when you're standing there in a chef's hat with a frying pan.

Eventually, you will change your self-perception to the culture of your new career—a process that is called "frame-shifting." For that to happen, you must get out of the habit of summing yourself up by what you did or who you were in the past. You might be tempted to neglect this step, saying to yourself, "When I get to my new career, I'll identify myself in a new way. Until then, I'll just use my old career; it's easier." Beware! Using your old career identity limits your options in two critical ways:

1. **It keeps you from moving on, intellectually and emotionally.** You run the danger of becoming one of those cartoon figures who stands alone by the punch bowl, saying, "Back when I was in vaudeville . . ." or the middle-aged man with a paunch who only wants to talk about his days as a high school football hero.

2. **It confuses people who might otherwise be of assistance to you in moving to a new career.** If Reggie had gone around saying, "I used to be a bigwig at FedEx," no one would have thought to alert him to the CDC job. What does a package delivery service have to do with a worldwide government initiative to stem disease? Actually, Reggie's skills were a great match with the new job. But it would have been hard to make the leap of cognition if he had insisted on being known as "the FedEx guy."

Relinquishing your old identity is one of the most painful things you will do when you reinvent your career. Your old identity is the last thing you'll want to let go of—*but it should be the first.* A successful career change depends on establishing and embracing a new identity right up front. That means leaving behind whatever ideas you hold about yourself that won't make sense in the place you're headed. Reggie treasured his twenty-three years of loyalty to FedEx, and it was hard at first for him to let that identity go. But once he did, new possibilities opened up.

It will be tough not to "be" anything for a while, but this is a necessary reinvention step. And it's not just about identity. You'll also have to let go of certain people or even places. You'll be relinquishing habits and ways of being that served their purpose in your old life but have no place in the next.

This is really about openness—an essential reinvention quality. You have to be open to new things in order to allow ideas, concepts, and people into your world. In particular, you must remain open to letting go.

Fundamental to letting go of your old identity is that you start seeing and thinking of yourself in a new way. Here are some tactics to get you started:

1. **Get a business card made that advertises your new career instead of your old one.** You can do this even if you're not sure exactly where you'll land, by thinking of your new field in broader terms. One of my clients, Katie, was working at a nonprofit but wanted to move into the food world. She had a card made up with the title "Gourmand." The well-known chefs, cookbook authors, and restaurateurs she met loved it.

2. **Start going to social events in your new industry.** By immersing yourself in its culture and becoming familiar with it, you will find it easier to picture yourself there.

3. **Put a temporary moratorium on hanging out with buddies from your old career.** You have to understand the nuances of this suggestion before you run out and cut all your ties with your old friends. I'm not saying to withdraw from everyone you know, but to ease off the ties and social activities that keep you living in the past and treading the same old ruts. It's important to move on emotionally, which will be difficult if you're still attending the regular Friday night margarita hour with the crew from your old job.

4. **Ask your friends and family to drop the old identity.** For purposes of how they describe you, ask them to drop your old career entirely and say that you're working toward the new one.

5. **Clean out your closet.** Get rid of any paraphernalia from your old career that will not be useful to you in the new one. A film critic who opened a day spa gave away thousands of screeners; a marketing executive who started a jewelry design business gave away her power suits.

6. **Redefine yourself.** When asked what you do, say that you're in the "new" field. If that feels too uncomfortable, say that you're working toward a position in the "new" field. Whatever you do,

don't say "I'm a [insert old job here], but I'm working toward [insert new field here]." The minute you say "but," it tells people not to take what follows seriously. If you're completely uncomfortable owning your new field, then when people ask you what you do, tell them "Nothing." This might be tough to say, but it is a great conversation starter!

Once you free yourself of the old definitions, you unlock your ability to use your skills—the tools of reinvention—in entirely different and surprising ways.

"Skills" versus "Jobs"

One of the pitfalls of identifying yourself by your job is that you fall into the trap of thinking that your skills and your job functions are the same. When asked what skills you have, you'll give a job function instead of identifying the skills used within that job function. Examples: If you're a lawyer, when asked what skills you have, you might say, "Drafting contracts and memorandums of understanding." If you're in finance doing buyouts, you might say your skill is "Doing due diligence for potential acquisition targets." If you're a real estate broker, you might answer, "Matching houses with buyers."

If those examples sound reasonable to your ears, it is because you are not totally immersed in the reinvention mindset. Actually, answers such as the ones in this example cause problems in many ways, not the least of which is that those job functions are particular to those industries and do not seem to translate to any other. If you're a real estate broker looking to move into the health and fitness field, matching houses with buyers won't be of any use. If you're a lawyer looking to switch to PR, writing memorandums of understanding won't be on the job requirement list. This causes despair among aspiring Reinventors. It looks as if their particular job functions have no equivalents in the new field, so they fear they have nothing of value on their résumé.

How to get around that? Recognize that *skills* are what you use to perform those job functions. And while job functions are local, valuable only within select slices of the professional world, *skills are global.* You take your skills with you wherever you go. They can strip you of your title, scratch your name off the glass door, and make you pack the contents of your desk in a box, but no one can take away your skills. They come with you when you leave your job. They're yours to keep for life. Reinventors think of themselves as a constellation of skills, not job functions, and they have learned to distinguish between the two. Let's reexamine the examples from above to illustrate the difference:

ROLE	"LOCAL" JOB FUNCTION	"GLOBAL" SKILL
Lawyer	Drafting contracts and memorandums of understanding	Writing
Finance	Due diligence for acquisition targets	Financial analysis
Real estate broker	Matching houses with buyers	Selling

If you're thinking about what you've done only in terms of job function, your toolbox for reinvention will look pretty empty. When you start thinking about what you've done in terms of the *skills* it took to perform the tasks, you'll see that you have plenty of tools at your disposal to help build a bridge to a new career.

Knowledge is also a part of your toolbox, and Reinventors think about how the knowledge they've acquired locally might be redeployed globally, in another field. Reggie knew all about logistics, about getting things from one place to another in a hurry, while tracking every step precisely. He could easily have used that knowledge within the same field, going from FedEx to UPS or DHL. Instead, Reggie understood that there was a broader use for his kind of operational skills. Getting packages to their destination on time anywhere in the world required the same knowledge as getting urgently needed vaccines to far-flung locations. He recognized that an expertise in logistics was just as important—in fact, more so—when it came to saving lives.

HIDDEN CONFLICT THAT COULD STOP YOU: NEEDING A FEW SPECIALIZED TOOLS FOR YOUR TOOLBOX

To reinvent your career, you'll need to find out which skills are most valued in your target career or business, and start matching them up with what you have in your toolbox. We call these "legitimacy points," and the more you have, the stronger your case for potential employers or customers. The stronger your case, the easier it will be to make a transition. Your goal, then, is to build as strong a case as possible by having as many of the necessary tools as possible.

The thing about legitimacy points is that you don't necessarily have to have all of them to make a switch. You just have to have enough, or at least enough of the most important ones. There are two specific kinds of tools that you need to pay close attention to in order to successfully make your case:

1. **Those that are absolutely required.** This is the price of entry. Without these tools, or legitimacy points, you'll have a tough time getting in the door. You won't be an M.D. if you haven't attended medical school. If every single person working in your target job has a Ph.D. in statistics, then the statistics are not in your favor if you skipped that class in college. These legitimacy points are usually clearly outlined by hiring managers in the position brief or job listing, although there may be some wiggle room if the other tools in your toolbox are strong enough. For example, maybe they won't require a Ph.D. in statistics if they desperately need someone with management skills, and you spent ten years running a multibillion-dollar company. You will have to gauge the required legitimacy points on a case-by-case basis.

2. **Those that seem to be required, but aren't.** These are excuses you tell yourself. It's really your fear showing up in the guise of imaginary requirements—usually large and practically impossible requirements—that you insist must be satisfied before you can pursue your opportunity. Something on the order of: "I

have to get a patisserie diploma from Le Cordon Bleu in order to open my cupcake business."

I had a client with a day job who wanted to become a full-time writer. She had published before, so this was not an unreasonable goal. I gave her some coaching requests to finish a few pieces and research the glossies—the major magazines—to become familiar with submission policies and what kind of stories they bought. At our next session, she showed up with a list, all right. But it wasn't a list of editors or magazines—it was a list of master's programs in creative writing. She already had a full-time job and kids, plus the demands of a busy life, but she talked about how she was going to apply to these programs and spend the next two years working toward a writing degree. Once she had this magical master's degree, *then* she'd be able to write full time.

I had one question for her. "Do editors require a master's degree before they allow you to submit your work?"

When your mind tells you that there's a big legitimacy point you must satisfy, you need to test if it's true or if it's a stalling tactic. Are they asking you for this requirement everywhere you turn? Is there really no other way you can try something without this one requirement? In the case of my client, the question she needed to ask herself was not "Would it be nice to be a writer with a master's degree?" The question was "Is it possible to write and be published *without* a master's degree?" Even if she truly did not know the answer, one conversation with an editor would have told her that not every published writer has an advanced degree (in fact, most don't). When you test this kind of assumption, don't skew the test question in a way that gives you the answer you want. Make it very simple: "Is there any way possible to do this, start this, or pursue this without the qualification that seems to be standing in my way?"

There will also be times when you analyze the tools in your toolbox and realize that you *do* need to add a few more. This usually happens when the case you make isn't quite strong enough to convince your target to give you a shot. Now you will need to go a step further and gain experience or learn something new that adds another skill to your toolbox. The most obvious way to add tools is through education, whether you take a one-off class, get a particular certification, or go back for a whole new degree. Another obvious way is to volunteer for projects at your office that expand your skill set beyond what you use in your current position.

There are less obvious strategies as well. The videographer for my wedding commanded top dollar (and he was worth it!), but that wouldn't have been the case if he hadn't any prior work to show. He had been managing project teams for a software company when he decided to start his new business, so he asked a friend if he could do her wedding video for free. The friend was certainly happy with the arrangement, and the fledgling videographer came away with a professional sample of his work to show other brides. By the time I came along five years later, he was booked up to a year in advance.

Sometimes giving away your services for free is the best way to monetize your time at the start of a new career. If you're an entrepreneur, doing a project or two pro bono is a good way to build legitimacy. If you're in a corporate career, volunteering is an excellent path for gaining experience in an unfamiliar area. Perhaps you're in sales but a local nonprofit lets you design their upcoming marketing campaign, or you can help the marketing team in your own company on your own time.

Reinventors don't try to overstuff their toolbox with the latest shiny and new gadget. They won't waste their time going for degrees in the latest trendy field, just to bolster their bio. But they will do whatever it takes to add the tools they genuinely lack and use them to build a pathway to their new career.

LIVING THE LAW: KNOWING YOUR SKILLS AND BACKING THEM UP

To be able to accurately assess what's in your toolbox, you have to be able to recognize the value of what's in there. This is the first step toward knowing what you already have that you can reuse, and what you don't have that you're going to need.

Start by simply making a list of job functions you've performed over your career. If you have an up-to-date résumé, this will be easy. If you don't, pull out the job descriptions from your last few positions and use them to make a list. Alongside each job function, list the skills you used to perform them. [11] Let's look at my Wall Street job as an example.

JOB FUNCTION	SKILLS USED
Negotiate contracts with sales agents	Sales, negotiation, business development, contract analysis
Oversee sales agents in foreign countries	Client relationship management, foreign language proficiency, cross-cultural ability
Train sales agents in company products	Writing, public speaking, teaching
Assist foreign sales agents in localizing and launching company products	Product development, marketing
Act as primary point person between sales agents and the company's internal departments	Internal and external relationship building, communications, leadership, advocacy

Job functions and skills are important, but they're not enough for building the legitimacy points you need. Job functions merely say that you did something, and it's not enough to announce that you've got the goods. You have to *show* that your skills and talents have delivered tangible, meaningful results, and you do that through listing your accomplishments.

From a reinvention perspective, accomplishments are crucial for showing that you have a history of getting results. But those results must be *meaningful to your target*. Reggie, with his expertise in operations and logistics and his time at the FedEx Leadership Institute, could prove he had a history of ensuring that items got to their destinations on time and that he had the leadership skills to inspire an organization; these results were meaningful to the CDC.

I cannot stress how important relevant accomplishments are. If you don't have them, you won't be able to make a strong case. (If that's the situation in which you find yourself, use the strategies laid out in the Hidden Conflict section of this chapter to bolster your experience.) Tailoring your accomplishments to your target is a crucial component of reinvention. Ultimately, you will use these relevant accomplishments

[11]Exercise on Page 235: Make a Skills List

to beef up your résumé or bio and in interviews and cover letters. You'll want to have a minimum of three to five to draw upon in order to prove a pattern of success.

Many people, eager to dive in and begin reinventing themselves, redo their résumés at this point and begin sending them out. Don't make this mistake! You don't yet understand the language spoken in your new career, and you'll need to translate all your materials so that you're understood. We'll be covering the how-to's of the translation process in Law 8 (Language), but right now, your focus is on gathering the data of your professional background and analyzing it.

Just as you did with your job functions, make a list of your accomplishments, along with the skills it took to accomplish them. [12] Don't try to skate through this by looking only at what you did in the past year or two. Take the time to come up with a complete list. The stronger and more complete your list of relevant accomplishments, the more legitimacy points you'll have for making your case, because you'll have a deeper well from which to draw. Dive deep to find any you may have forgotten.

To identify your accomplishments, use the "P.A.R." system:

P is for Problem: Start by identifying the problem you tackled (or the opportunity or challenge).

A is for Action: Figure out the actions you took to solve the problem.

R is for Result: Summarize the result by saying exactly what you accomplished in response to the problem, opportunity, or challenge. These results go on your list of accomplishments; try for at least three from your most recent position.

Also, keep in mind that each accomplishment should fit at least one of the following criteria:

Specific: "Developed a new fragrance for the tween market"; "Set up Brazilian subsidiary"; "Developed e-commerce platform for online store"; "Launched video product line in Europe"; "Implemented

---

[12]Exercise on Page 236: Inventory Your Accomplishments

financial database for all branch divisions"; "Created franchising guidelines for retail store division."

Identifiable: "Published articles on health and fitness in *O Magazine, Yoga Journal,* and *Shape*"; "Drafted speeches on Social Security reform for President Clinton"; "Managed accounts for Nike, Adidas, and Reebok"; "Presented Internet sales tax recommendations to Congress in 2004."

Quantifiable: "Raised $1 million in new donor funds in 2008"; "Reduced expenses by 20 percent, resulting in $500,000 annual savings"; "Organized annual holiday giving drive for three divisions"; "Increased sales by 20 percent in the first year"; "Put on a conference for more than fifty outside distributors"; "Brought in new client billings in 2009 worth $3.5 million."

Now you're ready to take these job functions and accomplishments, and the list of skills it took to do them, and analyze how what you've done in the past can be brought to bear on a new career or business. At this point in your reinvention, you won't be able to do this at a very deep level. You've just come up with a target path, but you haven't done more intensive research on it (Law 6) or spoken to a native (Law 7) to flesh out exactly how you'll be using your tools.

Keep in mind while you're gathering data and putting the next few Laws into practice that there are three ways of assessing what you've done in the past:

1. **Direct experience:** You have an accomplishment that matches what they're looking for in your target career. They want someone who sells copiers, and—that's right!—you have sold copiers.

2. **Similar experience:** You have an accomplishment that comes pretty close. They want someone who sells copiers, and you have sold personal computers. Both of them are types of office equipment, and the customer is the same.

3. **Causational skills:** You don't have a direct or similar accomplishment, but you can make the case that your skills will pro-

duce the desired result anyway. They want someone who sells copiers, and you have sold your services as a consultant. You'd make the case that your sales skills are transferable.

Sometimes you get lucky—you realize that you have direct experience relevant to a new career. For the most part, though, career reinvention relies on similar experience and causational skills.

A final point: In addition to having meaningful accomplishments, you'll want to demonstrate with an example from past experience that you know how to get up to speed quickly. There is always tension between an employer's desire to see a candidate hit the ground running and the reality that the candidate faces a steep learning curve. This is why employers tend to favor those with direct experience: less time spent on the learning curve. Entrepreneurs are under even more pressure in this regard from clients who have no investment or interest in you. All they know is that when they put down their money, they expect something immediately in return.

To allay fears that your learning curve will eat up time and money, come up with examples of how quickly you were able to get up to speed in past positions or situations. *Don't be tempted to deny there will be a learning curve.* That will be seen as the empty boasting that it is, and a prospective employer will have less confidence in you. There's also the implication when you insist it's a piece of cake that you're devaluing the work they're hiring you for. All you can do is assure them you've managed in the past and expect to do so again. Your honesty will be viewed as a sign of strength, and it puts goodwill in the bank. You'll draw on that account every now and then over the first few months, because learning curves don't disappear overnight, and more challenges await you.

You don't necessarily need a 100-percent match between the skills you have and the ones they want. You don't have to have every single accomplishment on their wish list. The point of this Law is to show that you have enough tools in your toolbox to handle whatever they throw your way in your new position or business. Now's the time to gather up everything you've learned so far—the dream lifestyle from Law 1 (Vision), tuning into your gut from Law 2 (Body), combating your fears from Law 3 (Excuses), your Reinvention Target from Law 4 (Road), and your tools from this chapter—and go get some help!

The Takeaway: Your tools are your skills and talents. Many of the same tools you used to build your current or previous career can be used in building a new one.

Watch Out for . . . The gap between the tools you have and the new ones you'll need.

Putting the Law into Action: Make a list of your previous job duties and successes and break them down into a list of the skills it took to perform them.

Something to Think About: What do I see when I look inside my toolbox? Am I willing to do what it takes to polish the old tools and get the new ones I need?

LAW 6

YOUR REINVENTION BOARD IS YOUR LIFELINE

I get by with a little help from my friends.
—The Beatles

In 1956 only a few girls at Rosati-Kain, a Catholic high school in St. Louis, couldn't afford the $60 annual tuition. Jeanette Reed was one of them.

Most black students at Rosati-Kain came from families of doctors and lawyers. Not Jeanette. Her mother worked in a laundry; her father was a bellman with the Trailways bus company. A wealthy donor covered Jeanette's tuition, and Jeanette worked in the school library to repay her scholarship.

Every so often, a nun would bring Jeanette's sponsor to the library to observe her at work. "It was like they were showing me off and saying, 'Here's the girl you're paying for,'" Jeanette says. "That was embarrassing."

There were other telltale signs of Jeanette's financial status, or lack thereof. She owned only two school uniforms, and the constant laundering grayed the white blouses. She was so distraught about a hole in her sweater that her mother relented and bought her a new one. The first day she wore it to school a nun accused Jeanette of stealing it, because another student had just lost one.

"How else can you explain it?" the nun said. "You don't have any money."

"My mother bought it for me."

Unconvinced, the nun sent Jeanette to the principal's office. Even after Jeanette's mother assured the nun that her daughter was telling the truth, the nun didn't apologize. "I always felt that I was looked at differently because I was poor and black," says Jeanette.

Later, when Jeanette was working the switchboard of the telephone company in Milwaukee, Wisconsin—newly married, her last name now Mitchell—she made herself a promise. Never, she vowed, would her three babies suffer the stigma of being pitied or thought of as poor.

Jeanette made a plan to make sure that wouldn't happen. She'd work her way up in the phone company by getting to know everyone who could help her, so she could protect her daughters from the ridicule she'd endured. She wanted her name to be so well known that when people saw her girls, they would say: "There go the children of Jeanette Mitchell."

I am the oldest of those children.

I I I I

Jeanette Mitchell is a remarkable woman—just ask nearly anyone in Milwaukee. They're likely to remember her past as a young, single, working mother raising three daughters, receiving welfare to supplement her small paycheck from the phone company (back in the day when that was still possible). And now, Jeanette Mitchell is an esteemed leader in the education field, a proverbial pillar of her community.

Growing up, Jeanette was the oldest of six. When she was a junior in high school, her parents lost their house because her father, Robert, was laid off from the bus company. A relative sent word that there were jobs in Milwaukee, so the Reeds moved there, leaving Jeanette behind to live with her uncle until she graduated from Rosati-Kain.

Jeanette was eager to spread her wings, but it wasn't considered proper for a young woman of nineteen to move into her own apartment. She joined the Army instead, and, in basic training, she met a handsome man named Samuel "Mitch" Mitchell, who tore up the dance floor. She married him in December 1962, and two years later Jeanette gave birth to their first daughter (that would be me). Ten months after that she delivered a set of twins, my sisters. Seemingly overnight she'd become the mother of three children under one year old—and her marriage was falling apart.

"I'm on my own," Jeanette thought. Her parents were still raising young children; they were in no position to help raise hers. "You need a good job at a gas company, a light company, or a telephone company," her mother, Jane, had told Jeanette a few years earlier. "Work there until you retire, and get a good retirement."

Jeanette took her advice. Prior to having her daughters, she had taken a job as a long-distance operator at Wisconsin Telephone, now known as Ameritech. After the birth of her children, instead of staying home with them as most women in that era did, she went back to work.

∎ ∎ ∎ ∎

How was it back then, Mom?

You couldn't make a long-distance phone call in those days without an operator physically patching you through amid a tangle of wires. Jeanette was one of those operators. One day, a coworker took Jeanette aside as if she were about to deliver a state secret.

"Set your sights higher," she whispered furtively. "Because there will come a day"—the woman looked around to make sure they weren't overheard—"when folks will be able to dial their own calls."

Light-skinned blacks usually got the plum positions, and Jeanette was darker-skinned. But she was newly divorced and had her daughters' futures burning a hole in her brain. For their sakes Jeanette was determined to do more, be more, and earn more. She started up the corporate ladder, climbing past the rungs that were roped off to women like her: "No blacks need apply."

Jeanette joined the company's speakers bureau and an informal group of woman managers. She made it her business to get to know the district managers in the department. She was often the only person of color at their events, so she joined the Progressive Managers Association (PMA), a professional support group for black managers. "When it came time for promotions," she says, "people would say, 'What about Jeanette Mitchell?' And somebody else would say, 'Oh, yes, I know her too.'"

All the while she was breaking barriers. "I was the third black person to be promoted to middle management. The other two were men." She kept climbing the ladder, earning promotions, getting the salary bumps she needed to make a life for her girls.

I I I I

When did it start to change?

"I'd lived my whole life for my children. Suddenly I realized that the day was coming when they wouldn't need me anymore."

Still working at the phone company, Jeanette decided to go back to school. She chose Alverno College in Milwaukee, where she could take classes in their weekend program to earn a business degree. The school was dedicated to empowering women, not just for their own benefit, but for their communities'.

Jeanette got more at Alverno than intellectual education. Her time there sent her on a journey of personal and spiritual growth. "The teachers there kept asking me, 'When you die, what will your tombstone say? Will it say that you made a difference in this world, or will it just say that you just walked through here?'"

After spending most of her adult life consumed with working to give her girls everything she wanted them to have—which is to say, everything—Jeanette felt the stirrings of a higher calling. She began volunteering and soon became well known around town as a person who was dedicated to giving back to the community. "I realized that I wanted my life to be about more than a telephone company."

I I I I

The minute Jeanette made it known that she intended to run for public office, her network lit up like an Ameritech switchboard.

Joyce Mallory, a member of the Milwaukee school board, called.

"There's an opening here," she said. "It's a part-time elected position, so you don't have to quit your job."

"The girls are all in college," Jeanette thought. "Maybe I can do this."

Jeanette won the election and sat on the school board for the next eight years. In classic reinvention style, she soaked up everything that job had to offer, developing skills and collecting relationships beyond the scope of the phone company. In her fifth year she was elected president of the school board. "I managed a million-dollar budget at work. But the school district was one of the biggest employers in the city, with a budget ten times the size of the one I was managing at the phone company, and I was governing that agency."

As it happened, education was the top initiative of Ameritech's community service outreach program. When Jeanette won the presidency of the school board, Barry Allen, the president of Ameritech Wisconsin, was delighted. In a stunning example of win-win, the company paid Jeanette's salary and let her work mostly full-time on the board because it tied in nicely with their education initiative. Ameritech would "lend" Jeanette to the community, all expenses paid.

During her time on the school board, the phone company was so impressed with how Jeanette balanced her corporate career with community service that she was promoted to district-level manager *and* sent through an executive M.B.A. program. She would stay with Ameritech for thirty years.

I I I I

When did you know it was time to leave?

"I was driving home from a meeting in Chicago in a snowstorm, going over the meeting in my mind, and all of a sudden the thought came to me: 'I really don't want to do this ever again in my life.'

"When you find that your soul isn't being filled anymore," Jeanette thought, "you know it's time to go." More than anything else, she wanted her joy back.

When she got back to Milwaukee, Jeanette called human resources executives Ray Kehm and Judy Boll to ask what it would take to retire.

"When I heard the numbers, I said I don't know if I can afford to do this."

In church that Sunday the pastor, Reverend Denise Lockhart, was preaching a sermon on faith. "There I was, a licensed teacher for this church, telling other people to have faith, but I was afraid to step out on faith."

On Monday morning Jeanette submitted the paperwork for her retirement.

Jeanette was fifty-two years old—a difficult age to be a job-seeker. But she put the word out among her informal advisors and found out that the Helen Bader Foundation, a Milwaukee-based philanthropic organization, was looking for someone to run their new education-funding program.

Jeanette wanted the job. But how could she get it? She had never interviewed for a job outside of the phone company, didn't have a résumé, and didn't know how to negotiate for the salary she wanted.

But the connections Jeanette had built over the years—at the telephone company, at Alverno, on the school board, in the Milwaukee community—had been woven into a tight web of support. She called Dr. Howard Fuller, a superintendent of Milwaukee Public Schools during her school board years, to get the scuttlebutt on the position. She also reached out to Bob Pietrykowski, a buddy from Future Milwaukee, a community leadership training group they'd both belonged to years back. Bob worked for the foundation, so he spoke with Dan Bader, its president. She landed an interview, and her daughter (that would be me) helped her prepare. Jeanette got the job *and* she got the salary.

For the next eight years Jeanette happily worked at her "dream job" at Helen Bader. During that time she went back to school for the third time, this time at Cardinal Stritch University. She earned her doctorate in leadership for the advancement of learning and service at age fifty-nine.

When she graduated, her dean, Tia Bojar, and mentor, Nancy Blair, recruited Jeanette to launch a new project. The university was opening a leadership center, and they wanted Jeanette, with the connections and the name she'd built for herself in the community, to run it.

"I thought to myself, 'Wow! That would be really interesting to do.'" Jeanette talked to her boss at Helen Bader, and he agreed to seed it for $1 million over five years and offered to help Jeanette move over to head it. "He said many foundations transition their top-level people into new jobs."

Now a highly regarded consultant, Jeanette still advises the leadership center she launched, as well as other education-related initiatives in the city of Milwaukee. Her life has exceeded her expectations by a magnitude once unimaginable to her or to anyone aware of her origins.

▌ ▌ ▌ ▌

Who helped you, Mom, and how?

"Bill Clayton was my mentor and boss for years at the telephone company. He was the clued-in colleague who was instrumental in helping me move up in the company. Ray Kehm was also a really good advisor. He had the Rolodex; he knew who could do what to help me transition out of the company successfully.

"Judy Boll was head of the human resources department. She helped hold my hand through that whole retirement process.

"On the school board, Howard Fuller was always there. He remains one of my mentors and advisors because I'm still involved in education, leadership, and people in this community.

"The warm and fuzzy friend role, Angie Ward plays that. Jane Ziol and Lavetta Torke also play that role. They are the friends I call on. I can always depend on them.

"I use my advisors to bounce my thoughts off of. Each person I talk to knows me in a different way, so they'll give me a different perspective."

She takes a moment to reflect on her journey from poor scholarship student to community leader. "As I look back at it, if you rely only on what you know, you don't know enough. Always being open to hearing other people's views and sharing with them keeps you growing, stretching, and learning."

Dr. Jeanette Mitchell then smiles, uttering what might be the understatement of the century: "I have a good sense about networking and people."

THE LESSON BEHIND THE LAW: YOU NEED A STRATEGY— AND HELP FROM OTHERS

At this point in your reinvention, you might be feeling a little overwhelmed. You've come up with a vision for your life, learned how to tune in to your body, given up your excuses, and ventured down the road less traveled. You've analyzed your background to uncover your skills and seen what tools will help launch you in your new career.

Now you need a strategy. This is the framework you'll use for conducting your search, and it will help you organize yourself as you move ahead. A reinvention strategy accelerates your progress by highlighting key areas where an investment of energy will bring solid returns. By sketching out your ideas now, you'll be sure to cover the key areas affecting your career reinvention and so make the strongest launch possible.

Are you stressing out? It's okay—many people do around now. You probably don't see how you can possibly figure out every single detail at this stage. You're right! You can't anticipate every single detail. But you don't have to. You don't even have to know exactly what you want to do yet, and you can still create a reinvention strategy. This is not a test where you have to have all the answers in order to get an A. In fact, it's not possible to have all the answers until the very end of this journey, because it is impossible to know in advance exactly how your reinvention will play out. Your strategy—like your reinvention—is a work in progress. No one expects it to be more than that.

Then there are those on the other side of the spectrum—the "I'm a free spirit, man, I don't do well with structure" types. Even *you* need to put a strategy in place. The career reinvention process is full of twists and turns, so planning ahead will guide you and give you a sense of order to help you keep your bearings on your journey.

Here are the hallmarks of a good reinvention strategy:

1. **It is flexible and open to change.** Your strategy is NOT meant to be set in stone! A good one is fluid; it evolves based on changing circumstances, situations, and information. It is nearly impossible to know at the start all the roads your reinvention will take. You may go down a path and find that it isn't for you, or

you may come across a more interesting offshoot that you hadn't previously considered. A successful strategy allows you to change course midstream.

2. **It acts as a benchmark.** Much of the confusion during reinvention comes from not knowing what to do when, or how to evaluate new information and opportunities. A good launch strategy can act as a point of reference from the very beginning, helping you keep sight of your ultimate goals and desires and providing a way for you to measure progress.

It's easiest to think of your reinvention launch strategy as a business plan: You're in the "business" of launching a new career. Here are the primary areas this strategy will address:

Research: You will be gathering information about new industries and companies, or about people who can help you. The idea is to identify what kind of research and development will be necessary for reaching your goal.

Operations: The nuts-and-bolts tasks and logistical details required for an efficient search. These could include making a business card with your new career or setting up a contact management system.

Funding: Ah, yes, the elephant in the room. Read on.

What About the Money?

Ed Diener travels the world looking for happy people. Then he sifts the data to find out *why* they are happy. Many years and scientific papers and extremely cheerful people later, Ed Diener has discovered: *It's not about the money.*

Diener—a professor of psychology at the University of Illinois— checked his results against other researchers, in 2004 when he performed a meta-analysis of 150 studies on happiness (in psychology, "happiness" is referred to rather grimly as "subjective well-being"). While there is no one magic ingredient that makes them the way they are, happy people all have two traits in common: *good mental health* and *good social relations.* Additional factors come and go, but having money is never essential. It's true what they say, then, that money can't buy happiness—even though some happy people also happen to be loaded.

Successful career reinvention depends, in part, on *not* focusing solely on money. A study we conducted at TRI in 2006 examined hundreds of Reinventors to isolate patterns that lead to success . . . or to failure. In terms of motivation, the most successful of the Reinventors—the ones who managed to get to the end of their rainbow—were first and foremost seeking a better quality of life, not just a pot of gold. Their top three reasons for reinvention:

- **Getting more passion and enjoyment from work**

- **Having a better lifestyle, and more freedom and flexibility in their schedule**

- **Doing something of value and having a greater intellectual challenge**

There is no denying that money is part of the attraction of working toward a new career, especially in economically challenging times. You don't go to all this trouble to reinvent yourself just to wind up in bankruptcy court. But Reinventors even use forced reinventions—the ones where you are one of five hundred people pink-slipped on a Friday as your entire industry implodes—as an opportunity to build a better, more secure lifestyle that provides rewards beyond just cash.

(By the way, plenty of people in the survey listed money as their top priority. They were the ones who stalled out.)

Just because money shouldn't be your only goal doesn't mean you don't need any. There are, of course, practical considerations. You need enough cash on hand to fund your reinvention, because a new career doesn't materialize overnight. While you work toward your goal, you still have to cover the basic overhead of daily life, such as food and rent. Electricity would be nice, too.

Other expenses will come up as you research your new career, such as for traveling to talk to people or going back for education or certification. You'll need ink cartridges or toner for your printer. You'll need Internet access. Some of you will need chocolate.

Back when I quit my Wall Street job without having anything else lined up yet, I blew through my entire 401(k) in four months. The tax hit wasn't pretty (those of you who've been unexpectedly laid off and had to go this route know what I'm talking about). If you don't map out the financial logistics, you could fall into two traps. One, clearly, is the risk of running out of cash before you land somewhere new. The other is just as important: the cloud of worry you will have about your dwindling finances. That will pull you out of the reinvention mindset, making it more likely that you'll abandon your reinvention and grab any job on the horizon—right fit, happiness, and long-term growth potential be damned.

It can be tough to plan your finances this methodically, especially if you've had or expect to have a sudden, calamitous change in your fortunes. In the case of my sorry experience with that 401(k), I had known for four years that I was unhappy with my Wall Street life. I could have used that four-year window of misery to build up a Reinvention Fund so that I could have made my move eventually without a financial crisis looming. The ideal scenario is to come up with a practical plan for funding your reinvention *before* you get started.

First, decide on the source of your funds. Here are the Big Three:

1. **Stay in your current job (if you have one).** Continue to collect a paycheck while exploring your new career on the side. This way, you only have to come up with enough extra money to cover reinvention expenses. Check also to see if your company pays for classes or educational degrees. Even if it doesn't, you might still stand a shot at getting them to throw dollars your way if you make a strong enough case that your schooling is a benefit to the company. This means you need to spend less from your Reinvention Fund to get that extra education. Jeanette was a master at this!

2. **Ask your partner (if you have one) to help carry the load.** Naturally, this is subject to your partner's consent. A shift in financial responsibility can lead to major relationship stress, but if you both keep your eyes on the prize, these temporary sacrifices will turn out to have been worth it.

3. **Tap your savings.** If you *have* any savings. If you don't, but you still have access to cash flow (see Number 1), start putting money aside right now for the leap. But do not max out your credit cards—many employers check credit reports as part of the hiring process.

What if you have access to none of the Big Three?

The "Plan B" Job

An additional source of funding kicks in after you have exhausted the possibilities of keeping your job, leaning on your partner, or siphoning off your savings. This fail-safe option is to *take a temporary job*—the less demanding, the better. This is your Plan B gig, just in case the money runs out sooner than expected. It can happen if you miscalculate how much to set aside or if your reinvention time frame takes longer than anticipated.

Did I say "if"? I meant "when."

Most people underestimate the amount of time involved in a reinvention. However long you think it will take, I recommend doubling that—at least from a funding perspective. Career reinvention requires an investment of six months to a year, minimum, of effort. Two years is fairly normal as well. Having a Plan B strategy in place will give you peace of mind and may even help you get where you're going faster—you never know who you're going to meet along the way.

I cannot tell you how many times I have seen people balk at the idea of taking another, lesser job, *temporarily,* to ease them through a cash crunch. From the way they carry on, you'd think I was talking about breaking rocks in the Gulag with a pickax. There was a woman who came to me and said, "I want to reinvent myself but I'm running out of money. I don't want to get a job in the meantime because it will block my reinvention. What do you think I should do?"

I told her to go out and get a job.

I knew that unless she got her cash flow going to meet her basic needs, she would be hard-pressed to make any progress on the reinvention front. The mental energy she needed to brainstorm ideas would be sapped by worrying about the rent. When my 401(k) money ran out after I left my Wall Street job, I moved on to Plan B and took an office-temp job. It was a painful, demoralizing experience. I was doing menial work even the assistants wouldn't touch. One day I found myself standing at the photocopier, reduced to tears—here I was, a former director on Wall Street, and my biggest task was making copies!

During my three months as an office temp, a friend of a friend offered me a job. I turned it down because it would not have taken me closer to the entertainment field, my goal. "Fine," said the woman. "When you give up your dream, you can come back and work for me."

Give up my dream? *Never.* I would rather stand at a copier fixing a paper jam.

Your Plan B job is *temporary.* It's *strategic.* Maybe I was collating and stapling, but I still had all the talent and skills and wherewithal that had gotten me that far. I was still *me*, even without the big title.

Two months after that woman told me to give up my dream, I started my wonderful new life in the entertainment field. When she heard I'd landed the job, she called me to try and work her way into the same company.

The last piece of your reinvention strategy plan is to activate your network!

As the overused saying goes, it takes a village. You will need the assistance of other people to reinvent your career. King Arthur had his Knights of the Round Table. Captain Kirk had the crew of the *Starship Enterprise.* Dorothy had the Scarecrow, the Tin Man, and the Cowardly Lion. Every great leader has a circle of experts, all focused on the same goal. Yours will be your Reinvention Board.

HIDDEN CONFLICT THAT COULD STOP YOU: BEING UNWILLING TO ASK FOR HELP

You can't go it alone. And you don't get extra points if you try. Even if you love the image of the rugged individual—the self-made success story in which someone forges a path in the wilderness against all odds—human beings, like dogs, are pack animals. We survive and thrive with the support of our crew. In career reinvention, trying to go it alone is crazy! You cannot possibly know everything there is to know about everything you need to know during your reinvention. It's true that we learn from our mistakes, but as my friend's mother liked to say: "You won't live long enough to make every mistake you need to make."

You don't have to learn everything "the hard way" if there are people in your life willing to let you benefit from their own failures and successes. You've heard the expression OPM—Other People's Money, the number-one resource by which rich people get richer? Consider this OPM—Other People's Mistakes. Learn from theirs so you don't have to spend time making all of them yourself.

When navigating a new road, plenty of people are reluctant to ask for help—men and women alike, even if it's so common among men that an entire genre of jokes has been created around it. (One e-mail purporting to tell women "the guy rules" put it bluntly: "Christopher Columbus did NOT need directions, and neither do we.")

Perhaps you were raised with the idea that "it's nobody's business but your own." Or you think it's impolite to pester people with questions. You could mistakenly believe that you're supposed to know everything already, and that asking for help is the same as acknowledging your failings. The entrepreneur Norm Brodsky writes in *The Knack* about his father's terse but unforgettable advice: "You don't ask, you don't get." To launch a successful career reinvention, you have to get comfortable reaching out and asking directly for support from friends, colleagues, and contacts. As Jeanette found out during her corporate climb and again when she moved to the education field, most people will be delighted to share their expertise—it makes them feel good to give back and share what they know.

The costs of being unwilling to ask for help are significant. It's much more difficult to build new contacts "cold." Without an introduction from a mutual friend, you'll spend too much time having to prove you're not a stalker. Without a drill sergeant to keep you accountable, you could spend weeks spinning your wheels. Without a native in the industry, you'll lack the inside track. *Without the help and support of others, you work harder, waste time, and get fewer results.*

What if you're uncomfortable being the center of attention or asking others to offer counsel without direct compensation? In such cases, try forming a circle of advisors whose members take turns helping one another instead of shining the beam on any one person for too long.

LIVING THE LAW: GET PEOPLE ON BOARD

As you sketch out ideas for your reinvention strategy, ▯[13] you'll want a crackerjack team to help you launch it. That is why you need a Reinvention Board. It is a handpicked coterie of advisors, each of whom has a particular skill or field of knowledge, all of whom have your best interests at heart. Even contestants on *Who Wants to Be a Millionaire?* are allowed to call a "lifeline" when they're stumped; this group is your lifeline. Like a traditional board of directors, this advisory group helps you brainstorm, facilitates your development, connects you with key people, and serves as an impartial sounding board. Its members are there to offer guidance and advice, wisdom and opinion; they can calm you down or stir you up as necessary.

One important point: Your board is there to help you analyze and vet your plans, not to address the big questions of your life. If you go to them with a "Should I . . . ?" question ("Should I turn down this highly prestigious job with a fat paycheck and move to Belize to become a dive instructor?"), they will help you analyze the pros and cons ("I have to admit, Belize is nice this time of year . . ."). But the yes or no decision is ultimately yours, and for that you'll have to use what you learned in Law 2 (Body) to tune in and see what your body says about which is the right path for you.

Your Reinvention Board can be more of a concept than an actual group that meets once a month. They don't each have to know the other members or be located in the same place. They're just the people you know you can call (or take to lunch) when you need help hashing out the details of your reinvention.

You'll want your board members to be successful enough and experienced enough to offer sound counsel. Ideally, they should have been through ups and downs of their own and lived to tell the tale. The

---

[13]Exercise on Page 237: Outline Your Reinvention Strategy

members of your board should all be helpful individuals who are rooting for you yet who are willing (and brave enough) to give you the unvarnished truth, whether or not you take it well. They're not afraid to tell you who you are. They keep you honest.

When forming your Reinvention Board, look for candidates who fall into one or more of these five profiles:

The Master Connector.

This is a champion networker with a golden Rolodex. Malcolm Gladwell in *The Tipping Point* says that such people "link us up with the world." They know everything and everybody, and everything *about* everybody. This is the member you call when you need a connection who can fill you in on a particular contact, or the one to go to when you're ready to pitch a company or set up an informational interview.

Jeanette's Master Connector for the education field was Dr. Howard Fuller, who was then the superintendent of public schools in Milwaukee. "He's a national figure in education," says Jeanette. "I call him when I need to know about somebody, when I want to connect with people, and for advice about where I might want to go and what I might want to do."

The Clued-in Colleague.

This is someone you have worked with, who has seen you in action in a professional capacity and therefore understands your strengths and weaknesses. Clued-in Colleagues—ideally a former boss who is supportive of your growth and is willing to be honest with you—can help analyze opportunities for how well they match your talents and work style.

I once served as the Clued-in Colleague for Linda, who had worked for me in a sales capacity. Linda made it a point to stay in touch long after we'd both left the firm, and she called when she was considering another sales position. I knew from experience that Linda was not cut out for sales. On occasions when she led meetings with clients—despite my presence as backup—she would crumble. I had to break it to her that a sales career was not in the cards.

"But I negotiated that Taiwan deal!" she said.

Ah, yes. The Taiwan deal, where I handed her every deal point and where she sent them on via e-mail.

"Remember the meeting we finally had after months of dealing with them long distance?" I asked.

"Oh, that," she said. "I was nervous."

"You froze. You went completely red in the face and couldn't answer their questions," I reminded her. "Afterward, you ran to the ladies' room and threw up. That goes beyond nervousness. That's terror."

In sales, nervous or not, you have to be able to think on your feet, not use them to run for the exit. Still, Linda had her heart set on sales. She felt it was a "safer" job should layoffs occur. My response: "Sales is only safe if you're good at it." As Linda's Clued-in Colleague, it was my job to be frank. Anything less would have done her a disservice. Often, your Reinvention Board is your last line of defense before possibly making a terrible mistake; if your board members won't set you straight when you try to take a job that's not a good fit, who will?

Warm 'n' Fuzzy.

This is a friend who is guaranteed to lift your spirits. When you're bleeding from the slings and arrows of reinvention, this person can apply the psychological Band-Aid and spread balm on your spirit by reminding you of your value: You were successful before and will be again. The Warm 'n' Fuzzies know just how to distract you during moments of despair and put you back in touch with what's good. They also take you out to do something fun every now and then.

Jeanette's Warm 'n' Fuzzy board members included Judy Boll in Ameritech's human resources department, who "helped hold my hand through the whole process of retiring." She also enlisted her friends Angie Ward, Mary Wacker, Jane Ziol, and Lavetta Torke. Jeanette's talented life coach, Sandye Brown—who specializes in executive and spiritual leadership—"helps me feel grounded."

The Drill Sergeant.

When you're stuck in a rut and paralyzed with false fears, it's time to call in a drill sergeant. Sometimes, the only way over the hump is a kick in the rump.

The Drill Sergeant, like your other board members, has only your best interests at heart. This person is fully supportive but without patience for whining and excuses. The Drill Sergeant's favorite phrase: "Get over it," followed closely by "Get it done!" or "Get over yourself!" Fill this slot with someone you admire but of whom you're a teeny bit afraid. You risk that person's displeasure if you don't step up and get going.

Jeanette says she's quite satisfied with her personal Drill Sergeant. It's someone who "tends to ask me the hard questions about where I'm going and what I'm doing."

You're welcome, Mom.

The Native.

Natives are familiar with the lay of the new land. They know who the players are. They know the scuttlebutt and the trends. They're the ones who can give you inside tips on how to mesh with the culture and speak the language as you'll learn to do in Law 8 (Language). They act as your guide and warn you away from danger.

Jeanette's Reinvention Board is full of Natives. Once again, here's Howard Fuller, his finger on the pulse of Milwaukee education. Also, there's Tia Bojar, the dean at Cardinal Stritch University who asked Jeanette to set up the leadership center, and Dan Bader of the Helen Bader Foundation.

As you can see from Jeanette's roster, it is possible that one person can fit two or more of these profiles. Your Master Connector can be a Native who, after hearing one excuse too many, morphs into your Drill Sergeant. It's fine to multipurpose your board members as long as they're flexible enough to switch hats. If you're lucky, they'll be able to suss out exactly what you need. Otherwise, you'll have to prompt them ("I'm stuck and I need a kick in the pants"). You can also ask a therapist or coach to alternate between Warm 'n' Fuzzy and Drill Sergeant.

Dina, a student in one of my public seminars who heard me talk about this concept, was inspired to set up her own board. She wanted to surround herself with mentors and strong females, so she used that as a jumping-off point for designing her board. At the time, Dina worked for a major New York publishing house. She was new to the industry, and was trying to decide whether it was a fit for her. Dina's board consisted of:

Elizabeth: Dina's Master Connector and Native rolled into one, Elizabeth is a publishing insider who could give Dina the lay of the land and put her in touch with a contact, all in one fell swoop. She helped Dina see that her first job in publishing—as an assistant for a senior executive in sales and marketing—was a great position because it exposed her to all aspects of the business and was perfect for a publishing newbie.

Katie: Another publishing insider who was Dina's Drill Sergeant. When Dina complained that she was working too many hours, Katie set an alarm on her computer to remind her to e-mail Dina at 4 P.M. every day to tell her to start wrapping it up to go home. She did this for a month, until Dina got the hint.

Yasmeen and Alana: Dina's Warm 'n' Fuzzy crew. Yasmeen, a free-spirited, stylish vegetarian, reminded Dina to stay connected with her instinct and soul. Alana and Dina were a mutual cheerleading team, sending daily motivational texts to one another ("P.S. Who's awesome? You are!"). Alana was also the Clued-in Colleague who recommended Dina for her current position.

Dina chose to have bimonthly in-person meetings with her board. They'd gather for a meal and swap strategies for all its members. Jeanette preferred to run hers like an informal network of resources, managing the relationships independently of one another and reaching out to her members individually for a meal, meeting, or call whenever she needed help. Take their example and set up your board in a way that best suits you *and* the people you're working with.

One VERY important reminder: Don't expect or ask board members to give of themselves in a way they simply cannot. Some people are fine about breaking out the Rolodex, but they'll tap a foot impatiently if you ask them to hang on the phone for an hour while you methodically scrutinize your latest fears. The Native who has only just met you may bristle at the thought of handing over a lifetime's worth of carefully cultivated relationships. If you ask people to give in a way that feels unnatural, they'll shut down, freeze, or stop taking your calls.

The *Do Not* Call List

You may be tempted to add certain friends to your board or hold open auditions to widen the field of candidates. Don't do it! There are plenty of people who have much to offer *under different circumstances*, but who are all wrong for your board. Now is the time to be discriminating, because your Reinvention Board has to be, above all, a safe space where you can hammer out the kinks in your plan. To be effective, its members (as in corporate boards) should have no conflicts of interest that could color their input. Anyone who puts their personal agenda above yours is likely to offer self-interested—or worse, downright awful—advice.

Here are a few people who should NOT sit on your board:

Your spouse or partner, who has an investment in every decision you make. It might sound unfair to make a restriction here, since this is the person who is supposed to be your main source of emotional support. But this is also the person who is the most likely to hyperventilate when you talk about chucking your law career to become a jazz musician. Anyone so affected by your every hiccup is going to have a tough time being impartial about your plans to change the status quo. In my seminars, I always run into people—at least one per class—who insist that their significant other is above such petty territorial concerns and should therefore sit on the board. I like to point out that it's not fair to such wonderful, sainted partners to expect them to ignore their own interests. Their needs should also come into play when you make decisions that affect both of you.

Your parents who, although they love you, remember the time they had to bail you out when you were stuck in Italy after college with no money, and that's why at forty-three you should not consider moving overseas to study with a sushi master in Tokyo. Your Reinvention Board is not the place for discussions about what you "should" or "should not" do. Even if your parents won't personally be affected by certain decisions, they're accustomed to having an opinion—and sometimes voicing it loudly—about everything you do.

"Frenemies," those secretly competitive types who find ways to undermine you while smiling angelically. Don't put them on your Reinvention Board no matter how powerful or well placed they are. They'll talk about how much they want you to succeed, but you know they'll do everything in their power to ensure you don't walk away with more of the marbles. Jeanette initially had such a person on her board before she wised up. We'll call this person . . . Cruella. This Cruella gal seemed sweet ("Jeanette, I so so so adore you, mwaah!"). She was popular (she was sleeping with the boss!). And she was totally thrilled with Jeanette's every promotion, right up until Jeanette got a promotion one rung above hers. The full moon of jealousy shone brightly in the sky as Cruella begged off hosting the customary congratulatory party for her "BFF" Jeanette. Seems that with winter coming, Cruella was going to be *very* tied up tracking down a new kind of fur for a coat she planned to have made.

Unhappy people who are frustrated with their lives or burned out and caught in a downward spiral. You want board members who are content, not bitter—and not only because it's a drag to be around party poopers. A study by Dr. Nicholas Christakis in the *British Medical Journal* showed that happiness is transmitted through social connections. If the people around you are happy, you will be, too. "Clusters of happiness result from the spread of happiness and not just a tendency for people to associate with similar individuals," concluded the study. A happy friend who lives within a one-mile radius gives a 25-percent boost in probability that you'll be happy, too. Although the *British Medical Journal* didn't mention it, we at The Reinvention Institute are certain that if Cruella lived within a one-mile radius, your plants would wither and die. Pack your Reinvention Board with successful, happy people, and your garden will grow.

One Final Point . . .

Before going any further in your reinvention journey, you'll want to pull together your board. ▯[14] As you do so, keep in mind that the Reinvention Board is based on the philosophy of "the circle of giving"—otherwise, it all becomes an exercise in selfishness and self-absorption. You're asking others to give to you, so to complete the circle you must offer the same help in return—although not necessarily to the same individuals. It's not always possible to repay in kind so directly, and that's why this is a circle. You "pay it forward" (a phrase popularized by the Kevin Spacey movie of that title) by giving freely to others. Person A helps Person B; Person B helps Person C; and so on. Anytime you can help your board members directly, I recommend you do so. But don't forget to help others, including strangers, in the same spirit in which you are being helped. Offer contacts, advice, and wisdom. I've personally found that this becomes a self-fulfilling prophecy: Those who give the most receive the most.

The Takeaway: Your reinvention strategy plans benefit from the help of a Reinvention Board, a coterie of advisors that acts as a resource for contacts, problem-solving, brainstorming, and emotional support.

Watch Out for . . . Becoming the Lone Ranger by being unwilling or too proud to ask for help.

Putting the Law into Action: Start the board selection process by reaching out to potential candidates.

Something to Think About: What opportunities can I create to "pay it forward" and truly give without any expectation of receiving?

THE 10 LAWS OF CAREER REINVENTION

[14]Exercise on Page 239: Assemble Your Reinvention Board

LAW 7

ONLY A NATIVE CAN GIVE YOU
THE INSIDE SCOOP

Success doesn't come to you . . . you go to it.

—Marva Collins

T he maternity-ward nurse placed the newborn in her mother's arms and tiptoed away to give them privacy for the first feeding. It was a lovely sight: Felina Rakowski-Gallagher in her hospital gown at 2 A.M. and Samantha, two hours old, at her breast. What words can possibly capture such a tender scene?

"You've got to be freakin' kidding me!" Felina muttered.

Not the Kodak moment you'd expect, but typical for Felina—a tough-as-nails former New York City cop. When things aren't right, Felina is first on the call button.

Except that the call button was, at this moment, dangling out of reach.

"So there I lay holding a newborn, having delivered this baby two hours earlier, and I couldn't call the nurse to ask, 'Am I doing this right?'" Felina recalls. "The baby is nursing—doing it wrong—and I'm getting sorer by the minute. You know the feeling of raking leaves without gloves on? Forty-eight hours later, I left the hospital holding my shirt out so it wouldn't rub against my nipples."

Women have managed to breast-feed their babies since time immemorial. Yet, somewhere along the way, one generation must have stopped sharing their secrets with the next. There are legions of new mothers with cracked skin, aching backs, and babies that won't latch on.

Really, someone should look into this. Felina just didn't realize that it would be her, and that the detective trail she eventually followed to solve the problem was giving her a road map to her reinvention.

Today, Felina owns and operates the first breast-feeding boutique in New York State. She named it—against everyone's advice—The Upper Breast Side, a pun on its location on Manhattan's Upper West Side. It's where pregnant and nursing mothers can find the products, advice, and hands-on instruction they need from people who are fluent in that sort of thing.

The shop is taller than it is wide, with boxes of nursing bras stacked to the ceiling, accessible by old-time rolling library ladders. Tousle-haired and in her mid-forties, Felina is surrounded by "My Brest Friend" pillows and herbal remedies for colic; she doesn't sell what she calls "crappy products," only the best in each category. But she couldn't have achieved this success without someone "on the inside" to guide her.

I I I I

Felina learned the number-one rule of entrepreneurship at Long Beach High School in New York, when she joined a club for future business owners: When you find a need that is going unmet, *go meet it.* That's how she found a job right out of college at SUNY Binghamton, spearheading the first pretrial release program in an upstate New York county. She performed background checks on people charged with misdemeanors and felonies. On the strength of her recommendation, many of those who couldn't make bail were released to their families—thus relieving overcrowding in the jails. The job spoke to two of Felina's passions: helping people no one else will help and finding practical solutions for vexing problems.

From there, it seemed reasonable to go into law. She took the qualifying exams . . . twice. "Don't ever have Chinese food with hot sauce for breakfast before you take the LSATs," she advises ruefully.

While helping out at her parents' art-deco jewelry business in Manhattan's Diamond District, Felina met Steve Gallagher, a dashing police officer from the city's mounted unit. She saw him on patrol so often that she began carrying apples and carrots for his horse, Fabian. Felina applied to the police academy as well and received a last-minute call in 1993 when a spot opened up; she wound up serving as an undercover decoy cop ("wearing uncomfortable stuff, and very little of it"), and finally made it to the mounted police unit alongside Fabian, her favorite horse. She married Steve, her favorite patrolman, in 1996.

The job had its drawbacks. "There were so many boring moments where you'd just sit on the horse and be asked the same question over and over again. Where is Battery Park? Where's the fish market? For some reason, when you're a cop, every answer is 'Two blocks and make a right.'"

By the time she was pregnant with Samantha, Felina was working for the chief of personnel. The work was interesting, if sometimes odd—like the time she had to arrange for the delivery of forty thousand new bulletproof vests. She fully intended to return to the job when her maternity leave was up; although they could get by on Steve's salary alone, "how would we ever move toward getting a place of our own, having savings, or taking a vacation?"

Things looked worse when Felina sat down to do the math. No matter how she sliced it, her paycheck would essentially be going into the pocket of the full-time nanny she would have to hire, with enough left over for the weekly Pampers bill. For this she was going to miss out on being with her baby?

Reinventing her career by going out on her own in a new business was starting to seem like more than a fantasy—it was a necessity. But who was going to explain to her how to pull off such an enormous feat?

George W. Anderson, Felina's former boss at the NYPD, observes that civil servants tend to be risk-averse after leaving the security and routine of the force. Felina was a different story; for one thing, she was already thirty by the time she entered the academy. "Felina had had other jobs, so she knew she could survive outside the police department," says Anderson.

Felina knew it would take time to formulate an exit strategy, so she returned to her old job while researching the idea of opening a breast-feeding boutique. It wasn't until Samantha was two that Felina felt confident enough to make it official: She would trade a secure job with benefits for an unknown future as an entrepreneur. To save on start-up costs, she would launch the business out of the living room of her one-bedroom walk-up.

In the year 2000, Felina Rakowski-Gallagher took a deep breath and made the leap from reassembling Glocks with her eyes closed to showing new mothers how to assemble the best breast pump on the market. She has never looked back.

I I I I

"There are women who think breast-feeding happens instantaneously, sort of like the planets and stars aligning," says Felina, recalling the first stirrings of the idea for her new career. "I wasn't one of them. I tried, and I fell flat on my face."

When Felina left that maternity ward in 1998, she knew she had a problem. She had the right equipment for nursing—a breast and a baby. But it was an agonizing, blistering experience, and her baby was practically starving. The nurse at the hospital had only barked out a quick set of instructions, and it seemed unfair to leave women hanging that way. She dragged herself, feeling "pitiful," to a breast-feeding support group at a local synagogue. That's where she learned that there is something in this world called a board-certified lactation consultant. Who knew?

She got a phone number for a lactation consultant, who advised her to buy a breast pump. She asked a physician friend to explain how to use it. The consultant made a house call to demonstrate the finer points of how to wrangle a nursing baby. Felina began to visualize a business built on helping other women solve the same problem. It seemed incredible that in New York City, home of millions of services, widgets, and improvements that catered to Manhattan's high-end demographic, there wasn't any one-stop shopping for breast-feeding advice and supplies.

That was the good news: There was no one in the area doing anything like it. No competition.

Now, the bad news: *There was no one in the area doing anything like it.* Felina didn't know what kind of business structure to set up for tax purposes. She didn't know about computer software like QuickBooks that make record keeping easier. She wasn't even sure what such a store would look like, since there weren't any in the area to visit.

It wasn't the first time Felina had been up that creek. Her family moved to New York City from West Berlin when Felina was six, and none of them spoke a word of English. Felina got the equivalent of a speed-learning course from her first-grade teacher, who was able to translate the schoolwork into Yiddish, a not-too-distant cousin of Felina's native German.

At the beginning of her career reinvention, Felina once again had need of a native speaker. With only twenty stores in the U.S. like the one Felina had in mind, there weren't that many Natives within reach. However, all twenty would be represented at an upcoming conference in Arizona.

Felina strapped Samantha across her chest in a blue and purple cloth sling and headed west. Despite the distractions of motherhood, Felina worked the room. She interrogated vendors, lactation consultants, and shop owners. Best of all, she introduced herself to Steve and Carrie Warburton, who ran The Lactation Station, a popular Salt Lake City shop where women could try various brands of breast pumps before shelling out $300 to buy one. Carrie was a lactation consultant and, as Felina later put it, Steve was "mysteriously very interested in the inner workings of breast pumps." They were conversant with the products, had a feel for the clientele, and knew how to run a successful small business. They were the real deal natives that had been living and breathing the career that Felina had in mind.

Once again, Felina strapped her baby to her chest and flew clear across the country—this time to Utah, where she practically moved in with the Warburtons. "They were pretty much complete strangers, but they invited me into their home and opened their world to me." The Warburtons wouldn't have agreed to open their books and lives to just anyone, but Felina wasn't just anyone. She was serious.

Felina watched the Warburtons in action and peppered them with questions. Who kept the books? How much staff did they need? What mistakes had they made? What made their customers tick? "I hired a high school kid to stay in the store to entertain my daughter so I could use both eyeballs simultaneously," she says. "I did that for close to a week."

None of the research that Felina did subsequently would have the impact of the cultural immersion of being right there with the Warburtons in the land of Felina's ambition, up close and personal.

❙ ❙ ❙ ❙

If you're a new mother who breast-feeds and happens to be in the neighborhood, stop by and shop at the Upper Breast Side. Felina will hand you a glass of water infused with slices of fresh fruit. Her mother, who helps in the fitting room, will give you a hug if you look like you need one. If it's busy, one or the other will shove a stack of baby photos at you—there are shots of Samantha, now ten, soothing nervous husbands as they wait for their wives, and shots of Jack, Samantha's little brother, playing with stacks of maternity books.

Felina started out in college with a vague idea about helping people and seeing justice done—and thanks to the help of some Natives along the way, that's what she ended up doing after all.

THE LESSON BEHIND THE LAW: YOU NEED ADVICE FROM EXPERIENCED PEOPLE

Felina did a lot of things right as she made the transition from cop to entrepreneur. One thing she did brilliantly was to go straight to the source: She sought out and learned directly from people who were already successful at what she wanted to do.

Getting the lay of the land from a Native increases the odds of a successful transition. Whether you're looking for a job or planning to become an entrepreneur like Felina, start by making the effort, no matter how much or how little, to talk to people in your prospective industry. Don't leave out this crucial step!

Locating a Native

How do you find contacts in your target field? Where are those Natives hiding?

They're not. They know perfectly well where they are. You just have to look in places you haven't looked before, and you can start by consulting your network. One of the members of your Reinvention Board (Law 6) is a Native who can introduce you to others in the field. But you don't always need to rely on a go-between. One client was a master at getting people in high places to talk to her. She would write them cold, expressing her admiration for their work and her desire to learn how they'd done it. She followed up every letter with a call. Those who met her in person were so taken with her energy that they gave her entrée to their personal networks.

There are other creative ways of mining your contacts for Natives, including such online tools as LinkedIn or Facebook. If you've exhausted your circle of contacts, try attending an industry conference, checking your alumni network from all the schools you've attended, or writing to someone you've read about from that industry (you'd be surprised how open people can be when approached this way). Felina pitched herself at conferences and asked around until she found someone who would talk to her. You have to be willing to take your efforts to that level. Ultimately it is a numbers game: The more Natives you approach, the higher your likelihood of success.

Handling a Native

Most people have a natural inclination to help others, but Natives aren't going to waste time discussing their careers with "tourists," people who are "just looking" before going back to their old lives. You have to demonstrate that you're determined to become a Native your-self, and that you'll go to serious lengths to make that happen.

As a new mother, Felina had a great excuse to stay home. She was overworked and sleep-deprived. But Felina realized that "I'm a new mother, so I can't . . ." was an excuse, and that she didn't have to let it stop her. Instead of staying home bemoaning her lack of sleep, she took several cross-country research trips with her newborn daughter in tow.

The Warburtons in Salt Lake City had never opened their doors to anyone in this way before—and they have no plans to do so again. But they could see that Felina was no tourist. Anyone who traveled clear across the country with a newborn was determined. The take-away from Felina's story is that it's up to *you* to prove how deeply in-vested you are in your journey. It's that dedication that usually gets people to respond with help. One way to show it is by going beyond the easy and convenient. *This level of commitment increases your chances of convincing a Native to help you.*

Commitment alone does not guarantee success. It is the rare Native who will greet you at the arrival gate with a bouquet and a chauffeur-driven limo to take you on a private tour of your new land. Show respect and consideration for those who agree to help you by accommodating their schedule to your needs. Felina didn't expect the Warburtons to come to her in New York or sit on the phone with her for hours; she flew out to Utah. She didn't park her baby with the store staff; she hired a local sitter so she could make full use of the access the Warburtons afforded her. Felina made it easy for them to help her, instead of expect-ing them to make it easy on her.

Too many people seeking information and assistance have it back-ward. They're doing the asking, but they expect the Native to jump through hoops to answer. A blogger once sent me an extensive list of questions and asked me to respond by e-mail. I told her I preferred to speak by phone, as I didn't have the time to draft so many replies. The blogger e-mailed back that a phone conversation was "too much work." I turned her down—if she wasn't willing to make an effort, why should I? Then there was the student in one of our Career Reinvention Boot-Camps who felt frustrated and angry when a former high-school acquaintance, someone who had made it to the top of my student's target industry, didn't respond to a request for career advice. Although resentment in such a situation might feel justified, it is unreasonable. You can never know the real reason(s) you're not getting a response— They're on vacation? At a funeral? Your e-mail is in the spam folder? They have amnesia? You're the hundredth person to have asked them for advice today?

Not everyone can or will help you. Nor are they obliged to. And that's okay, because there are always others who will come through. Shake off rejections and nonresponses and keep moving forward. While you are figuring out if the career or business you've chosen is viable, you're simultaneously testing how well you tolerate the strains and frustrations of the reinvention process. *Giving up just because you're discouraged by a rejection means giving up on your reinvention.*

A Native by Any Other Name . . .

As you begin locating Natives you'd like to contact, don't assume they're all equal. "Anyone is better than no one" is a great philosophy when you're stalled on the highway and need jumper cables, and a terrible philosophy when you're seeking a Native for specific information. *Only speak to contacts who are doing well in your target career and who enjoy what they do.* Burnout cases—those who have been at it too long, who are by nature pessimistic, or who are not where they want to be in life—will needlessly skew your perception of what your new life would be like.

Happy people say, "I love this career, although I can tell you right now that if you don't want to deal with x, y, and z, then this isn't for you." Burnouts say, "Why would you want this stupid job anyway?" or "This business sucks." Happy people are more likely to be objective, because they don't have an ax to grind. Burnouts are more likely to put a negative spin on things. Studies have shown that you can "catch" the emotional states you observe. So, if you see a burnout lumbering toward you with a sour look and a list of complaints, look away! Spare yourself!

Burnouts are caught in a vortex of negativity. You can identify them by their sarcasm and by the nature of the details they share. They think they're being "realistic," but all they see is the glass half empty. I ran into one when I first started The Reinvention Institute. I was interested in learning more about coaching, and a friend put me in touch with Ann, who had been in the field for many years. Initially, I was thrilled to talk with her, but my excitement quickly gave way to dismay. The first thing she did was warn me how tough it would be to earn a living. Then she mentioned how hard it was to get clients to respect boundaries. She went on to say that the paperwork was a nuisance. Finally, she cautioned that loneliness was a way of life for a coach— there was a tendency to withdraw socially because people were always asking for advice. I guess that included people like me, but I was sorry now that I'd asked for any.

"Is there *anything* you can recommend about coaching?" I asked this killjoy.

Her reply: "Helping people."

Your dream of a new career is still tender and in need of nurturing, so you are vulnerable to downbeat people right now. If you inadvertently find yourself in the company of one, watch out! Their depressing comments can put a damper on your momentum and trigger old fears (and a few new ones you didn't even know you had). Don't share your nervousness about your reinvention with a burnout, because they'll be only too happy to reinforce your anxieties while suppressing any positive data that would have put your concerns in a more encouraging light. My advice to clients who run into sourpusses is to gracefully redirect the conversation to neutral territory. You could say, "I have already done my homework on the industry's problems. What do people report are its benefits?" Asking about what "people" think is a way of taking it out of a personal framework, and that may elicit a more impartial answer.

If nothing works, thank them for their time and move on.

It's not only the burnouts who can steer you wrong. Anyone with an agenda that conflicts with yours—a secret saboteur—is likely to offer advice designed to derail you. A friend I worked with during my years in entertainment was interested in purchasing an office-cleaning franchise and planned to ask the advice of another franchisee in her city. As we discussed her strategy, I discovered a disturbing detail: There were only two franchise licenses available for her city, and the man she intended to contact owned one of them. I immediately recommended that she not make that person her first stop. In the franchise world, the fees usually include exclusive rights to a particular territory. "Right now, he's picking up the business from your region without having to pay for it," I said. "He has an incentive to discourage anyone from buying the other franchise."

My friend took my advice. The first Natives she spoke to—franchisees in territories outside her city—painted a glowing picture of the industry. She finally went to the local franchisee; he was the only one who complained about the business. "If I had gone to him first, I probably wouldn't have gone any further," my friend told me.

Today, her franchise pulls in $3 million a year—and she's talking about buying out the guy across town.

HIDDEN CONFLICT THAT COULD STOP YOU: FAILING TO BANISH YOUR MYTHS AND FANTASIES

Now that you're busy dodging burnout cases and secret saboteurs, you might be reluctant to raise your own doubts about your chosen business. Perhaps you think that such questions are too negative or that the answers should be obvious. But beware: Refusing to ask sufficient questions now invites disappointment and disillusionment later. As you check the myths and fantasies you came up with in Law 1 (Vision) against the real-life experience of people who already have your desired career, you'll get the real deal about what actually happens there on a day-to-day basis. Find out who your coworkers are likely to be, what downsides to consider, and what makes for success in that industry. Here is a list of questions to ask a Native:

1. Are there any negative effects on your lifestyle or your ability to pursue personal goals?

2. What hours do you work? Are they flexible, or can you make your own schedule? Do you frequently have to change personal plans at the last minute?

3. What is the earning potential in this business? How long do you estimate it takes to reach that level?

4. What kinds of people do you interact with frequently?

5. What qualities do you think it takes to be successful?

6. What does it take to reach the top? How much time, energy, and money (if you're willing to share) did it take for you to get to where you are?

7. How much travel is involved? When you travel, is it mostly overnight or do you have to take longer trips?

8. What would you say are the downsides of this career? What are the unavoidable things that are the "price of entry" to get to do this?

Asking a Native these questions up front can forestall a lot of trouble and misunderstandings. I had a client, Randi, who was tired of freelancing and wanted a "regular" job. I asked what that meant. What would a "regular" job look like? What would be involved in doing it? She had never worked in an office, had never been assigned a cubicle, had always set her own schedule. Once she went out and started talking to people about what happens in "regular" jobs, she realized to her horror that she would actually have to show up *every single day*.

Amazingly, this had never occurred to Randi, at least not enough to visualize and see how it felt. That's what happens when you don't fill in some facts and details at the hazy borders of your reinvention. She had been entranced by the idea of a regular paycheck, but all of a sudden, the reality of having to show up every single day at a certain hour for fifty weeks of the year hit her full blast. In her next session Randi said, "You know what? I'm not so sure that a regular job is the job for me." She wasn't willing to give up her cherished autonomy.

As you learned in Law 1 (Vision), when we're unhappy, we have lots of fantasies about what it's going to be like someplace else. Then we get there and it's: "Well shoot, I don't like the people." Before I moved to the new terrain of the entertainment field, I knew only of the upside: business-class travel to exotic locations, meals in fabulous restaurants, high-level deals with CEOs. But there was a downside too: extended time away from home, long flights, constant jet lag, and the obligation to socialize with clients from morning to night. I was willing to accept that trade-off—at least for a while. But if you aren't prepared for the downside (and there's *always* a downside), it's possible to land in your new career with a *thud*, realizing for the first time that "international travel" also means being in a different country every day—not for sightseeing, but to oversee licensing deals. You get up at 5 A.M., pack, fly to a city, check in at a hotel, attend a meeting, go back to the hotel to make calls, leave for a client dinner, return to the hotel, work till midnight to catch the end of the U.S. workday, and go to sleep. Get up the next day and do it again. For twenty-one days in a row.

Glamour? Yes. Also exhaustion. And missing out on birthdays, anniversaries, and just plain fun with loved ones back home.

An international career rarely includes seeing the sights and relaxing. You don't have the freedom you have when you're on holiday. The big joke in my family is that when I took my mother along on a business trip to Asia, she came home with photos of me surgically attached to my laptop, or with a cell phone sprouting from one ear. I don't appear in any of the "fun" photos.

"Didn't you vacation with your daughter?" her friends asked.

"No, she was working."

There is a shot of my mom by herself in front of Mount Fuji. There's a shot of her by herself in downtown Tokyo. The only relaxed photo of the two of us—in front of a blossoming cherry tree in Kyoto—was taken on a national holiday, my one day without meetings.

It's time to shatter your myths and fantasies and understand exactly what you're getting into. Different kinds of work call for different temperaments. If you don't know the downside of a career in advance, you won't be able to judge whether it's right for you. Only by asking the tough questions up front will you be able to make informed decisions.

In order to reach a pool of Natives, you'll need use the time-tested skill of networking. Many people are uncomfortable with the idea of networking, but the discomfort is usually born of run-ins with what Keith Ferrazzi, author of *Never Eat Alone,* calls the "networking jerk." That's the one "with a martini in one hand, business cards in the other," and eyes darting "in a constant search for a bigger fish to fry." It's the "insincere, ruthlessly ambitious glad-hander you don't want to become."

What the "networking jerk" forgets is that networking is about *relationships.* It's a tool that helps you forge long-term, mutually beneficial connections. Landing a job is NOT the goal of networking. You won't get the deal or the offer simply by exchanging business cards with someone. Setting a goal for a networking event to show up at a gathering where you don't know anyone and come home with a signed employment contract is not only unrealistic, it adds so much pressure that potential contacts will sense your desperation and avoid you like the H1N1 swine flu virus.

Networking is a relationship-building tool. Its primary objective is to get an in-person meeting. It is much more effective to meet people face to face than through the anonymity of e-mail. By attaching a face to your name, you ensure that others are less likely to forget you. BFFs, marriages, and long-term work collaborations often start over a cup of coffee. Now, isn't that a more reasonable expectation for an evening of networking than reeling in the big one?

Networking Goal 1: Land an in-person meeting. To achieve this objective, remember that *you* drive the action. It's not enough to get someone to promise a meeting—you also have to take responsibility for making it happen by asking for the business card and initiating the follow-up call or e-mail. This is not a game of musical chairs where your efforts to land the meeting stop when the networking event is over.

Networking Goal 2: Add to your knowledge. Now that you have scored an in-person meeting, it's time to use it to enhance your understanding of your target industry. This stage of networking is an excellent opportunity to learn about what positions are available and what skills, talents, and qualities you'll need to be successful there. More important, it is a chance to learn about the other person's likes and dislikes and how you might be able to return the favor of their assistance. You didn't think this was all about *you*, did you? Networking is about building relationships, and healthy relationships go two ways. Keep the other person in mind and think of ways to be helpful. You could send an article, provide industry information (which you are gathering anyway during your rounds of informational interviews), or even recommend restaurants, books, and movies.

Networking Goal 3: Get yourself passed along to other Natives. You've gotten an in-person meeting, you've shared information through simple conversation, and now you want access to more Natives with whom you will do the same. You are entering a different field and the more people you know in it, the better. You will still need to call on your network, even after you personalize your shiny new desk with a photo of the family. The more Natives you know, the more people to tap into who can help you succeed in your new career.

That's right—when it comes to successful networking, landing the position is the *by-product* of successful relationship-building. If you think of networking only in terms of finding new work, you will open every conversation by telling people you're looking for a job—which limits the number of in-person meetings you'll get. Contacts who don't have an open position are less likely to agree to meet with you, which turns into a vicious cycle: Fewer meetings mean less access to information and other contacts, and fewer strong relationships that could have helped you land a job further down the line.

I I I I

When you reinvent your career, you want to be strategic about how you network. Make a list of the Natives and other helpful people you'd like to meet and/or the organizations where you're likely to find them. ▌[15]

---

[15] Exercise on Page 241: Make a List of Natives

SOME TIPS FOR PLAYING THE NETWORKING GAME

1. **Use both e-mail and telephone when trying to reach contacts:** For ongoing communication, honor the style preferred by the people you approach. Some prefer e-mail, others prefer phone, and some still prefer the old-fashioned way: in person. Ask or figure it out, and shift your approach accordingly.

2. **Pay attention to timing:** Your target contact is on "work time"; you're on "search time." Give people an appropriate window in which to get back to you. It will probably take longer than you think.

3. **Alternate your method of follow-up:** Call one time; e-mail a week or so later. This creates the feeling of staying in touch without feeling like a pressure tactic to your contact.

4. **Always be cheerful and polite:** When leaving messages or speaking with your target (or an assistant), make sure you're courteous and pleasant, even if you've contacted them multiple times without success. Keep in mind that no one wants a guilt trip. If you come with attitude, they really won't want to help you.

5. **Use the Rule of Four:** As general rule, if you don't get a response after four tries over the course of a few months, move on. Caveat: Let this guideline be driven by how much you want or need this opportunity, because persistence often pays off. If you really want to speak to someone who does not respond to calls or e-mails, get more creative. Send something, like a gourmet treat or an interesting book. See if the person is due to speak somewhere and show up in person. Get a mutual contact to arrange a lunch for the three of you.

6. **Keep your options open:** Even if you really want to reach a particular person or organization, don't get fixated on one path. Often the "perfect" contact or company turns out not to be what you imagined (another myth!), whereas your ideal position or most helpful contact can come from completely unexpected quarters.

7. **"Close" each networking interaction:** Don't leave a networking session without knowing your next step. Ask for the names or the cards; schedule the follow-up call or the get-together.

8. **Express your thanks:** Make sure you take time to send a quick thank-you after each interaction. E-mail is sufficient, but keep in mind that since it's about building relationships, it's better to do something special if you can. There was someone I'd taken time for who followed up with a $5 gift card to Starbucks and a short thank-you note: "Have your next cup of coffee on me." Simple and memorable, and of course I will take her next call!

The Takeaway: Natives can provide useful information on the pros and cons of your target industry, along with an invaluable insider's feel of what it is actually like to work there on a daily basis.

Watch Out for . . . Burnouts who drown you in negativity and saboteurs with hidden agendas who deliberately steer you wrong.

Putting the Law into Action: Set up networking meetings with at least three Natives over the next three weeks.

Something to Think About: What are the downsides I'm willing to deal with in order to have the upsides of my new career?

LAW 8

THEY WON'T "GET" YOU UNTIL YOU SPEAK THEIR LANGUAGE

The limits of my language mean the limits of my world.
—Ludwig Wittgenstein

I t was 1996, and Julie-Anne Horton had three days in which to learn to speak "golf." She had grown up around country clubs, but tennis was her sport. She was a journalism student at the University of Central Oklahoma in need of a part-time marketing job, and the American Golf Corporation happened to be hiring.

She spent the next three days poring over golf glossaries— "Believe it or not, there are such things"—and watching instructional videos. "I just wanted to get a basic sense of the outline of a conversation about golf and understand the game itself. I was trying to pick up some of the lingo. I wrote down a couple of key words that I wanted to somehow incorporate into the conversation so I could sound more knowledgeable."

Just in case she was asked whether she played, Julie-Anne had a carefully researched answer at the ready: "I'm not a scratch golfer; I'm kind of a hack like everyone else." In journalism, a "hack" is an unoriginal writer, but in the language of golf, "hack" is an accepted term of modesty.

After three days of total language immersion, Julie-Anne went to her interview. Sure enough, she was asked, "Do you golf?" She knew just what to say. Her intensive studies had paid off, and she got the job. For the next three years, Julie-Anne created a marketing and brand strategy for AGC, managed a budget of $2.4 million, and exceeded revenue goals by 30 percent. By the age of twenty-one, she was driving a Jaguar. "My father loved to let me chauffeur him around. He'd pull down the tray table and use the Grey Poupon commercial language. He was such a ham."

The Jag wasn't merely a luxury or a by-product of Julie-Anne's success. It was essential in a culture (and parking lot) of Mercedes and BMWs. "It certainly went along with the country club lifestyle. It was looking the part as much as knowing the lingo. That included driving the right car."

Julie-Anne sold the Jag in her third year at the University of Oklahoma College of Law, but she never forgot the lesson she had learned, career-wise, about the importance of speaking the language. *Theirs.*

I I I I

Julie-Anne Horton (now Selvey) was born in 1975 in Shawnee, Oklahoma, a suburb of Oklahoma City, where everyone knew everyone. The Hortons, originally from the Carolinas, raised their four children the Southern way: lemonade and watermelon on the porch, summers by the lake with the cousins, football-this and football-that. And, of course, Mrs. Horton's famous pecan pie.

Both parents were liberal-arts professors, yet they observed strictly traditional roles. Julie-Anne's mother, a former opera singer with a master's degree, was responsible for the cooking, the house, and seeing to Julie-Anne and her three older brothers. Her father, Dr. William L. Horton, was "a proper South Carolina man" who had two master's degrees and a Ph.D. He made all the family's decisions, right down to the dinner menu.

Dr. Horton was forty-five and fairly set in his ways by the time his daughter was born, but Julie-Anne's defiant streak was always working to pull him out of his 1950s mentality. As a teenager, she announced from the back seat of the family's big white Cadillac that she wanted to become a doctor *and* a lawyer. Her dad shot her down with: "I think you would make a great secretary or nurse."

"That didn't sit well with me," says Julie-Anne. "I was one of those students who made straight A's. If I made a 99, I wanted to know why I didn't make a 100. That was frustrating to have him limit the realm of possibilities."

Her father later came around. He had grown up in the South Carolina town of Rock Hill—so named for a mound of stubborn, sedimentary flint that nearly prevented the Charlotte and South Carolina Railroad Company from completing an important rail line. Bill Horton's life followed a similar trajectory: stubborn and flinty, with late-stage mellowing.

I I I I

Julie-Anne hedged her bets in college by taking a cross-section of the classes she would need to become either a doctor or a lawyer, but she found what she wanted when she heard about a friend's father, a patent attorney. "I was so fascinated," she says. "This was the technical background I was looking for. This was the legal background. I just knew with laserlike focus that I didn't want to be in any other type of law."

Julie-Anne stayed close to home for college and law school because her father's health was declining. Then, with his blessing, she moved to New Hampshire for a master's in intellectual property at Franklin Pierce Law Center. After finishing her degree she settled in the D.C. area, taking postgraduate courses at Johns Hopkins and working for the University of Maryland Biotech Institute, a hub of five major research centers. Her job as the legal director of business development was basically about translating between the guys who invented stuff and the business and legal departments who protected it with patents and trademarks. "The challenge of that position was learning how to crack the code, to speak the language and interact with Ph.D.-level scientists."

Next up was managing the intellectual property portfolio for Digene, a company that develops, manufactures, and markets RNA and DNA tests for human diseases. She loved the work, "but it was heavy. I was bringing home very serious subject matter on my shoulders."

That brought her to a career crossroads in 2005—that, along with Kenton Selvey, whom she'd met through mutual friends. Kenton negotiated licensing deals for Discovery Communications and was the rare romantic prospect who eagerly engaged in discussions of biotech patents. When New York–based menswear designer Joseph Abboud offered Kenton a job, Kenton wouldn't go to New York City without Julie-Anne. And that was that.

I I I I

In New York, Julie-Anne decided to bring her legal skills to bear on music, "something that was young, vibrant, energetic, and current." Kenton says admiringly of his wife that she has a knack for "bending her career to fit what she wants."

Still, it was a tough nut to crack. "I didn't have a concept that to work in the music industry in particular is so sought after that people will do anything," says Julie-Anne. "People will work for free. You're talking about coming from this background where I've got four degrees to my name. What do you mean I can't have the job that I want?" The hurdles made Julie-Anne even more determined to climb over them.

Julie-Anne came to The Reinvention Institute to learn how to reframe her background in the language of her new target industry. When we polished her materials, we made sure to highlight the big-name brands she'd worked on at American Golf such as Nike and Ping (a big name in the golf industry). "If you're talking about a patent résumé, you're talking in very technical terms," says Julie-Anne. "I went through and changed a lot of the language. I played up the entertainment aspect of American Golf. That helped me establish some legitimacy."

One day there was a "blind" ad posted online whose language and style told Julie-Anne it had to be Warner Music Group. The wording sounded much like the copy on that company's Web site; viscerally, Julie-Anne recognized their accent. It took six frustrating months to get the interview, but Julie-Anne's hard work in the career language lab paid off—her accent was flawless. She got the job.

Julie-Anne's reinvention story doesn't end there. Reluctantly, she decided to leave Warner Music Group after several years. Her daily commute from Westchester to the Manhattan office was too much now that she and Kenton wanted to start a family. She discovered that IAC/InterActiveCorp, a NASDAQ 100 company with about four thousand employees, had an office in White Plains, close to where she lived. IAC bills itself as an "interactive commerce company," with so many Internet properties in its portfolio—including Match.com and Ask.com—that it gives the impression of owning everything-dot-com. It seemed like a worthy successor to the Warner job, and today, Julie-Anne is corporate counsel at Mindspark Interactive Network, a division of IAC.

I I I I

Dr. William L. Horton died in 2005 after a series of strokes. He and Julie-Anne had a routine when she visited during college. He would greet her with: "You look smarter!" and point to his head for emphasis. When he lost the ability to speak, he would point to his head, wordlessly.

"Do I look smarter?" Julie-Anne would ask, and her father would nod.

The moral of Julie-Anne's story: It's not difficult to learn a new language when there is so much you want to say.

LESSON BEHIND THE LAW: YOU HAVE TO KNOW THE LINGO

One of the biggest pitfalls in reinvention is when people try to skip this Law. In their rush to get started and reinvent themselves *now*, they see an opportunity and shoot off their résumé without adjusting it to explain, in the target industry's language, how their experience is relevant. They're often shocked when the only thing they hear in response to a job for which they were "perfect" is the sound of crickets.

In the best of economic times, pitching yourself for a position in a different industry without bothering to translate your background is a low-return strategy. In a tough job market, it can lower your chances to nil. If you don't do any translation, yet clients or hiring managers "get" you anyway, it's a sign that you are probably pursuing a traditional job change: same words, similar work parameters, just a different signature on the paycheck.

This Law—learning to speak the language so that those in your new career understand you—is at the heart of the reinvention process. Don't underestimate its importance. Since *you* are the one who wants a shot at something new, it's up to you to be bilingual and help others understand what you have to offer.

When you reinvent your career, you're asking people to take a chance on you. You could have the best track record in your current industry—but elsewhere, you're an unknown quantity. When you speak the language of a new field, its members are comfortable that you understand their needs. It's this sense of security that encourages them to take a risk on hiring you or engaging the services of your business.

Learning to Speak "Reinvention"

How do you learn the vocabulary of a new industry? There are no handy Berlitz tapes or cheat sheets, but there are plenty of resources for clues:

1. **The Internet:** The first place to begin every search. Google key words, check out industry blogs, and surf the Web sites of the top players in your target industry. This strategy can turn up interesting details and even job leads. (*The Wall Street Journal* recently reported that employers are moving away from online job boards in favor of their own Web sites when searching for candidates.)

2. **Industry Trades:** Made for insiders, industry trade publications are filled with the jargon of their target audience and are a veritable gold mine for the vocabulary you need. They are also a good source of profiles on industry leaders. Whether you're

looking for a particular job or planning to strike out on your own as an entrepreneur, these background pieces offer insight into how others achieved success or solved the problems you are facing.

3. **The News:** Less helpful for specialized vocabulary, but critical for catching trends and other information affecting your target industry. By reading *The Wall Street Journal, The New York Times,* business magazines, and local papers, you will gradually recognize your target's key players, grasp its new technologies, and understand where the profit is made.

4. **Specialty Products:** When the golf opportunity suddenly popped up for Julie-Anne, she took a crash course in its language by watching golfing videos—the career reinvention equivalent of those "learn French in a week" tapes. If you're targeting an industry where consumers need to learn in order to use its products, check to see if there are any learning videos or guides that you can review.

5. **Classes:** Depending on the industry you choose—especially if it's trendy—there might be classes offered. A client of ours wanted to break into online ad sales and found several places that taught courses in that subject. A great source for finding such classes is the target industry's trade association. They often offer webinars and seminars as learning opportunities for their members.

Going Beyond the Words

An old Czech proverb says: "Learn a new language and get a new soul." Moving to a new career goes beyond just learning its words; it means adopting its customs and understanding its unwritten rules. In effect, reinvention requires you to become bicultural.

Tossing off an impressive phrase or two won't cut it. The Natives in your new career will immediately see through that ruse, because speaking a language is also about understanding the unspoken nuances associated with that world. It's these nuances that help build rapport and solidify relationships; that help you "fit." As she planned her pitch for the golf job, Julie-Anne didn't just learn what the terms *scratch golfer* and *hack golfer* meant. She went beyond the definition to grasp the cultural nuance—that it is important for golfers to demonstrate modesty where appropriate. Her words showed the hiring managers at American Golf that she had her information correct, but her *usage* of those words let them know she would fit in with the culture.

Julie-Anne became bicultural in other ways, too. Although she never became an avid golfer, she made sure to master the game's basics. She often dressed for her job the way golfers dress, right down to the cleats. She drove a Jag because it helped her fit in with the country club lifestyle. Casual clothes and fancy cars were a part of the cultural language of her job, and Julie-Anne was determined to stay fluent.

Cultural immersion is the quickest way to become bicultural. To get up to speed in the unwritten mores of your new career, hang out with its Natives, read its trades, attend its industry conferences, and follow the flame wars on its blogs. Pay attention to what you observe, and check your interpretations with your Native board member.

The Art of Translation

When I sold entertainment game software overseas, we would "localize" it to suit individual countries, a process that involved not only changing the language but adapting the cultural framework of the game as well. One of the games involved a hunt for the best beer. When we launched it in Germany, we translated the game into German, naturally. In addition, all instances of the phrase *eis klat* (translation: "ice cold") were removed, because that is a country that traditionally serves beer at room temperature.

Making a seamless translation of your experience—"localizing" it—is an art that is essential to successful reinvention. You'll be reworking and rephrasing the content of your background to bridge the cultural divide between the career you're leaving and the one you want, while ensuring that the translation remains culturally consistent.

Back when I was on Wall Street, my job involved working closely with what we called "agents and resellers." In the entertainment industry, where I wanted to go, the word "agent" means something else entirely—that's the guy who takes 15 percent of your earnings—and there didn't seem to be any particular entity known as a "reseller." I ran it by a friend who worked for the Motion Picture Association of America.

"I've been researching the field and I don't see my title anywhere," I said. "I'm wondering whether these terms exist. If not, what terms should I use?"

My friend asked me to describe what I did in my capacity as director of agency and reseller sales.

"We have partners overseas who represent our products in their countries," I said. "We also take our content and sell it to companies who turn around and resell it through their own channels."

That's how I found out that in my new land, "agents" are "licensees," and "resellers" are "distributors." The division where I was heading was known as "licensing and distribution."

As long as I had him on the phone, I also asked my friend about the culture of the entertainment world. What kind of people would I encounter? What were the personality traits of those who were successful? What mattered to them?

"They have egos," he said. "Very big egos."

Outsized ego was one of the things I liked least about Wall Street. But I figured I could deal with it in entertainment because I would be more interested in the topics those egos would be holding forth on— and this proved to be the case.

Another detail my friend shared during that phone call was that people in entertainment were seriously social creatures. In the culture of Wall Street, there was plenty of wining and dining, but the point of schmoozing in entertainment was to build a strong web of relationships, not primarily to boast about who made money for whom.

When it was time to interview in my target field, I explained that I worked in "licensing and distribution of financial information." This they understood. By staying away from "agents and resellers," I didn't have to waste time explaining what I did and they didn't have to consult a reference library. I also made sure to mention the strong relationships I'd built with our international partners and how I'd been responsible for the wining and dining when they came to town. This showed I would fit in with the new culture—which in turn made them feel comfortable taking a chance on me.

HIDDEN CONFLICT THAT COULD STOP YOU: LEARNING TOO MUCH OR TOO LITTLE

There are two ends of the language-learning spectrum, and neither one is good news when it comes to reinvention.

Perfectionists

At one end are perfectionists, who won't try out the new language until they're completely fluent. This turns into a never-ending delaying tactic, since perfectionists agonize over every word, concerned that they're missing something. They tend to get hung up at this stage over their perceived lack of proficiency. Perfectionists are afraid that since they don't understand 100 percent of the nuances, they're destined to make a cultural faux pas. As a result, they often lose momentum before they can get their reinvention going. It's like building a boat and never sailing in it—there's always one more coat of paint to apply.

Here's how to tell when you're falling prey to perfectionism:

1. **Procrastination:** If you find yourself regularly saying, "Next week I'll make that call," or "Next time there's an event I'll go," you're using perfectionistic procrastination to weasel out of your responsibilities to your reinvention. In this situation, you're putting off steps that would bring you into contact with Natives— ostensibly because you're afraid of saying the wrong thing, but really as an avoidance technique. Another version of this is when all the learning you do is online, never testing your learning on people or in the "real" world.

2. **Self-criticism:** You continually beat yourself up for your lack of fluency, making it difficult to get any traction. This creates the impression among the Natives that you're insecure, which makes them lack confidence in your ability to deliver in the new industry. One of my clients, Shelly, found herself in this position. She wanted to get into the fashion field, and lucked in to a meeting with a highly placed Native. During their talk, Shelly flubbed the name of an up-and-coming designer, and the Native made a point of correcting her. Instead of admitting she was learning and laughing off the mistake as she should have, Shelly apologized several times for the error. In her next three coaching sessions Shelly continually brought up this mistake, and it was a couple of months before she could bring herself to meet with another Native. She had no energy for moving forward because she had used it all in beating herself up.

3. **Anxiety:** You are so worried about making mistakes that it keeps you up at night or your mind continually races. This is another form of energy drain that makes it difficult to progress.

4. **Hopelessness:** You're sure that you'll never be able to realize your reinvention because you've decided that you just cannot master this step. Instead of e-mailing a Native to try to get a meeting, you finish off those final two boxes of Girl Scout Thin Mint cookies.

5. **Secrecy:** You refuse to share any mistakes you've made with Natives who could have explained where you'd gone wrong, because you don't want to admit your weaknesses. When asked if you need any help, you say: "I've got it under control." Which is so not true.

The solution for perfectionists: Get out into the real world! The key to the fluency you seek is *practice*. Without practice, you're chasing a pipe dream. If you're procrastinating or feeling hopeless, set a goal to schedule a meeting with a Native and enlist a friend to give you a pep talk and make sure you've followed through. If you're struggling with self-criticism or anxiety, understand that making mistakes is a natural part of learning a new language, and give yourself permission to make a few. It only takes "good enough" to get where you want to go. And if you're hiding secrets from Natives who could help, gather up your courage and share just one. Most likely you'll hear, "Been there, done that."

Cultural Elitists

At the other end of the spectrum from perfectionists are cultural elitists who can't be bothered learning a new language because they think that their old one *rules*. Cultural elitists assume that everyone speaks their language, so there's really no need to learn any new vocabulary, much less make adjustments in behavior to "fit" into a new field. The reactions to their monolingual and ethnocentric outreach efforts range from polite rejection to deafening silence.

Here's how to tell if you're falling prey to cultural elitism:

1. **Bragging:** If you are continually talking about how fabulous you were in your old career and what a star you were, you're bragging. People in your new career only care about what you can do for them *now*, not how wonderful everyone thought you were then.

2. **Nostalgia:** Are you continually talking about how good it was back in the day? Are you missing and mourning the way it was? Like the image on the "5 of cups" tarot card, you spend all your time turned backward, looking at the cups that have spilled, instead of at all the full ones waiting right in front of you.

3. **Know-It-All-ism:** This is when you find yourself telling Natives how things should be done, despite your lack of experience in the new career. One of our BootCampers, Ted, was prone to this. Laid off from a job as general counsel for a major telecommunications firm, Ted had connections up the yin-yang. In fact, Ted was in our BootCamp at the recommendation of one of those connections, who knew that he wanted to make a change. Ted

set his sights on getting another general counsel position within a different industry—from a reinvention perspective, a fairly straightforward task. But although Ted could easily get meetings, nothing seemed to pan out for him. Several months after BootCamp ended, I ran into the acquaintance who had first sent Ted to The Reinvention Institute. I asked whether Ted had landed yet; unfortunately, the answer was no. Ted had torpedoed his latest opportunity by telling the hiring firm, point by point, what they were doing wrong in their business. He had so offended them that they'd put the word out among others in their industry to avoid him.

The solution for cultural elitists: Open up to the new! If you haven't been getting a lot of response or traction, it's a signal that you need to work harder at bridging the cultural divide. If you've been bragging or indulging in nostalgia, recognize that where you're headed is just as good as where you've been, and make it a point to combat your cultural elitism by looking for ways in which your new industry might actually be better than the old field. If you've fallen prey to know-it-all-ism, be willing to admit you *don't* know it all, and be open to learning.

LIVING THE LAW: POSITIONING YOURSELF IN YOUR NEW NATIVE TONGUE

Many times you will not have direct work experience for each aspect of your target industry or for starting up a business. As you learned in Law 5 (Tools), you may have to rely on similar experience and causational skills—transferable talents that will produce the desired result—to make your case. The easiest way to make a strong case is by revising your reinvention materials, which include the practical building blocks of a traditional job search (résumé, cover letter) or the start-up gear of the entrepreneur (Web site, promotional literature, business plan).

Your Reinvention Résumé

At The Reinvention Institute, we recommend creating what we call a Reinvention Résumé (or, if you're in business for yourself, a Reinvention Bio to use on your Web site or when soliciting investors). This is different from the traditional résumé and bio in that it uses the language of where you're going to highlight the skills and talents of where you've been.

Reinvention Résumés differ from regular résumés in several ways. A major difference is that they *always* contain an overall candidate profile section right on top—a valuable piece of real estate for showcasing your transferable skills and talents.

When Julie-Anne came to The Reinvention Institute, we made a number of subtle changes in her materials to demonstrate that she knew what people in the music industry cared about. Julie-Anne had perfectly transportable skills, but the language she was accustomed to using made her seem an unlikely candidate in a field packed with music aficionados. In fact, her vast technical experience in the sciences and in patent law could be considered a problem from the point of view of an entertainment company. What did biotech have to do with the latest hot artist? How would filing patents translate to defending trademarks for a boy-band singing sensation's clothing line? This is why it was important for Julie-Anne to highlight the skills she used in biotech, rather than her specific job functions. As you learned in Law 5 (Tools), *skills are global. Job functions are local.* The way job functions are described in one industry does not always compute in another.

Here are two examples of the actual changes we made in her materials:

BEFORE: Experienced leading cross-functional teams, including representatives from sales and marketing, in developing profitable co-promotional and joint development agreements.

AFTER: Savvy negotiator, expert at structuring agreements to maximize profits and brand exposure while identifying and minimizing corporate risk.

The first example simply says what Julie-Anne did in her previous role. The second example focuses on the translatable skills Julie-Anne possessed to do those functions. To develop a profitable agreement, you must be a savvy negotiator. And the skill underlying the mountains of legalese found in contracts? Minimizing risk for the company.

Here's another example:

BEFORE: Nine years of negotiating licenses and contracts in the U.S. and abroad.

AFTER: Nine-year track record of negotiating profitable licenses and contracts in competitive markets in the U.S., European Union, and Asia.

In the second example, we made sure to highlight two things that would catch the eye of any music executive: profitable licenses (the Holy Grail for most entertainment firms) and her experience in the competitive European and Asian markets.

A few examples from my own background:

BEFORE: Media professional with fifteen years' experience.

AFTER: Seasoned executive with extensive experience in launching and building major media brands overseas.

The first example merely provides information—what industry I've worked in, and for how long. The second example highlights the talents I have in launching and building brands in foreign markets—a skill translatable to a number of industries.

BEFORE: Business development salesperson for entertainment properties.

AFTER: Influential relationship manager with a network of top-level decision makers in "blue chip" media companies.

Business development is a task. Relationship management is the skill underlying the task.

BEFORE: Manage staff of twenty-five and department budget.

AFTER: Highly energetic and effective team leader with staff management and P/L responsibility.

The first example focuses on job function. The second example illustrates the skills it takes to perform those functions. To manage staff, you must be energetic and an effective leader.

A Few More Points . . .

Regular résumés usually lead with job titles, whereas Reinvention Résumés tend to highlight companies (if you lead with job title, you risk being pigeon-holed into a particular role—the kiss of death to any self-respecting Reinventor). If Julie-Anne had started each listing with "patent attorney," it is unlikely that anyone hiring in the music business would have read further. Instead, she prominently positioned the well-known sports brands she worked with in some of her positions, such as Nike and Ping.

Finally, a Reinvention Résumé is always accompanied by a cover letter (or e-mail), which is a powerful tool for explaining more deeply, yet conversationally, how your background is relevant. Don't be lazy and skip this step! Taking the time to write a strong letter gives you the opportunity to demonstrate your passion for the industry in a meaningful way, not to mention your communication skills. For example, Julie-Anne could have used her cover letter to mention to Warner that her parents had been musicians and that music was in her blood—details that didn't properly belong in her résumé, but that Warner might have found relevant.

Pulling It All Together

The first step in creating a Reinvention Résumé or Bio is to know what skills are necessary and valued in the new land. Go back to the legitimacy points you collected in Law 5 (Tools) for your target field; these will give you the types of skills and talents that are needed for your new role, the yardsticks that measure success there, and the minimum qualifications for making the first cut. Next, pull together a "translation list" or phrasebook of common terms in your target industry ▯[16] and have your Native board member vet it. Redraft your résumé or bio, describing your skills, talents, background, and accomplishments in the language of the new industry. Make sure your translation is smooth enough that it is clear to potential employers or clients how your background is relevant.

One important point: When you're doing this step, don't go translation-crazy. You cannot change the title you held at your previous job, even if it sounds better in translation. The human resources department at your old company needs to be able to confirm your employment should someone call to check your credentials. When I created my Reinvention Résumé to switch from Wall Street to entertainment, my title remained "Director of Agency & Reseller Sales" even though it had no meaning in the new field. That way, when they checked out my background, everything would be consistent.

To combat possible confusion caused by nontranslated titles, pepper the narrative paragraphs in your reinvention materials with terms that employers (or, if you're an entrepreneur, customers or potential investors) can easily grasp. Make sure you describe every one of your previous roles using the new terminology. This will draw a connection between your background and their goals, and it will comfort them that you are not such a long shot after all. You might not have a traditional background, but you already speak the language.

Focusing on the skills with which you performed your old functions will also strengthen your marketability and show potential employers or customers that you possess valuable talents, regardless of your previous title. Use this same principle when reworking your cover letter (or bio, if you're an entrepreneur).

To see how this works in action, you can download, for free, a detailed example of a Reinvention Résumé or a Reinvention Bio from our Web site at www.reinvention-institute.com. If you want more in-depth instructions about writing a Reinvention Résumé, including how to break down your own job functions into skills and translate them, you can also buy our Reinvention Résumé Rx Kit on www.reinvention-institute.com. It provides step-by-step directions on how to rework and reword your own reinvention materials.

It takes time to gain fluency in a language, and it takes effort to

---

[16]Exercise on Page 243: Learn the Lingo

translate your materials. I encourage you not to shortchange yourself by trying to rush the process. Take the time to make a clear, artful case for how your experience can help hiring managers and potential clients achieve their goals. You'll be rewarded when the Natives in your new industry welcome you into their fold as one of their own.

The Takeaway: Fitting in when you travel to the land of your new industry requires learning the language on two levels— verbal (words, phrases) and nonverbal (cultural expectations).

Watch Out for . . . Going to the extreme of perfectionism or minimizing the importance of learning a new language.

Putting the Law into Action: Rewrite your résumé, bio, or pitch letter in your new language.

Something to Think About: What level of effort am I willing to put in to become fluent in this new language?

LAW 9

IT TAKES THE TIME THAT IT TAKES

Patience and shuffle the cards.

—Miguel de Cervantes Saavedra

There are certain red wines you can drink right from the bottle the minute you buy them, but connoisseurs prefer the ones that need to age for months, even years, to develop complexity and release their full splendor. That's how it was with Marianne Hee's career reinvention; it needed the seasoning of time.

The job she eventually landed at Atlantic Wine & Spirits was worth the wait, because they entrusted her with an enviable portfolio. Few newcomers to the clubby world of spirit sales get to represent some of the most renowned wines in the business: Newton, BV, Sterling, and Acacia, along with the champagnes Dom Pérignon, Veuve Clicquot, Moët & Chandon, and Krug.

For connoisseurs, the wait is part of the fun.

I I I I

The thing is, Marianne was supposed to become a doctor. The house calls she would make would be to the sick and ailing, not to fancy Manhattan nightspots where drink orders are filled by "mixologists."

She'd carry a doctor's little black bag, not wheel a fifty-pound case of liquor samples.

In the small Malaysian town of Tampin where Marianne was born in 1971, no one doubted her destiny. By fifth grade, every one of Marianne's schoolmates—as well as her two siblings—was settled into one of three tracks: A, B, or C. The A's went into medicine or business— preferably medicine, because "business" carried the taint of "merchant." The B's became . . . well, it doesn't matter what they became. Marianne's father was a doctor and her mother was a nurse, so Marianne was born to be an "A."

"It's as if you're predestined and your occupation is already chosen for you," says Marianne. "Since my mom and dad were an important part of the community because my dad was a doctor, a bar was set for all of us. We couldn't be anything less than A students. That was it. We didn't have much choice."

Marianne rarely saw her father. "He was working like a madman," she says. Even when the family moved into a railroad apartment right above his practice, he barely stopped by for lunch. "He would sit down for literally ten minutes and then get called downstairs."

When Marianne was eleven, the family relocated to the U.S. and somehow wound up in tiny Dunedin on the west coast of Florida. They chose Florida because Marianne's mother laid down the law: "I don't do snow." Why Dunedin wasn't as clear. Settled by Scots in 1899, the fifteen square bricked blocks of downtown Dunedin are steeped in all things Scottish, from the pipe-and-drum corps at the schools to the sign on Edgewater Drive that welcomes visitors with a life-size Scot in kilt and bagpipes. The town's big event is the annual Highland Games.

Needless to say, culture shock. Marianne's English was acceptable— she spoke Malay at home but had learned English at school—but her accent marked her as an outsider. Despite seeing that American students were free to pick their own careers, she and her older brother and sister wound up sticking with the tried and true. "It was premed, engineering, or accounting," says Marianne. "They were the 'Asian professions.' We had choices now, but I still felt that my parents moved here and sacrificed everything for our education and our lives. I couldn't just go off and be a soap star."

At the University of Florida, her sister went for engineering, her brother for accounting. "Is no one going to carry the family torch?" wondered Marianne. Her father, well aware of the demands of a doctor's lifestyle, pleaded with her not to go into medicine. Marianne finally took a few business classes "for fun," and something clicked. She liked the practical applications, the "real-world tangibility" of what she was learning.

Marianne's siblings took jobs with Salomon Brothers in Tampa, but Marianne decided to take her chances in New York. In the fall of 1994, she packed her trusty red Nissan Sentra with cooking utensils and sesame oil and bottles of hoisin and oyster sauce. "It was hilarious," says Marianne. "Most people would have packed their clothes. If I had broken down on the side of the road, I could have cooked for myself. I had my rice cooker and bamboo steamer. Have wok, will travel."

It took about two months to land a job with Shareholder Communications, a small private firm that provided shareholder consulting services to corporations and mutual funds. Through a later merger, it became Georgeson Shareholder Communications. Marianne was thrilled to be on Wall Street. "I got there and was excited. I was a bright, young, starry-eyed kid who thought, 'Wow! This is really cool.'"

As Marianne plunged into the world of governance analysis and proxy solicitation services, "starry-eyed" turned to bleary-eyed. "I worked like a dog. I worked twelve-hour days and would forget to eat lunch."

Over the next eight years, she rose through the ranks. In 1996, at work, she met the man she would marry: Robert Brennan, who today is an executive vice president there. They found that seeing each other on the job and again at home was just too much togetherness.

"We needed to choose our careers or us," says Marianne, who decided it made sense for her to take the career hit.

She left Georgeson in 2003 at the age of thirty. "It felt like I was leaving the place where I grew up. Then I had to figure out what I wanted to do next. By the time I left, I just needed to decompress and go somewhere."

I I I I

For a while, Marianne taught Pilates, then traveled overseas and unwound enough to decide she didn't want to be "that nutso person," the workaholic with no time for a life. She came to The Reinvention Institute not so much to reinvent herself onward and upward as to learn how to slow down and let her next steps unfold.

"It was just so full-throttle for me. I was only seeing things one way, which was climbing, climbing, climbing. I was missing the emotional connection to my life."

Marianne's coaching encompassed not just her career, but her life as a whole. She worked on strengthening her relationships with her family, acknowledging her achievements, zeroing in on what she wanted out of life, and learning to feel comfortable enough to pursue it. During one session, I asked her this: *What would life be like if you didn't apologize for what you wanted in your world?* She came back with: "I wouldn't feel guilty, and I would nurture myself more."

Marianne was learning the difference between "being" and "doing" by focusing on being who she wanted to be, and allowing herself to venture outside her boundaries. She spent six months sorting out options that might bring balance to her life. As a hard-driving person used to making things happen right away, she was practicing letting the process develop in its own time.

After a while, she got itchy and started pushing to get her career moving again. In March 2005, she took a job with Lipper, an investment analysis firm, hoping for a compromise between the intensity of corporate finance and the more leisurely world of Pilates. After spending so many years working steadily toward her goals, she understood that—like fine wines—some careers take time to ripen. But after a year, it seemed that her life in finance was like one of those wines that, if left too long, turns to vinegar.

"I was struggling because I wanted to be excited about my job," says Marianne. "I wanted to build something. It had gotten to where I went to work just because I went to work. There was nothing behind it."

She poured out her troubles to a friend in the wine-and-spirits business.

"You've always been so passionate about food and wine," he said. "Why don't you consider switching industries?"

That sounded about right for a woman who had once packed her car with spices and cooking utensils in the event of a roadside culinary emergency. But before jumping in, Marianne had to ask herself the classic question that everyone must ask before attempting a career reinvention:

"Is this insane?"

I I I I

Giving a reinvention time to mellow can feel like a tug of war between the emotional, intuitive right brain and the analytic left brain. "Part of me was excited and a part was scared," says Marianne. "I was putting myself out there. I wondered, Is this viable? Can I make it work? Am I crazy for even thinking this?"

Marianne started to plan her reinvention. A key piece was the funding; she knew her earnings would take a temporary dip. Her career switch would take time and require an investment in additional training. Fortunately, Rob's salary was enough to provide the financial cushion the couple needed.

She learned that jobs for wine-and-spirits distributors had very slow turnover. "Once the salespeople have established their account base, they don't really go anywhere. Some of these guys have known each other for ten-plus years." She would have to wait till opportunity showed up.

Marianne used the in-between time to build new skills and prepare. "I had to get up to speed by going to work at a restaurant. Being on the client side, you learn what goes through their mind, why they buy what they buy, and how they carve together the wine list for their restaurant. By the time I went to interview, I could speak the language."

She spent six months doing an informal internship as a sommelier at Artisanal, a Park Avenue restaurant with its own fromagerie and gated wine cellar. To bolster her appeal among hiring managers, she enrolled at the American Sommelier Association.

Then her friend in the business found out that Atlantic Wine & Spirits was planning to expand its line and thus needed to add a salesperson. "It was all timing, and the tip from my friend."

Even after she interviewed for the job, the patience she was learning to cultivate paid off. "They liked me, but said they couldn't bring me in until October."

By waiting until the right moment, she was able to reap the full bouquet of what Atlantic had to offer.

Marianne is still developing a taste for her brand-new career. The first casualty was her favorite pair of designer black-leather pumps with "crazy three-inch stiletto heels" that she wore when she was sitting behind a desk. Now that she walks around town visiting restaurants, she wears a comfortable pair of dark brown ankle boots from Clarks. "They have a nice rabbit toe and a cushy bedding. There's also a chunky heel that's only about a half-inch tall. It's not sexy, but it works."

Marianne has also reached another phase in the evolution of her life: She and Rob want to start a family. She will have another opportunity to apply what she learned from her career reinvention: It takes the time that it takes.

THE LESSON BEHIND THE LAW: YOU HAVE TO GIVE IT TIME

One of the most frequent complaints I hear at The Reinvention Institute is about how long the process takes. Student after student comes in, each with a "reinvented by" date in their heads. When they're still in the thick of the process as that deadline comes and goes—which inevitably happens—they're shocked and frustrated. They begin to think all is lost; nothing is happening and nothing will *ever* happen. The truth is that progress does occur—in its own good time.

It's not that I haven't told them up front (as I am telling you now) that reinvention will take much longer than they imagine. But many potential Reinventors believe themselves to be the exception and confidently set out to prove me wrong. They sometimes think that a complicated process is easy, or assume that labor-intensive tasks will take no time at all.

You might think—oh, that would never be me, I know how much time and effort is required. But when you're busy envisioning yourself draped in glittering Olympic gold, the last thing you want crowding that image is the thousands of hours of hard work it takes to have a shot at the medal.

This Law, though, is immutable: Reinvention takes the time it takes. Like trying to harvest a garden four weeks after planting the seeds, or inducing birth five months after conception instead of the usual nine, forcing an artificial timeline on a natural process courts disaster.

The New Oprah

I'll never forget the attractive young woman who came to me years ago for a consultation. She was energetic, clearly intelligent, bright-eyed, and ambitious. She also had a whopper of a reinvention goal.

"I want to be the new Oprah," she announced.

She wanted to be the most famous TV talk-show host in the land—except a younger (she was in her midthirties), more down-to-earth version of the reigning queen of daytime TV. (This was before Tyra Banks grabbed that younger, more down-to-earth-Oprah niche.) Hers was a very big dream, but people have them all the time, and that is a good thing (even Oprah wouldn't be "Oprah" if she'd hadn't had a huge dream). I encourage our clients and students to pursue the biggest vision their heart holds and consider it my duty to help them turn that image into reality. Still, I was a bit taken aback by the enormity of her objective so I decided to probe more deeply.

"Do you have experience as a talk-show host?" I asked.

No, she didn't. But she had done some work in TV—not on-camera, mind you, but in very, very close proximity to people who had. She was familiar with the ins and outs of the television business from the production side, and hankered to be in front of the camera.

"My friends all say I'm like Oprah," she explained. "So tell me, how long will this take?" This is probably the most frequent question I get from prospective clients. They are hoping to launch their reinvention quickly, and I dread this moment because I know I am about to burst their bubble. I held out hope, though, that this girl—given the sheer size of her reinvention goal—would be the one-in-a-million Reinventor who understood how much time she'd need to invest.

"You can absolutely make a TV personality career happen," I said, "but you've got to build your case first. You have to identify what you have to say, explain why people need to listen to you, and come up with a strategy to assemble the portfolio to back that up." This would require a detailed plan, which, I figured, would take about six months to fully sketch out.

"Six months?" she gasped. "I was thinking more like six weeks."

Thank goodness I hadn't placed any bets. Most people think it takes about that long to lay out a plan for their reinvention because they don't account for the time it takes for research, analysis, pondering, and brainstorming. They also believe the myth that they can work on their reinvention full-time when the truth is they must fit its tasks into an already overfull schedule. Both of these factors make six months a much more realistic and achievable timetable for any aspiring Reinventor, never mind one who intended to topple a legend.

I don't believe in selling false hope, so it was time to reality-check Ms. Wannabe Oprah. "At six weeks, you'll have some ideas on paper. It'll take the next few months to test whether those ideas will have traction in the marketplace. At six months, if you're lucky, you'll have your angle down and be ready to take action on your plan. Each of these stages takes time, and you don't want to rush through them."

She wasn't buying it. Aswirl in the fantasy world her well-meaning friends had created for her, the fact that it might take more time and effort to lay out a strategy was completely unappealing. I wasn't willing to promise a quickie reinvention, and she couldn't imagine that there wasn't a way, somehow, to speed it up.

That was the last I saw of her, either in the real world or on TV.

The Illusion of Control

While they're not as bad as The New Oprah, most of my clients come in with an unrealistically short deadline in their heads. As accomplished professionals who are used to being in charge and running the show, they believe they control 100 percent of the reinvention process. Many think there is a direct correlation between their level of effort and the speed of the outcome, and that more effort automatically brings faster results. Very quickly they learn the brutal truth underlying this Law: It takes the time that it takes. Reinvention is a mix of elements you can control and elements you can't.

What's under your control when you reinvent your career? The prep work you do and the time you put into revising your materials, learning new skills, establishing credibility, and making connections. But there are a number of important things that affect the timeline of your reinvention that you don't control:

1. **When people get back to you:** You can call, e-mail, or send notes by carrier pigeon, but you can't force someone to respond to you within a certain timeframe. Maybe the contact you called is on a three-week sabbatical at an ashram in India. Telepathic skills or spells on the new moon won't help: They will get back to you when they're done meditating.

2. **When meetings happen:** Reinvention requires you to meet with people, and although you may have all the time in the world for others, they have limited time for you. When you're reaching out to busy people, it could—and often does—take three weeks or more to get on their calendar.

3. **Life events:** Newbie Reinventors often labor under the illusion they're going to stop their lives to reinvent themselves. But the fact is that you must juggle reinvention's tasks while you're living your life. The amount of time and effort you have available to put in is subject to what's going on in your world. If you get sick or your in-laws come for a visit, if there's a family vacation or a demanding project at the office, that two-week project to pull together your reinvention materials can take three or more (especially if your in-laws arrive to take everyone for a surprise trip to Disney World just as you're sipping a cup of Theraflu and e-mailing your boss to say that you'll get that crisis communication plan to her within the next twenty-four hours).

4. **World events:** If you were planning to reinvent your career in New York City in September 2001 or in New Orleans in August 2005, your timetable was going to take a major hit. Beyond unforeseeable disasters, knowable world conditions also affect your timeline, and these are the ones eager-beaver Reinventors tend to ignore. In the summer of 2009 *The New York Times* reported the story of a man who was laid off from a database marketing company for economic reasons. He was confident that with his qualifications, he'd land another job within a few weeks; two months, at most (this, in the worst economic downturn since the Depression). He was stunned that it took six months—three times as long as he expected. He fell into the same trap many Reinventors do: believing that their will alone makes them immune to the realities of what's happening in the world.

5. **When opportunity arrives:** Although you will take steps to create opportunity, you don't control when it actually shows up. Your outreach to Natives may not uncover any openings. This doesn't mean an opportunity won't eventually appear on the horizon, but you can't influence what time it emerges. Sometimes you're pitching a company and they love you, but they won't have the budget to bring you on for another four months. Another example, from my own experience: I'd been in contact with the CEO of a company who, although he liked my background in international licensing, didn't have any positions that were a fit. So I went about my business but touched base with him every few weeks. One day, I happened to call just as opportunity arrived, and I was hired as an international vice president pretty much on the spot. Between "there's nothing available" and "wait a minute, there might be something that's right for you," the CEO had gone to a conference of the company's international publishing partners. They were eager to jump into the burgeoning dot-com boom and pressed him to create local Web sites for their countries. He didn't have anyone on staff with the right background to handle that initiative; I called a week or two after he got back.

A whole chain of events may have to happen behind the

scenes before your opportunity sails into view. Even if you stare fixedly at the horizon and throw white flowers into the sea to entice the gods to do your bidding, it will still arrive in its own good time. What you can control is your availability—make sure those who pilot the ships of opportunity know that you're on the embarkation deck, ready to make the trip. While you're waiting for your ship to come in, take a page from Marianne's playbook and use the time to develop your skills, get additional training, make connections, and steep yourself in the environment of your new industry.

All the uncontrollable aspects of reinvention fall squarely under the category of our old friend ambiguity. And as we learned in Law 4 (Road), humans are hardwired for "ambiguity aversion," an inability to cope with the unknowable. To combat the uncomfortable feelings it brings, you'll naturally resist taking in any information that contradicts the illusion of complete control. In career reinvention—and life—we want certainty. But reinvention, like gardening, requires you to surrender to its timetable. It is a mix of not trying to rush the things you do control—overfertilizing and overwatering can kill your seedlings—and allowing enough breathing space so that opportunity develops (if you don't leave enough room between plants it stunts their growth and limits the harvest). In order to relinquish the illusion of control and maintain your sanity while you're waiting for fresh basil and tomatoes, you'll need to manage your expectations.

HIDDEN CONFLICT THAT COULD STOP YOU: UNREALISTIC EXPECTATIONS THAT CAUSE A CYCLE OF PAIN

In the first century A.D., the Greek philosopher Epictetus said: "People are disturbed not by things, but by the views which they take of them."

The man was truly ahead of his time. Twenty centuries later, studies would prove that our perception of pain is highly subjective, and influenced by our past experiences and our expectations for the future.

In other words, if you think that your career reinvention should take six months and it ends up taking longer, your expectation that things should be moving more quickly will cause you pain.

Unrealistic expectations about how much and how fast you can work, or how much time your reinvention will take, can sabotage you. They may lead you to give up too early or feel like a failure. I often see clients stuck in a cycle of self-recrimination because of this. They hold themselves to an impossibly high standard and then feel so badly about not reaching their lofty goals fast enough that they just give up.

This almost happened to my client Alyssa. A former nurse who'd held high-level executive positions in the U.S. health care industry, she embarked upon her reinvention determined to pursue her goal of improving the health care outcomes of poor, underserved populations on a global level. To do that, she chose international health care management as her target. Alyssa had some great tools in her toolbox—a clinical background, lots of related experience, and a web of supportive contacts—but there were a few important ones she needed to add (including brushing up on her French, the language of international relief work). Alyssa, being a type-A, highly motivated, somewhat control-freak executive, immediately set a deadline of landing her new gig within six months.

Well, six months came and went—of course—and Alyssa was despondent. She continually beat herself up because she hadn't met her date, and questioned her value and the wisdom of her path. Never mind that she'd had the unfortunate luck of starting her reinvention a few months before a recession. She couldn't shake the feeling that because she hadn't met her timeline, she was a failure.

It took a lot of coaching to get Alyssa to see that her reinvention wasn't in error, her expectations were. She had to admit that yes, market forces were at play, and that yes, people got back to her at their convenience, and yes, she had chosen to berate herself for missing an artificial deadline instead of acknowledging the inherent ambiguity of the situation. She also had to own up to the fact that yes, she was getting traction in her reinvention, and no, she didn't want to go back to her old field. So rather than giving up in defeat, she decided to change her expectations. She gave up the illusion of control and surrendered to the natural timeline of her reinvention. She kept doing the work, but instead of trying to rush things she allowed space for opportunity to show up. It took another seven months, but Alyssa landed a job with an AIDS organization that is right on target for her reinvention.

Changing Your Expectations

I'm not suggesting that it's as simple as "change your mind, change your life," but there is a scientific basis behind the idea that your thoughts influence the pain you feel. Positive expectations can powerfully reduce the subjective experience of pain, while negative expectations amplify it. Even feelings of uncertainty about an outcome (ambiguity again) can ramp it up.

You have a choice about how you perceive the timeline of your reinvention, and how you view it can have a dramatic impact on your emotional well-being. You can say, "Good things take time" or "It's taking too much time." You can think, "I know it'll all work itself out, I just don't know when" or "I'm not sure if it'll work itself out." You can say, "Not knowing is *not* the same as not getting" or "Not knowing means the odds are not in my favor." One thought causes pain, the other soothes your soul. It's up to you to determine whether the time you spend reinventing your career is a hard, painful slog or an exciting, ever-evolving journey.

Expectations out of line? Here are some useful reality checks:

1. **Test for magical thinking.** In uncertain economic times, companies are more cautious about hiring employees or doling out contracts to entrepreneurial providers. This slows down the opportunity-creation cycle and lengthens the amount of time it takes to get to "yes." Have you accounted for this in your timeline, or are you sure you're going to be the exception? If you think it's reasonable that others might experience a delay but you (because of your experience, background, baby blue eyes) won't have to go through one, you're under the spell of magical thinking. Deciding that in this case you most likely

won't be an exception will cause you to plan for a longer time-table and forestall stress down the road.

2. **Make a "control" list.** Mentally sort your reinvention steps into the things that are within your control (such as locating a class) and outside your control (when that class is scheduled). Under-standing up front what you can't control minimizes the pres-sure you'll feel when something delays your original plans. A member of one of our Reinvention Team coaching groups signed up for a semester-long course in interior design, her target field. The school canceled it a week before the start date. This threw a monkey wrench into her timeline, but because she understood that this turn of events was beyond her control, she refused to obsess over it and decided to take several one-day seminars as an alternative. Eventually, she was able to take the original class when it was offered at later date.

3. **Keep Plan B simmering on the back burner.** Much of the pain of dashed expectations comes from putting your eggs in one basket and experiencing the tension of a looming deadline with no backup. Having an alternative strategy—a psychological (and literal) fallback plan—gives you a cushion just in case things don't go according to your original timetable.

4. **Let go.** Redirect your focus to enjoying the journey instead of reaching the goal. Slow down and take pleasure in the learning; tap into the excitement of doing something new and breaking fresh ground in your life. If you happen to be between jobs, allocate some time for hobbies and family time and other enjoyable non-work-related activities. Consider the time off a gift, and do some-thing fun to take advantage of it. Later you'll wish you had.

LIVING THE LAW: KEEPING YOUR MOMENTUM GOING

Career reinvention is a process of building momentum. Like the magic of compound interest, small investments made over an extended timeline can pay off in a hefty return. But just as compound interest doesn't give you a large amount of money in a short period of time, so you can't build momentum overnight. For the biggest return in your reinvention, give yourself enough time to tap into the power of compound actions.

Thoughts + Feelings = Action

Actions are the result of thoughts and feelings. They do not happen in a vacuum. Getting momentum from compound action requires you to consciously manage your thoughts and feelings.

There's a saying in the New Age community that "What you focus on expands." Many people dismiss this truism; they think of it as permission to ignore problems that, the moment they're put out of mind, will explode and create a mess. But numerous studies have shown that ruminating repetitively on negative thoughts can interfere with problem solving, concentration, and motivation—the very things required to get you out of a negative thought loop. Giving too much attention to pessimistic beliefs takes mental energy away from constructive thought. Doing this can keep you from being able to see your way to moving in a positive direction.

Thoughts are a choice, and you have far more control over them than you think. You can decide what you want to think about something, how you want to think about something, and how much you want to think about something. Managing the timeline of your reinvention forces you to practice controlling your thoughts. You will continually have to choose between thoughts that sap your energy ("It's taking so long, it'll probably never happen") and ones that inspire you to take action ("I've got this extra time, so let me volunteer at this organization and polish a few of the tools in my toolbox").

Emotions also matter, since they have a symbiotic relationship with thoughts. Thoughts give rise to emotions and vice versa, so actively striving to experience positive feelings helps control your thoughts. It is not possible to go through reinvention (or life) without experiencing negative emotions, but research by Dr. Barbara L. Fredrickson, professor of psychology at the University of North Carolina at Chapel Hill and author of *Positivity*, has found that the ratio of positive to negative feelings makes a difference. She recommends that for "every heart-wrenching negative emotional experience you endure, you experience at least three heartfelt positive emotional experiences that uplift you." Drop below this "positivity ratio" of three to one and you run the risk of falling into a downward spiral and into a rut. Surpass it and you spiral upward into a creative, growth-oriented mode and flourish.

The first step in managing your thoughts and emotions is to become aware of them. Take a "Thought/Emotion" survey to see what you're thinking and feeling every day, and assess the balance of positive to negative thoughts and emotions. ▯[17] Run through your thoughts about what happened each day, and match them with the emotions you felt at the time, as in the example here.

A quick tally will reveal the ratio of positive to negative emotions behind your thoughts; if this were your chart, your positivity ratio would be two to one (the number of positive thoughts proportionally to the number of negative ones). Don't be alarmed if you initially see that you fall below a ratio of three to one; most people sit at two to one—a state where they are just existing in life, neither moving creatively through new levels of growth nor falling into the abyss of depression. Shooting for three to one is not about being permanently happy, just seeding more positivity into your life. Test your ratio on a daily basis; when the balance of your thoughts and feelings tips toward three to one, it'll be much easier to accomplish the daily tasks that are consistent with your reinvention goal and take action to make changes for the better.

Your Reinvention Tactical Plan

In Law 1 (Vision) you came up with a vision for your life and brainstormed career ideas that could deliver that lifestyle. In Laws 2 (Body) and 3 (Excuses) you learned to tune into your body, give up the excuses, and manage your fear. In Law 4 (Road), you opened your mind to explore options down the road less traveled, and in Law 5 (Tools) you surveyed the tools in your toolbox to see how you could build a path to your new career. In Law 6 (Board), you came up with a strat-

[17]Exercise on Page 245: Thought/Emotion Survey

THOUGHT	EMOTION	POSITIVE?	NEGATIVE?
I didn't have any meetings scheduled today. My reinvention will never happen.	Sad, angry		X
If I don't have any meetings scheduled today, I might as well read the paper. Maybe I'll learn about a company that would be a good for my target list.	Excited	X	
Have to give a call to one of my Board Members. I'm sure they'll help me brainstorm a few ideas.	Hopeful	X	
I volunteered today—it was nice to spend time helping others.	Happy	X	
Everybody's talking about the difficult economic situation. Maybe I should consider going back to my old career.	Scared		X
Caught up with an old colleague. Thank God I'm not doing that anymore.	Grateful	X	
Total		4	2
Positivity Ratio		2	1

egy for your reinvention and assembled your Reinvention Board of advisors, and in Law 7 (Native) you reached out to Natives who could act as your guides. In Law 8 (Language), you learned to speak a new language and translated your background so that it would be understood in your target field. Now you know you have to put in the time—and now is the moment to put that time to use.

A Reinvention Tactical Plan 📘[18] is a list of practical tasks that you'll do on a daily, weekly, and monthly basis to put your reinvention in motion. Like most tactical plans, it begins with goals; I recommend setting monthly ones that are practical, realistic, and doable (you can get an idea of how to lay them out from the workbook exercise). Don't try to tackle the "big picture" every day (e.g., goal for today: reinventing my career)—you'll feel overwhelmed. Instead, pace yourself (e.g., goal for today: I'll make three phone calls, write two letters, and find a new industry newsletter to read). Setting smaller objectives will increase your chance of completing them.

Next, break down the monthly goals into weekly action steps, then into a task list to work into your daily schedule, as in the following example for landing a new job or clients for a new business:

MONTHLY GOAL: PITCH COMPANIES A, B, C, & D

WEEK 1 ACTION STEP: CONTACT COMPANY A

Task list:

Craft pitch letter

Call Master Connector Board member to see if he can connect me personally with someone who works at Company A

Surf networking Web sites to see what other connections I might have to Company A

Call Native to get the scoop on Company A—reputation among peers, dish on company principals, newest strategic alliances, high-priority initiatives

Research latest news stories about Company A and industry trends

The challenge is to work those tasks into your already overstuffed to-do list. Here are some suggestions:

1. **Make them manageable:** Break tasks into fifteen-minute increments (I will spend fifteen minutes surfing the Web sites of my target companies to check for new job postings). If you don't like doing something but must (e.g., drafting a cover letter), set

[18]Exercise on Page 246: Create a Reinvention Tactical Plan

a timer and give yourself permission to quit when it goes off. Where can you find fifteen minutes? Turn off that *Law & Order* rerun early—you already know how it ends! Tell your friend you can't stay on the phone because you have something to do. Surf your favorite blogs for thirty minutes instead of an hour. Look for other time stealers in your day and cut back on them.

2. **Make them consistent:** Small steps taken on a regular basis are better than overloading yourself. You may feel ambitious, but if you put too much pressure on yourself to accomplish a big task all at once, you can burn out quickly. You don't run all twenty-six miles of the marathon the first day you lace your sneakers; you run every day and build your mileage slowly over the course of several months.

3. **Make them fun:** Enjoy yourself while you power through your task list—listen to your iPod or Internet radio, curl up on the couch with your laptop, or decamp to the neighborhood coffee shop. If you're not able to make the work fun, give yourself a reward for each accomplishment. Go for a workout and steam, treat yourself to a movie, or meet a buddy for the half-price margarita happy hour. Incentives are a good thing.

4. **Make them optional:** If the pressure is killing your initiative, give yourself an "out clause." Decide you will take action toward your goal for a month; after that you'll revisit your choice and see if you want to continue. This psychological trick helps diminish the feeling that there's no turning back. Knowing that you only have to take action for a few weeks before you get to decide again lowers the stress.

Keeping the Momentum Going

Reinvention is a journey that has a long-term payoff but very few short-term rewards. You will often put in lots of effort without seeing immediate results. If your only goal is to land the job or "have" the new business, you'll be less likely to reward yourself for the intervening steps. When that happens, it's easy to lose faith. Feelings of discouragement top the list of reasons why some Reinventors quit midstream.

So that this doesn't happen to you, use the following tactics 📖[19] to help keep you moving forward:

1. **Build in daily, weekly, and monthly rewards.** Create an incentive system for your interim targets—your monthly goals, weekly action steps, and daily tasks—and reward yourself when you hit the mark. Your rewards can be monetary, time-based, or activity-based. They should be fun and pleasurable; treat yourself nicely after every hurdle you jump. Here are some examples: *After I make the call to my Board Member, I'll go get a cup of coffee. If I get the pitch letter out to Company A this week, I'll treat myself to a massage. Every time I hit my monthly target, I'll reward myself with a day off at the beach.*

2. **Set up formal accountability measures.** The flip side of rewarding yourself is holding yourself accountable for achieving your goals. Reward without accountability is like gorging yourself on chocolate every night and not stepping on the scale—it tastes sweet in the moment, but you'll feel bitter when it comes time to zip up your favorite jeans.

   Accountability works best when you don't rely on your own internal motivation. It can be difficult to push yourself to take action—especially if it's something you don't like to do—so it's best to enlist outside help. Ask a trusted friend or your Drill Sergeant board member to give you a call about your progress. Assemble an informal group of like-minded Reinventors into a Reinvention Team (we run formal ones at TRI), and convene for weekly check-ins.

3. **Set up your tracking system.** You will need a system to manage the details of your career reinvention. As you launch yourself, you'll be introduced to new contacts, come across organizations you'd like to investigate, or hear intriguing ideas you'd like to explore. If you don't have a way to track all these details, you may get overwhelmed.

[19]Exercise on Page 248: Create a Reward and Accountability Plan

Your system doesn't have to be complicated—in fact, the easier, the better. Some of my clients prefer an electronic tracking system; others write everything in a notebook or keep things in a folder. The idea is to create a home for all your career reinvention information.

4. **Do one thing that challenges you every week.** As you learned in Law 1 (Vision), the career (and life) you seek is just outside your comfort zone. To make it to the finish line of your reinvention, you'll be forced to step up your game. Taking on one challenge every week will push you to do, be, and have more. This might mean making a phone call to a new contact, asking a few friends to become part of your Reinvention Team, or writing that letter to your dream company. The more you get used to going beyond your boundaries, the more opportunities open up to you.

You can bet that your reinvention will take longer than you think. You can also bet that you'll get where you want to go, as long as you don't try to rush it. Focusing on the journey—feeling a sense of accomplishment at completing each task, celebrating every time you jump over a hurdle—gives you a chance to hone your talent for transformation. You'll then know what all Reinventors understand: This is not something you do in a moment or for a while—reinvention is a way of life.

The Takeaway: The reinvention process has its own timeline; let it set the pace. You can control the amount of effort you put in, but you cannot control when opportunity shows up. Your role here isn't to control but to be ready.

Watch Out for . . . Unrealistic expectations that skew your perspective and cause you to feel like a failure.

Putting the Law into Action: Set up a plan to reward yourself when you complete a reinvention task or hit a monthly goal.

Something to Think About: What enjoyable activities can I pursue while I'm on my reinvention journey?

LAW 10

THE WORLD BUYS INTO AN AURA OF SUCCESS

*The real distinction is between those who adapt their
purposes to reality and those who seek to mold reality in the
light of their purposes.*

—Henry Kissinger

errie Williams sat in the back of a taxi speeding through midtown Manhattan, headed to an awards dinner at which she was to be the honoree. Tonight wouldn't be the first public celebration of her accomplishments, and it was unlikely to be the last.

Terrie was a public relations powerhouse, a successful African-American woman in a business dominated by white men. Not so long ago, she'd been too shy to join coworkers for lunch. Not so long ago, people in the industry had been scandalized to learn that this newcomer—a hospital social worker who'd taken two courses in PR—had landed Eddie Murphy, the biggest unsigned celebrity of the day, as her first client. Since 1988, The Terrie Williams Agency had been a Who's Who of brand-name celebs, including Janet Jackson, Russell Simmons, Lionel Richie, Sean "P. Diddy" Combs, Stephen King, the Reverend Al Sharpton, and jazz legend Miles Davis.

Terrie's schedule was packed from morning to night with meetings, strategy sessions, and public events. She was known for her ability to be "on" at a moment's notice, and for the handwritten notes she sent and personal phone calls she continued to make, even as her career soared into the stratosphere.

On paper Terrie's life was beyond perfect. She had the high-profile business, the high-earning career, the high-end lifestyle, the respect of her high-flying clients and peers. But as the cab neared the hotel where an adoring crowd awaited her, Terrie stared out the window at the blur of nighttime streets, asking herself as she often did, "Why do I feel so low?"

The taxi driver pulled into the hotel driveway, jumped out, and opened Terrie's door. *Show time.* Terrie checked her reflection in the window. She was dressed impeccably as always, her makeup artful, her close-cut natural hair flawlessly shaped. Putting on her game face, Terrie asked herself another question. Wouldn't a normal person in her situation be delighted? Nervous? Excited?

Not Terrie. As usual, she was empty inside.

I I I I

If Terrie's childhood were set to music by her beloved client Miles Davis, the score would be his 1955 album, *Blue Moods.* Because blue she was, as a child, growing up with her parents and younger sister in Mount Vernon, New York, literally on the wrong side of the Metro-North train tracks.

On May 17, 1954, five days after Terrie was born, the Supreme Court overturned a lower court ruling in the *Brown v. Board of Education* case, paving the way for remapping Mount Vernon's school system. Terrie (along with her schoolmate Denzel Washington) would be sent to school across the tracks as part of the city's compliance with the new integration laws.

Being a guinea pig in this social experiment left its mark on Terrie. It made her determined to save the world, even though she had no idea how to start.

Her parents, Charles and Marie, had been sharecroppers who worked the fields of North Carolina. Both came from fatherless families, and both were raised to soldier on without complaint. Marie was the only one of nine siblings to finish high school; she went on to earn a master's degree in social work after her daughters finished school. Charles had been forced to drop out early to help his mother raise his four siblings. When Terrie was fourteen the trucking firm that employed her father went bankrupt. In a decisive act that would echo through the next generation, Charles and a coworker left the company and started their own.

To most black folks back then, including the Williams family, education was the ticket out of poverty. If you went to school, worked hard, kept going no matter what, you'd make it: That was what it took.

Terrie's grandmother lived with the family, and she reinforced the message that black mothers everywhere passed down to their daughters: When you get knocked down, you get back up. You *always* find a way to make it through. "No doubts, no inadequacies, no mistakes were allowed," says Terrie. "That's what shaped me."

I I I I

These high expectations were tough on Terrie. "I learned early on that I had to be the very best student," says Terrie. "But that's not what I was."

In the Williams family you didn't have a choice; you simply achieved. To compensate for her academic shortcomings, Terrie needed to find a different way to excel—and she did. She plunged into school leadership activities and became a student of the human condition, and her own. "I became intrigued with psychology. I wouldn't say that I knew I was depressed back then. What I knew was that I couldn't express my feelings."

Her first save-the-world strategy was to become a nurse. "But then I realized I couldn't stand the sight of blood." When Terrie entered college she planned to earn a doctorate in clinical psychology. She had to drop that idea when she failed one of the prerequisites—twice.

Terrie graduated cum laude from Brandeis University after majoring in psychology and sociology, and got her master's of science in social work at Columbia University in 1977.

Her first job was as a medical social worker at New York Hospital (now Weill Cornell Medical College). "I worked with a lot of terminally ill patients," Terrie says. "There was sadness all around."

Terrie was the youngest woman on staff and the only African-American. "I felt very lonely. I had this routine—every day I'd go out for lunch and have a cheeseburger, fries, and a milkshake. Then I'd go back to my office and take a nap on the couch. Other people asked me to lunch but I never went. I was shy and in pain and didn't know how to express it."

One day Terrie decided that her solitary routine was "pathetic." She vowed that the next time someone asked her to lunch, she'd force herself past the shyness. "That's how I began to break the shell."

I I I I

Terrie didn't know it then but at age twenty-two she was about to enter her Miles Davis *Milestones* period—literally.

She was on duty at New York Hospital when she heard that Miles had been admitted for hip surgery. Miles Davis! Terrie couldn't let her shyness deprive her of this opportunity; she just couldn't. To her own surprise, she marched into Miles's room and introduced herself.

"I started visiting Miles every day," she says. "He became a friend. We had nothing in common, but somehow we had a really strong connection." They talked about life. They talked about clothes. "He was a real clothes horse."

One day Miles turned to Terrie and stared at her until he had her undivided attention. And then he said, in his raspy, low-key, matter-of-fact way, "You don't belong in this job. You're meant for greater things."

Terrie was stunned. "Here was this legend saying to me that he saw some promise, some spirit that needed to pursue different horizons. It gave me confidence, a real boost. It was amazing, a man like that giving me advice."

Miles never mentioned the subject again, but he'd planted a seed. A few weeks later Terrie was reading the black-owned *Amsterdam News* when she noticed a small ad for a public relations seminar. "*That's* what I want to do," she thought. With Miles's words ringing in her ears, she signed up for the seminar.

I I I I

She hated it.

She hated the class. She hated the teacher who taught it. But she was still intrigued with PR. So she did what her mother and her grandmother had raised her to do: She got back up and found a way through. She tried a second seminar, this time with better results.

Terrie kept her job at the hospital for two and a half more years. But she moonlighted, too, doing publicity for WWRL radio, making connections. In 1980 she got her big break. Filmmaker Warrington Hudlin offered her a job as program administrator of his fledgling Black Filmmaker Foundation. She took it, and the former shy girl made the leap to full-time publicity.

"I was scared, but my mother said, 'Don't worry, I'll be your net,'" says Terrie. "I left the safety of my hospital job on a Friday afternoon. I woke up Monday morning in my new life."

The foundation position was the first in a series of paid and volunteer PR jobs that Terrie took as she gained experience and contacts. No matter how many new relationships she built, she made sure she never abandoned the old ones.

Which is why in 1986, five years after she became his hospital buddy, Miles invited her to his sixtieth birthday party on a yacht on the West Coast. Terrie bought herself a ticket and went.

I I I I

It was on that yacht that Terrie did *not* try to chat up Eddie Murphy.

Marie Williams had brought her girls up right: You always extend hospitality and you always make everyone feel honored. "You introduce yourself to the other person," Terrie says, "the one who's alone, the one no one's paying attention to."

So as she wandered the yacht, enjoying the jazz trio playing Miles Davis songs, checking out the partygoers' designer outfits, watching the waves of the Pacific yielding to the boat's hull, Terrie didn't gravitate toward the crowd surrounding Eddie Murphy, who was basking in his *Beverly Hills Cop* and *48 Hrs.* stardom. "Everyone on the planet wanted something from Eddie Murphy," says Terrie.

Instead she approached the members of Murphy's entourage who were otherwise being ignored. She struck up a conversation with his crew, a conversation that—Terrie being Terrie, and Terrie being Marie Williams's daughter—continued after the yacht docked and the party lights dimmed.

She kept in touch with "Eddie's Boys" the way she did with everyone she met, sending them newspaper clippings of interest and attending parties at Eddie's place when they invited her. Although they were used to fending off the advances of the opportunists who wanted to be close to Eddie, Terrie's new friends seemed to sense her integrity. "People can spot bullshit a mile away," she says. "If that had been my reason for getting to know them, it wouldn't have worked."

One year after the yacht party, Terrie heard that Eddie Murphy was in the market for a press agent. While the big, established, glam PR firms fell all over themselves trying to win this plum client, Terrie made up her mind: This was her moment. She was going to get her own, starting with Eddie Murphy. "I want to make money in this lifetime," Terrie thought. "Big money. Legally."

She was ambitious, not crazy; she knew the odds were slim. She didn't have the flashy office or the flashy connections that her competitors had. She was unknown in Hollywood. She knew nothing about running a business. She didn't even *have* a business; she was working for Essence Communications at the time.

Terrie, remember, was also her father's daughter, raised to believe that "God loves the child who's got his own" by a man who started his own company when his employer went out of business. And she did have this: the inner knowledge that she had something of value to offer. And she had relationships, too—relationships that came naturally to her to build. "I didn't know I was going to have my own agency," says Terrie. "But I always knew I would have my own *something*."

She decided to pull a David-and-Goliath: the untried underdog fighting the powerful PR giant. She'd been to parties at Eddie's house, so she knew his home address. She gathered her courage, put together a pitch package outlining how she would handle his public relations, and sent it to him. The next time she was on the phone with one of his boys, Eddie heard that it was Terrie calling and picked up the phone.

"I got your package, and I'd love to have you represent me," he said.

"I cried," says Terrie. "I just cried."

❚ ❚ ❚ ❚

"I have a very deep and abiding faith," says Terrie. "When Eddie said yes, it was God saying that this was what I should do. But I was really scared."

Terrie called Miles to tell him the good news. "Sign me up, too," he said. The singer Anita Baker was next. As Nelson George wrote in *Billboard*, there had never been this much black star power concentrated in the hands of an African-American publicity pro.

Terrie Williams—a woman with no formal training in PR or business, and with virtually no money—opened her agency on the strength of that first triumvirate of clients, all A-listers. She was in business.

On a roll, Terrie went for her next big dream. She'd always wanted to have a book to her name, so she gathered up her parents' wisdom about relationships, and her own, and wrote one: *The Personal Touch: What You Really Need to Succeed in Today's Fast-Paced Business World*.

Her first book became a business bestseller, so she wrote another one, the inspirational *A Plentiful Harvest: Creating Balance and Harmony through the Seven Living Virtues*.

That one worked, too. So she wrote *Stay Strong! Simple Life Lessons for Teens*.

"I didn't say, 'Oh, I hope I can be an author one day,'" she says. "I said, 'I'm *going* to be an author.' I didn't know when or how. I just spoke it. I claimed it."

Terrie claimed it all. She went to the awards dinner that night with her game face on. Her plate was full. But her heart . . .

Her heart was numb.

❚ ❚ ❚ ❚

The lack of feeling that Terrie experienced the night of that awards dinner was nothing new. "I'm not really feeling. I'm just doing" is how she describes her inner life of that time. "It was so sad. I got so sick and tired of being honored."

She kept signing clients, big names, but none of it meant anything to her. Just as she was beginning to connect the dots of her life, the depression that had been circling like a shark beneath the surface made a sneak attack.

The years of pretending and isolation finally caught up with Terrie. After that awards dinner she spiraled down into a personal crisis, precipitated by several life-changing events. A beloved aunt died. Her parents split up and sold her childhood home. She sold her agency, although she continued to run it along with her new business partner. Her office lost its long-time lease. Even the comfortably familiar phone number for The Terrie Williams Agency had to change.

"I couldn't get out of bed for nine months," she says. "I know now that I'd been burying myself in work. I was overwhelmed, but I just kept on going.

"The trauma, the secrecy, and the lies of slavery shaped me. I was never abused, but something was wrong. I was confused because I wasn't in touch with what it was."

Terrie's depression had a profound impact on her business. Revenue fell. Clients drifted. The success she'd built came to a crashing halt.

I I I I

As always, Terrie did get up and find a way through. The predictable next chapter of the story would have her staging a comeback, becoming an even more successful, more famous PR pro with even more famous clients. But life had another plan for Terrie, so she took a different turn.

The sound track of this phase of her journey would be Miles Davis's sober but ecstatic *Black Giants.* In June 2005, Terrie published a first-person essay in *Essence* magazine that provoked more than ten thousand responses. The story of her nearly lifelong struggle with depression touched a nerve in the black community, where the subject is virtually taboo.

Reading the heartfelt letters, Terrie felt she'd been called by God to take a new direction. She decided to honor the feeling. The gift of her breakdown was a new book, *Black Pain: It Just Looks Like We're Not Hurting,* and a new career helping African Americans break the cycle of silence and pain that persists from the days of slavery.

Terrie spends most of her time now as a mental-health advocate, working with The Stay Strong Foundation, a national nonprofit organization she cofounded in 2001. She still rounds up the boldface names that filled her PR Rolodex—but the calls she makes now are to publicize her campaign to give voice to depression in the African-American community.

As Terrie tells her story now, she cries freely. The old pain is still close at hand. But she sits up straight and makes eye contact as she shares it, unbowed, unashamed.

The world is drawn to Terrie's aura. The light of her intention is so powerful, she doesn't have to look for people to fuel it. People come looking for Terrie.

"I am a woman on fire," she says with simple conviction. "I'm not playing."

THE LESSON BEHIND THE LAW: CONFIDENCE COMES FROM BELIEVING IN YOURSELF

There are numerous books on the self-help shelf that push a confident attitude as the elixir for success. Mix a few of the titles—take 1 pint of total self-confidence, 2 tablespoons of maximum confidence, a pinch of extreme self-esteem—throw in a little determination, stir in a few drops of daily affirmations and—poof!—a magical new you, ready to slay any dragons in your path. This secret formula gives you superhero-sized powers to barrel through anything, take the world by storm, climb any mountain, win friends, and influence people. In short, once you drink this special brew, the world falls at your feet to do your bidding.

But the problem with that cup of confidence is that its effects are only temporary. It doesn't bring about permanent change; it just makes you feel good in the moment. Its potency lasts a day or two; if you're lucky, perhaps a week. You quickly build up a tolerance for this particular fix, and it takes more and more of it to get that same high. And the lows, when you come down off it, are soul-crushing. Worse yet is that the world knows, somehow, that you're under the influence: The self-assurance you project just doesn't seem *real*.

The Real Magic Brew Behind Confidence

The aura of success that people buy into doesn't come from the surface trappings of confidence; it comes from an inner *knowing* that you have something of value to offer. You recognize this knowing in yourself by the emotion-based feeling of power that pours forth from your heart. If your heart is empty—because you're unhappy, don't really believe in yourself, or doubt yourself—and your emotions reflect that, no concoction of self-help slogans is strong enough to blot out that truth.

The research has been done and the data is in: This is one area where you can't fake it till you make it. Science has shown that being happy matters in a job search. In one particular study, over a period of three months students who had "low positive affect" (aka were unhappy) were less likely to have been invited for follow-up interviews than those students who had high positive affect. No matter what words you use or how much effort you make to conceal your lack of belief in yourself, the way you really feel will seep out.

I learned this the hard way, during one of the most painful periods of my life. I'd just graduated from Harvard, yet my feelings of self-worth were in the toilet. This was from an accumulation of factors. One was that I had entered college from a small Catholic school in Milwaukee where I had been at the top of my class, the proverbial big fish in the little pond. At Harvard I was in the biggest pond of them all, an academically elite and competitive environment, and I was swimming with the minnows. A few A's and B's in language classes weren't enough to stem my feelings of shame over a flood of C's and once, shockingly, a D.

Worse still was the fallout from a huge mistake I'd made. In my senior year, I was the manager of a popular coffee house in a library on campus. It was an all-cash business; we didn't take credit cards, and the nightly earnings were logged by hand into a notebook. I was not good with money; I didn't even know how to balance my own checkbook. So, although I was meticulous in my monthly reports to the administrative liaison in the university's office, I kept track of cash flowing in and out "in my head." Over time that led, embarrassingly, to a $400 shortfall. I paid it off promptly when it was discovered during a routine audit;

nonetheless, I was subject to disciplinary proceedings. I was allowed to graduate, but I had to petition formally for my degree.

They gave it to me, but I returned to Wisconsin emotionally devastated. I had legitimately done the work to earn a Harvard degree, but I felt like a fraud. I threw myself into interviewing for international banking jobs in Chicago and New York and although I always got an audience because of my credentials, and I always talked the talk, I just couldn't get that second interview. Nobody would hire me. I was reduced to taking a temporary data-entry job at a local manufacturing company, working the 4 to 11 P.M. shift.

I look back at that phase of my life as the time when I took my psyche apart and rebuilt myself. Like Terrie when she decided to focus on excelling in areas where building relationships—something she had an aptitude for—mattered, I needed to construct the foundation of my confidence on the things I knew in my heart I was good at. I had to learn to rely not on external credentials of success, but on a fundamental belief that I had something valuable to offer.

As I mended my belief in myself, results began showing up in my life. I left the temp job and got a much better position at a local but nationally prestigious insurance company. I decided to apply to graduate school, something I'd avoided because I was still embarrassed about my grades. This one required a leap of faith; I knew that although the Harvard name carried weight, it didn't cancel out the fact that I didn't meet the GPA requirement of the program I had chosen. Though interviews weren't a part of the application process, I requested an audience with the dean of admissions and flew to Arizona to make my case. I believed I would be a valuable addition to their student body, and this time my words and my feelings matched. It worked: I got in.

How to Get that "Inner Knowing"

Believing in yourself is infectious. *Not* believing in yourself is also infectious. Which attitude would you like others to pick up on and mirror back to you?

Reinvention requires getting people interested in what you have to offer; if *you* don't believe, deep down, in your value they'll pick up on that. It will be impossible to convince potential employers or clients to hire you unless you feel in your heart that you are worthy of what you seek. This "inner knowing" is the real magic potion. Even those with "more" (smarts, connections, Gummi Bears) won't get far without it.

People naturally respond to the person who radiates an aura of success. Science backs this up; studies have demonstrated that individuals who experience more positive emotions—joy, satisfaction, contentment, enthusiasm—receive more social support from the people around them. Having a respectful, heartfelt, compassionate view of yourself, and truly believing in the value you bring to the world, gives you a sparkle and an energy that people are drawn to. This quality is far more attractive to hiring managers or prospective customers than vast industry knowledge or a massive network of contacts.

When you have this inner knowing, your belief in yourself is heard in the force of the emotion behind your words. This is the rocket fuel that powers the launch of your reinvention. But how do you fill that tank? Those two years I spent in the trenches restructuring my psyche taught me the best ways to move the needle from empty to full:

1. **Focus on your natural talents.** I spent a lot of time at Harvard trying to force myself into an unnatural box, academically speaking. This caused me to miss some important data: I got A's and B's in my language classes. (*Hello?* Natural talent to the left!) When I began to focus on my A area by switching majors and choosing an MBA program built on foreign languages and cross-cultural competency, success followed—first in my GPA, then in my career. Instead of pining for the resources and contacts she didn't possess, Terrie used the natural talent she already had for building strong and authentic relationships to attract some of the biggest names in entertainment to her PR firm as clients, and to enlist their support when she moved on to become a mental health advocate.

2. **Do the emotional work to heal.** I sometimes find in my work with clients that their shame about past mistakes affects their

ability to believe in themselves. Leslie fell into this trap. She'd been a senior executive at a transportation company notorious among its peers for its treacherous politics. Leslie was devastated when she was let go after only eight months on the job, even though that was the average tenure of several of her immediate predecessors. Despite having a stellar reputation in the industry and nearly twenty years of experience, she had a hard time getting over the humiliation of not having made that particular position work. This showed up in her continual apologies in interviews for the blot on her résumé. Of course no one else wanted to touch her, not because she was a bad candidate—the rest of her résumé attested to her fabulous experience—but because she believed she was a terrible prospect. Sensing this, they were hesitant to take a chance on her, and that fueled her insecurity even more. Her strong belief that she was damaged goods had become reality.

It took Leslie nearly a year to get over the blow to her ego; when she finally did, she landed another position.

It is important to spend time healing those painful episodes that inhibit your progress. Find a safe space and air your private concerns—whether to a trusted friend, therapist, or coach—as a first step in letting them go. If you feel particularly devastated, don't be afraid to take a time-out from your reinvention to focus on your emotional work. As you restore your faith in yourself, you will start moving forward again naturally.

3. **Acknowledge your past successes.** A curious phenomenon I've noticed in my coaching is that people tend to overlook their own achievements. Clients will show up for sessions claiming to have done nothing, but after deeper discussion it always turns out that they've had many successes. A variation of this is that they will remember what they've done, but minimize its significance. One of my clients buried her Pulitzer Prize on the second page of her résumé under "Other Awards."

    As you learned in Law 5 (Tools), accomplishments are the foundation on which you build your reinvention. Forgetting about them or deliberately lessening their importance erodes your self-esteem. To combat this tendency, one of the standard requests I make of my clients and students is that they keep a Daily Success List to recall the good things they've done. Regularly reminding yourself that you've succeeded in the past will strengthen your belief that you can succeed in the future.

4. **Surround yourself with people who believe in you.** As you saw in Law 6 (Board), career reinvention is a team effort, not a one-person game. Your Reinvention Board acts as your advisory committee; but an ongoing support group is the squad you'll call on to brainstorm ideas, elevate your vision, help you through the rough spots, and keep things in perspective. We created the Reinvention Team coaching groups expressly for this purpose. Weekly calls build a tight circle of like-minded people who aid one another in their efforts; one participant called it "part career laboratory, part flight simulator, part graduate seminar on steroids." An informal circle of good friends meeting regularly for dinner could also provide you with the consistent support and encouragement you'll need while you're in the throes of your reinvention.

Do You Really Believe?

Along with inner knowing of your value, you also have to believe that what you want to accomplish is possible and that *you will do it.* Having that kind of faith—despite the naysayers, the effort, the trials, and the terror—shows a level of determination and belief in your abilities that will contribute to your success. Everyone wants to sign on to the winning team. The opposite is also true: If you don't believe you can reach your reinvention goal, people will be much more reluctant to come on board. Eddie Murphy and Miles Davis weren't going to sign with a PR agent who wasn't 100 percent sure of her future success. Why would they risk it?

I often have students in my classes who say they're certain they will reinvent themselves when, in actuality, they don't believe that at all. How can I tell the difference? I listen to the words they use when they talk about their goals; their true feelings always sneak through. *You may not hear yourself speaking, but others do.* They know how likely you are to reach your objective by the language you use when you discuss your reinvention. You think you're talking a great game—Yes, *of course* I'm making it happen!—but your word choice communicates ambivalence. When you don't fully believe that you can do something, it comes through. Here's a list of words that illustrate the difference:

"BELIEVING" WORDS	"AMBIVALENT" WORDS
Know	*Think*
Will	*Maybe*
Sure	*Doubt*
Positive	*Try*
Can	*Can't*
Have	*Lack*
Trust	*Might*
Certain	*Wonder*

The believing words communicate a feeling of confidence, faith, and strength of conviction that is an integral part of an aura of success. The ambivalent words convey the message that "there's *always* a chance it might not work out." Those who sit in that space often feel like they're being more "realistic," when in fact they're just pessimistic about their chances.

HIDDEN CONFLICT THAT COULD STOP YOU: MISTAKING PESSIMISM FOR REALITY

There's an old joke that's told about a little boy who was, shall we say, extremely determined to look on the bright side of things. His parents were worried that he was *too* optimistic; after all, life is hard and you can't go around expecting to get what you want. Having an abiding faith that life will deliver your goals and dreams was surely a recipe for failure.

After much discussion, they decide to take their son to a psychiatrist. Said psychiatrist came highly recommended; he had a wall full of diplomas and appeared frequently on the TV morning shows to discuss his latest groundbreaking studies showing that repurposed byproducts from barn animals could empirically be shown, when used correctly, to improve the level of reality-based thinking in humans.

After a short consultation with the boy, the psychiatrist reported the scary news to his parents: Yes, he suffers from an excess of belief in the possibility of success and the most drastic measures are required to dampen his spirit. The parents nervously give their okay—they only want the best for their son, and he has to learn how to deal with reality. The psychiatrist leads the boy away to another room piled high with nothing but horse manure. . . .

You know how this joke ends: with the boy digging in that pile of crap, looking for a pony. But I'd bet a million bucks that if we checked in with that boy when he was fifty, he would probably be president, a captain of industry, or at the very least riding his horse to yet another Kentucky Derby win.

In the ebb and flow of a reinvention, there will be times when it seems like you're standing in front of nothing but a pile of crap that looks like "reality." In those moments, ambivalence about whether you can make your reinvention happen can slip into pessimism. You might find yourself saying, "I'll try it, but I don't believe it will work." But career reinvention requires you to believe that something can happen before you see hard evidence of it—before you find the pony in the pile, you must have faith that it's there. *If you refuse to believe in the possibility of success, you will never see the proof.*

When I first moved to Miami, my neighbor across the way stopped by to say hello. Juan worked for a commercial real estate company as a financial analyst; when he heard that I was a career coach, his ears perked up.

"I'm ready to do something different," he said, excited by the idea of some free coaching.

"If you could have any kind of job, what would it be?" I asked.

Juan longed to do a very specialized kind of job—the details of which were so complicated and involved that even my experienced coaching self got bored.

It was clear, though, that he had some transferable skills, so it was time to speak to a few Natives and assess the opportunities. "How about reaching out to a few people who are doing that job and taking them to lunch?" I suggested.

There was one small problem with that strategy, he told me: That position didn't exist in Miami where I live so there wasn't anyone to network with locally.

"No one at all?" I asked. Nope—he was sure.

Now Miami isn't New York City, but it's a city nonetheless. The chances were extremely slim that there wasn't someone down here doing that kind of work.

"If you believe that the job doesn't exist down here, then for you it doesn't. I'll bet you a *cortadito* that there are several people in town happily doing it. Doesn't stop those guys from already having what you say doesn't exist."

My response wasn't exactly welcomed with open arms. Juan told me I wasn't being "realistic" about the opportunities down in Miami; it just wasn't possible for him to land the job he wanted as long as he stayed in town. But I held firm: Tell that to the guys who are already doing it.

He avoided me for the next couple of months, so I was surprised to pick up the phone one day and find him on the other end of the line.

"Guess what?" he said.

"Okay, I'll bite. What?"

"That job I was telling you about—I met a guy who does that here in Miami. He told me there were a few others as well, and I'm getting together with all of them for lunch."

I was happy that Juan finally got it: He just wasn't looking hard enough for his pony in the pile.

LIVING THE LAW: OVERCOMING THE CHALLENGES OF REINVENTION

The power of inner knowing and your belief in yourself is a source of strength and courage. It draws people to you and gives you the fortitude to seek out opportunity. But an aura of success doesn't inoculate you against the challenges you'll face during reinvention. Your quest for a new career won't end in victory unless you pass a few tests along the way.

I've helped thousands of Reinventors through this process, and here are the four most typical challenges I've seen:

1. **I'm losing faith.** This usually occurs after a big setback. An important meeting with a Native you've been looking forward to finally happens and doesn't go well. You find out that you're missing an important skill and must add another tool to your toolbox. One of your family members expressed a lack of faith in your abilities. You crossed an artificial deadline in your reinvention ("I thought *for sure* I'd have landed by now") and are disappointed that more time and effort is required.

   A crisis of faith causes you to question the wisdom of the entire journey. At times like these, you'll feel a mix of intense sadness and fear. You'll wonder if you should quit in the face of the "evidence" you're seeing and/or hearing. A loss of faith in reinvention is a dark night of the soul.

   Solution: Write about your values. [20] Writing about your deeply held values reminds you of your higher purpose. It broadens your vision, boosts your sense of security, and quiets your sensation of being tossed about by life. In fact, studies have shown that writing about life goals is associated with feeling less upset and more happy, and getting sick less often. Periodically journaling about your highest desires helps to remind you why you're on this journey. Why did you want to reinvent yourself in the first place? Ask yourself about the vision for your life and what important things you expect to accomplish. Ask yourself how you'll feel five years from now if you didn't give it your best shot.

2. **I can't find the "right" opportunity.** This occurs when you've been presented with several options that were good, just not good enough. You've explored a few paths down the road less traveled

[20]Exercise on Page 249: Values Journal

and none of them seemed to be the best way to go. You've compared your reinvention with that of others, and yours is lacking. You're looking for "the one"—the perfect opportunity—but what has crossed your plate thus far hasn't been quite right.

When you've been doing the work of reinvention but the right opportunity seems elusive, you'll get discouraged. You may feel disappointment or despair. You will wonder whether it's too much work or even worth doing at all. When the perfect opportunity doesn't show up, you feel like you're chasing a pipe dream.

Solution: Do an analysis to see how well the opportunities you've been presented with fit with the life vision you laid out in Law 1 (Vision). [21] If there's a mismatch, adjust your strategy to target opportunities that are more on point with your goals. If they are a match but you can't stop searching until you find "the one," check to see if you're trying to review too many options by answering yes or no to the following:

When I'm looking for something to watch on TV, I'll surf through all the channels to see everything that's available before I choose what show to watch.

I have a hard time buying clothes because I just can't find any I really love.

When I'm ordering in a restaurant, even if there's an entrée that I think I might like, I wait to hear what others choose before I decide.

If you answered yes to two out of the three above statements, chances are you're what researchers at Columbia University and Swarthmore College call a "maximizer." This means that you seek the best and will exhaustively research all available possibilities before making a choice. To go back to our example of the Baskin-Robbins ice cream counter in Law 4 (Road), as a maximizer you'd want to taste every single flavor—even the Ox Tongue, favored in Japan—so that you'd know, for sure, that vanilla was the best. You just won't make a

---

[21]Exercise on Page 250: Opportunity Analysis

selection until you've tasted every one, never mind that you're lactose intolerant and should only have a few bites anyway.

If you answered no to at least two of the statements, you're most likely what that same study calls a "satisficer"—content to choose after reviewing a couple of suitable alternatives. As a satisficer you're okay with "good enough"; you'll search just long enough to find an option that crosses the threshold of acceptability. If you were standing at that ice cream counter, after a couple of tastes you'd figure you'd tried enough, and pistachio would be just fine for today. While your maximizer buddy is still sampling every flavor, you're hanging out at the café tables in the sun enjoying your ice cream cone.

If you can't find the "right" reinvention opportunity despite being presented with several good options that fit your life vision, you're probably a maximizer. The research showed that although maximizers often do better financially in job searches (the determination to find "the best" means you'll seek out more options, period), they do worse in terms of overall satisfaction. On the whole, maximizers experience less happiness, life satisfaction, and optimism, even with more choice. To break this tendency, borrow a page from the satisficer playbook: Stop looking for the best, look for "good enough," and get on with enjoying your life.

If you're a satisficer, you probably didn't even get this far. You read just enough to know it didn't fit, and moved on.

3. **I'm not getting traction.** This happens when you are doing the work of reinvention—responding to job postings or pitching clients with your translated materials, reaching out to Natives, and attending events in your target industry—yet seem to be getting nowhere. There are two ways lack of traction shows up: In one, you're landing in-person meetings and phone calls but nothing's happened yet; in the other, you're getting no response at all.

When you're not getting traction, it looks as if you're putting in a lot of effort with little or no return. You will feel frustrated and angry. You'll resent the amount of work you're doing and want to dial back your efforts. You think you're spinning your wheels dreaming of reinvention, and you're tired of wasting your time.

Solution: Analyze the type of response you're getting. If you're not hearing anything back at all—no meetings, no callbacks, no conversations—chances are there's a problem with your reinvention materials and the way you're pitching yourself. Go back to Law 5 (Tools) and redo your skills and accomplishments assessment. Make sure you're highlighting the talents that matter to clients and hiring managers in your target industry and showcasing the successes that back up your claims. If you are missing critical tools or are lacking accomplishments, suspend your outreach efforts and focus your attention on getting tangible experience to bolster your case. You may need to volunteer in your target industry or do a few pro bono projects to build legitimacy. These solutions also apply when you're landing in-person meetings, getting callbacks, and speaking with Natives but the feedback you're getting is not so good.

On the other hand, if you're landing meetings, getting calls, and speaking with Natives and getting great feedback though nothing has panned out just yet, then it's probably a timeline issue. Go back to Law 9 (Timeline) and check your expectations. Perhaps you're trying to control things you can't (like when opportunity shows up) or indulging in magical thinking ("It will only take a couple of weeks to land a new position in the middle of a recession"). Work on changing your expectations, and make sure you're rewarding yourself for hitting interim targets instead of waiting for your ultimate reinvention goal.

4. **I'm running out of time.** This is usually a euphemism for running out of money. There's no—or not enough—cash coming in and you're feeling the pressure of a dwindling bank account. You start looking for change between the couch cushions and wondering whether electricity is *truly* essential. Your Reinvention Fund is just about tapped out, and you're wondering how you're going to survive.

When faced with a looming deadline—real or imagined—you hit the panic button. Your body goes into a fear-based "red alert," and you cycle through worry, anxiety, and stress. You will feel pressured by the lack of money or lack of support from the people around you. When you think you're running out of time you'll be tempted to make a spur-of-the-moment decision to abandon your reinvention.

Solution: First, STOP. When you are feeling full-blown fear, your brain shuts down access to the very creative and problem-solving functions you need to get through this moment, which increases the likelihood that you'll make a decision you will later regret.

Second, BREATHE. Do something physical that drains the anxiety from your body and redirects the focus of your mind. Bake a cake, shoot a few rounds of golf, go for a sail or for a run, take a salsa lesson. Fun, mentally absorbing activities improve your attitude and outlook and give you a much better frame of mind from which to figure out your next steps.

Third, ACT. Six months before the needle hits "E," dust off your Plan B job from Law 6 (Board). It's time to get a temporary gig to keep the cash coming in so that you have the time, space, and peace of mind to keep working on your reinvention goal. Also look at ways to free up extra cash by cutting back on nonessentials. A roof over your head is essential. You cannot cross that off your budget, even when it involves rent, mortgage, property taxes, and other fixed costs. Food is essential, although eating it in three-star restaurants is not. Clothing is essential because there are laws about that; still, you don't have to fill three walk-in closets with clothing hot off the Paris runway. The right classic pieces are all you need.

After those essentials, what's left? Mostly it's stuff that makes your life nicer. I am not suggesting that you give these things up entirely—just dial back. Cook at home more often. Have a facial monthly instead of weekly. Instead of downloading $60 worth of music, cut a few songs from your playlist. The money you've freed up buys you peace of mind.

The Very Last Challenge of Reinvention . . .

I'm not ready. At long last you've hit your reinvention goal and are standing at the entrance of your new life. You've got the job or landed the client, and now it hits you: This is *real.*

When this moment arrives—and it will, if you've done the work of building up your inner knowing and believing that it would—you feel elated, relieved, and, yes, scared. You will recognize that it's time to move from believing to living. And you will have one last flash of doubt. . . . *Can I really do this?*

Do not go to your intellect for help—it will be panicking. You won't be able to turn to your body either—it will be right there with your mind, on full red alert. Tune out the people around you; their joy at your good fortune will only increase your fear. Don't turn to your journals; putting that question in writing will intensify your uncertainty.

When you stand at the border, about to cross over into the new world you've created, and you're wondering what to do, remember this last bit of advice:

In Terrie's words, "Just speak it. Just claim it."

Just say *yes.*

The Takeaway: When you cultivate your "inner knowing," belief in yourself, and faith in the possibility of attaining your goals, others will be drawn to you.

Watch Out for . . . Pessimism about your chances masquerading as "reality."

Putting the Law into Action: Remind yourself of past challenges you've overcome and give yourself credit for getting through them.

Something to Think About: How determined am I to succeed in my reinvention quest?

EPILOGUE:
THE LAST TAKEAWAY

We are near the end of our journey through this book. We stand together at the threshold of your new career. You now have what I was missing so many years ago—the Laws of Career Reinvention to guide you. You have a vision for your life and are tuning in to your body's instincts. No more excuses!—you are ready to set out on the road less traveled, tools on hand and team onboard. You are learning a new language and letting the Natives guide you. You are in it for as long as it takes, and people are magnetized by your determination and light.

As you begin crafting a new path, use the principles of these Laws as your blueprint. And now that you are joining the ranks of Reinventors, I send you off with words of counsel and one last story:

1. **Remember that you have two careers.** Your first job is what you do to earn a living and your second job is to continually develop yourself and your skills. Do not neglect your second job!

Keep your eyes not just on the speedometer in front of you but also on the road ahead. Stay plugged into trends, keep abreast of the news, don't take your finger off the pulse of what's happening—not just in your industry, but in the world. Adjust the speed and the strategy of your reinvention according to what you see.

2. **Make a habit of being happy.** Science has demonstrated the importance of a positive attitude in tapping into creativity, problem-solving, excitement, and engagement—all qualities you need to reinvent yourself. Cultivate routines—write down your daily successes, take regular relaxation breaks, pursue hobbies—that bring joy to your world.

3. **Don't make your reinvention bigger than it needs to be.** It is about shaping your career into something you love. Sometimes you need a radical overhaul; other times, small tweaks. Do not use a power saw when pinking shears will do.

4. **You will change your mind.** What you want out of your career will shift according to the cycles of your interests. What works at one stage or age of your life may no longer fit when you reach the next. Always stay primed for change. Keep your toolbox on hand, its contents up-to-date, sharp, and ready. When you decide that it's time to move on, even from a career you have loved, you will be prepared to go.

I I I I

One month before my thirty-ninth birthday I walked away from my glamorous entertainment career to start The Reinvention Institute. I turned down an offer for what would have once been my dream job—a posting in London as head of international brand strategy for a well-known media company, big salary and perks included. I sold my loft in Manhattan's trendy Tribeca neighborhood, said good-bye to my many friends, called in the movers to pack up my things, and left.

Three months later I stood in a rented townhouse in Miami—whose patio was triple the size of my kitchen in New York—surrounded by the remains of a lifestyle I no longer led. Four Saturdays after that, I celebrated this most recent of my reinventions by doing something completely at odds with anything I had ever done: I held a yard sale.

I wasn't raised to discard things from the past. Growing up in Wisconsin, my mother filled the gap left by my missing father with relatives; if we ever wanted to get rid of something that had outlived its usefulness, there was always a cousin who would happily take it. In my family, not only did things stick around, so did people. When I got accepted to Harvard—the first member of my family to go to college— I knew I'd have to break tradition and move more than fifteen minutes away from the two people I'd seen nearly every day since I'd entered this earth: my grandparents.

Robert Lee Reed was my mother's father, who managed to escape farm life in the small town of West Point, Mississippi, by enlisting in the Army. As a result, he never finished high school. Eventually he earned his GED and became a garbage collector.

When I was growing up, Granddaddy would find books among the garbage he picked up in the predawn hours on the cold streets of Milwaukee and save them for me. I'd be playing in the yard and he would call me off to the side to slip me the latest treasure he'd discovered—children's stories when I was little, Harlequin romances when I was eleven, novels when I was in my teens. He knew I'd exhausted the resources of the local library and he didn't want anything to stop my quest for knowledge. The day I was accepted to Harvard, he slid my high school picture into his worn brown wallet, where it stayed.

Years later, when I was out in the world in my high-flying jobs, I traveled to many countries and shopped for beautiful things at every stop. And in every country I visited, I dashed off a postcard to my grandfather.

I was traveling in Southeast Asia when I got word that he had taken ill. I flew thirty hours to get back to Milwaukee, but I arrived too late. I said good-bye to him as he lay in his coffin, his face permanently still.

After the funeral, the family went back to his apartment to sort through his possessions. Sitting on a low wooden table in the living room was a woven rattan box from Hong Kong I had given him one Christmas. In it was every single postcard I had ever sent him—except for the one postmarked Laos, which was sitting in his mailbox, unread.

It's funny how one person's garbage is another person's treasure. The books Granddaddy saved for me from the scrap heap helped get me all the way to the Ivy League. Sorting though my possessions to prepare for the yard sale, I felt as if I were watching a slide show of my life. As things sold and pieces of my old self disappeared out the patio door, the sadness I felt over parting with my history gave way to a sense of freedom.

The one thing I kept from that era that was worth more than any expensive knickknack I had bought on my travels was the last postcard I had mailed to my grandfather, the one that arrived too late to reach him. In his honor, I keep it in my office at The Reinvention Institute. It is my bookmark.

The last takeaway? As you reinvent yourself through the seasons of your life, let go of what no longer works and take only your most cherished things from the past with you into your future.

This companion workbook is designed to give you practical exercises to help you put the Laws into practice. Although the exercises are organized in a linear fashion, your reinvention may not fall so neatly into a step-by-step process. You may already have selected a Reinvention Target or have scheduled a meeting with a Native. No matter where you are in your reinvention, I encourage you to read through every Law so that you are familiar with the building blocks of the process, but feel free to complete whichever exercises you most need.

This workbook is a self-guided tool; you can complete some exercises as you read along in the book. Others you'll need a few days, or even several weeks, to do. Work through them according to your own requirements and timetable. *Follow the process that works best for you.*

If you'd like to go even deeper into the reinvention process, visit our Web site at www.reinvention-institute.com to download a free companion guide to this workbook that contains extra exercises.

IT STARTS WITH A VISION FOR YOUR LIFE

CRAFT YOUR IDEAL LIFESTYLE

STEP 1: MYTH BUSTING AND FANTASY CLEANUP

Myths are unquestioned beliefs you hold about the world around you, like "I've been doing my job for so long, I'm stuck in this industry" or "My life will be better when I change careers." Identify the myths and fantasies that you could be harboring about your reinvention by taking a moment to answer the following questions:

What problems do I think will be solved by my reinvention?

Examples: *I work too much. No growth opportunities in my current industry. I'm bored by my job.*

1. _____

2. _____

3. _____

4. _____

Once I've reinvented myself, what things will I finally get that I've been waiting for?

Examples: *Relaxed lifestyle. Passion about what I do. Feel happier about my life.*

1. _____

2. _____

3. _____

4. _____

What are the top three barriers I think will stop me from reinventing my career?

Examples: *I'm too old. I don't have enough money. I don't have any connections.*

1. _____

2. _____

3. _____

4. _____

What are the cool things I'm looking forward to in my new career?

Examples: *Meeting celebrities. Traveling to exciting places. Getting paid to pursue my interests.*

1. _____

2. _____

3. _____

4. _____

What won't I have to deal with once I switch careers?

Examples: *Egotistical people. Pressure on the job. Working so hard.*

1. _____

2. _____

3. _____

4. _____

STEP 2: VISUALIZE YOUR IDEAL DAY

Create a detailed picture in your mind of the kind of life you're shooting for.

In the morning:

Where are you?

_____

_____

_____

_____

What does the room look like?

_____

_____

_____

_____

Who's with you?

_____

_____

_____

_____

At work:

What does your workplace look like?

_____

_____

_____

_____

What is the atmosphere like?

_____

_____

_____

_____

Where do you go at lunchtime?

_____

_____

_____

_____

Continue visualizing the details of your day and write them here:

_____

_____

_____

_____

_____

_____

_____

_____

_____

_____

Optional:

Create a vision board. This is a homemade collage that represents the life you'd like to create with your career reinvention. Leaf through magazines and see what pictures and words catch your eye. Choose images and phrases that speak to you instinctively, that inspire feelings like: *Wow, I really want that. Those words capture exactly what I want to have in my life. Just looking at that photo makes me happy.* Cut them out and hang them up, tape them to a piece of posterboard or paste them into your journal. Make sure you put your vision board somewhere that you'll see it often: Keep the visual of your ideal life front of you!

STEP 3: BRAINSTORM CAREER IDEAS

Come up with a list of careers that have the potential to deliver it. Get your creative juices flowing by answering these six questions:

1. When am I in flow?

What do I do that is so effortless and joyful that I could happily do it for hours?
Examples: *Gardening. Programming apps for my iPhone. Cooking new recipes. Talking about leadership with my staffers.*

Make a list of your "flow" activities:

_____

_____

_____

_____

2. What feels "easy" to me?

What feels as natural to me as breathing? **What do my friends tell me I'm so good at?**
Examples: *Analyzing life issues. Recommending cool new restaurants. Shopping for the latest fashions. Advising on the best electronic gadgets to buy.*

Make a list of the things people say that you're good at doing:

_____

_____

_____

_____

3. What seems "obvious" to me?

What is so abundantly clear to me that I wonder why others don't see it or do it? What unique ideas do I have about how things should be done?
Examples: *Why doesn't my company take orders online instead of by telephone? Why doesn't somebody teach people how to change their résumé if they want switch industries? Why doesn't somebody make jewelry from broken china pieces?*

List a few "obvious" things you think should be done:
Why isn't there a company that _____?
Why don't businesses do this: _____?

4. What are my inexhaustible interests?

What things spark an unending sense of curiosity in me? What can I never get enough of?
Examples: *BlackBerry apps. Reality TV. Sailing. Self-help books.*

Make a list of your inexhaustible interests:

_____

_____

_____

_____

5. What do I gravitate toward in my current career?

What parts of my job work for me?

Make a list of the things you enjoy about your current career:

_____

_____

_____

_____

6. What do I think should exist in the world but doesn't?

What do I think people should be able to buy or eat or read that is not out there right now?

Examples: *An airline that solves all the problems that bug you about flying. A service that delivers movies to your mailbox and eliminates late fees. A company that teaches people how to reinvent their careers.*

Make a list of the businesses you think should exist in the world:

_____

_____

_____

_____

How do your answers to these questions compare to the life you want to lead?

Brainstorm a few possible careers that match your interests and can provide the lifestyle you envision.

Some possible careers to explore:

_____

_____

_____

_____

_____

_____

_____

_____

YOUR BODY IS YOUR BEST GUIDE

TUNE IN TO YOUR BODY.

STEP 1: ANALYZE YOUR DECISIONS

Record five simple decisions you made today. Examples include what you decided to eat for breakfast or lunch, when you decided to read your e-mail, whether or not you decided to go to dinner with friends, work out, or lie on the couch and watch the latest episode of *Ghost Hunters*. Analyze what your intellectual side said about each decision vs. the "gut instinct" side. Indicate which one carried the day.

DECISION	WHAT MY GUT SAID	WHAT MY INTELLECT SAID	WHICH ONE I FOLLOWED

What did you notice? Did you listen to your gut, or did your intellect talk you out of what your gut said? Or was there a balance between the two? Take a moment to write some observations about what you learned:

_____

_____

_____

_____

_____

STEP 2: PRACTICE TUNING IN TO YOUR GUT

Try hourly tune-ins for a couple of days to get a more precise picture and see what patterns emerge. When do you listen to your gut? When do you ignore it? For example, you might feel okay following your gut when it comes to personal decisions like what to have for a meal or what to wear, but ignore your gut when it comes to work decisions like staying late at the office or taking on additional assignments. Take a moment and list your patterns:

I LISTEN TO MY GUT WHEN . . .	I IGNORE MY GUT WHEN . . .
Ex. I decide what to eat for lunch and dinner	Ex. I get asked by coworkers to pick up some of their tasks

Are there areas of your life where your body is sending you signals but you're ignoring them? Examples might include not admitting that your current job is making you miserable, that you dislike the city you live in, even that you're bored with the same workout routine. Make a list here:

BODY SIGNAL	WHEN DOES IT SHOW UP?	MESSAGE I'M IGNORING
Ex. My teeth clench	Every time I hear a siren in the street	I hate living in New York City

PROGRESS BEGINS WHEN YOU STOP MAKING EXCUSES

GIVE UP EXCUSES

STEP 1: MAKE A LIST OF YOUR EXCUSES

Make a list of your fallback excuses: the reasons you're stuck or unhappy, unable to make a change or progress in your reinvention. The top three barriers you listed in the Law 1 (Vision) myth section could also count as excuses.

Examples: *I'm over fifty—no one will hire me. I don't have enough money. I don't have a degree. I'm too busy raising kids.*

Make a list of your five most frequently used fallback excuses:

1. _____

2. _____

3. _____

4. _____

5. _____

STEP 2: BRAINSTORM SOLUTIONS FOR YOUR BIGGEST EXCUSE

Choose your biggest excuse and brainstorm three ways to solve the problem.

Examples: *Excuse: I don't have the degree I need. Solutions: Check company options for tuition reimbursement. Check into auditing courses at a local college. Check into financial aid or special grants.*

Your turn:

Biggest Excuse: _____

Solutions:

1. _____

2. _____

3. _____

STEP 3: MATCH YOUR ACTIONS TO YOUR WORDS

Ask yourself the following: *What does my mouth say I want? And when I shut my mouth, what do my actions say I want?* You may be surprised by the disconnect between what you say and what you do.

WHAT I SAY I WANT	THE ACTIONS I TAKE (OR DON'T TAKE)	WHAT MY ACTIONS SAY
Ex. Start an interior design business	Keep planning to research classes but haven't gotten around to it	I'm not serious about starting an interior design firm

LAW 4:
WHAT YOU SEEK IS ON
THE ROAD LESS TRAVELED

PICK A REINVENTION TARGET

STEP 1: BODY BRAINSTORM

Spend a day or two pondering this question: *Of all the things in the world I could choose to do for a living, what would I ask for if there were no limits?* As ideas come to you, tune in to your body and see what makes you feel excited, makes your heart sing, makes you feel relaxed. Write your thoughts here:

_____

_____

_____

_____

_____

_____

STEP 2: CREATE AN "EXPLORE" LIST

Pull out the list of possible careers you brainstormed in Law 1 (Vision). See what matches there are between that list and the question above and put those ideas on this list.

Careers for my "Explore" list:

1. _____

2. _____

3. _____

Extra brainstorming questions:

Of the ideas from my Law 1 (Vision) list and what I came up with by tuning into my body, which one seems like the most interesting path?

_____

What have I always wanted to do but never felt I could?

_____

If I didn't have to earn money, what would I do?

_____

When I was ten years old, what did I want to be when I grew up?

_____

STEP 3: BRAINSTORM THE "HOW"

Looking at the options on your "Explore" list, ask yourself: How can I make these work? List ideas in the following chart:

IDEA FROM MY "EXPLORE" LIST	HOW I CAN MAKE IT WORK
Ex. Starting an organic farm	Take a class in organic farming techniques.
	Start an organic garden in my yard and try to sell some of the produce at the local farmer's market.
	Take a "working vacation" on an organic farm.
Ex. Become a restaurant critic	Write reviews of local restaurants for the city paper.
	Start a blog about local restaurants.
	Take cooking classes with local chefs.

STEP 4: PICK A REINVENTION TARGET

Choose a goal from among the options on your "Explore" list.

My Reinvention Target: _____

My Backup: _____

YOU'VE GOT THE TOOLS
IN YOUR TOOLBOX

KNOW WHAT YOU HAVE TO OFFER

STEP 1: MAKE A SKILLS LIST

Make a list of job functions you've performed over your career. Use an up-to-date résumé or job descriptions from your last few positions:

JOB FUNCTION	SKILLS USED
Ex. Manage software product development team	Ex. Project management, negotiation, team-building, programming
Ex. Train customer service reps in company products	Ex. Writing, public speaking, teaching

STEP 2: INVENTORY YOUR ACCOMPLISHMENTS

Make a list of your accomplishments, along with the skills it took to achieve them:

ACCOMPLISHMENT	SKILLS USED
Ex. Signed million-dollar joint venture partnership in Germany	Ex. Sales, negotiation, business development, contract analysis
Ex. Created and presented three-day broker training program for over 500 sales agents	Ex. Writing, public speaking, teaching

YOUR REINVENTION BOARD
IS YOUR LIFELINE

OUTLINE YOUR REINVENTION STRATEGY

STEP 1: FIGURE OUT THE LOGISTICS

Sketch out a few ideas for the following areas of your reinvention strategy:

Research: Background information you need; e.g., market trends, industry information, leading companies, contacts who can help you. Take a moment to answer the following questions: *What ideas must I investigate? What information do I need? Which potential contacts or Natives must I reach?*

_____

_____

_____

Operations: The logistical details of search: e.g., getting a new e-mail address, signing up for job boards or online networking sites, setting up a contact management system. Take a moment to answer the following: *What tasks must I accomplish? What items do I need to pull together?*

_____

_____

_____

Funding: The money you need to live plus the money you must put aside for reinvention-related expenses (e.g., classes, travel, networking lunches). Take a moment to answer the following: *What financial resources do I need for my reinvention, and where will I get them?*

_____

_____

_____

STEP 2: IDENTIFY YOUR PLAN B JOB

My Plan B gig: _____

✶✶✶✶✶

> **Note:** If you want to learn how to map out a more comprehensive Reinvention Strategy, you can buy our Reinvention Strategy Planning Kit on our Web site at www.reinvention-institute.com.

STEP 3: ASSEMBLE YOUR REINVENTION BOARD

Brainstorm who you can enlist to play the various roles you need on your board:

My Master Connector: _____

My Clued-in Colleague: _____

My Warm 'n' Fuzzy: _____

My Drill Sergeant: _____

My Native: _____

LAW 7:
ONLY A NATIVE CAN
GIVE YOU THE INSIDE SCOOP

NETWORK WITH INDUSTRY INSIDERS

STEP 1: MAKE A LIST OF NATIVES

List the Natives you'd like to meet (people you know personally or have heard about in the industry that you'd like to connect with):

1. _____

2. _____

3. _____

4. _____

5. _____

STEP 2: PLAN YOUR OUTREACH

List where you're likely to find them and how you plan to reach them:

NATIVE	WHERE I'LL FIND THEM	BEST WAY TO REACH THEM
Ex. Industry Bigwig	Delivering the keynote address at the upcoming conference	Sit in front row and introduce myself after the talk

THEY WON'T "GET" YOU UNTIL YOU SPEAK THEIR LANGUAGE

LEARN THE LINGO

Make a "translation list" of industry terms to use when drafting your Reinvention Résumé or writing your Reinvention Bio (you can download samples of both from our Web site, www.reinvention institute.com):

_____

_____

_____

_____

_____

_____

_____

_____

_____

_____

_____

_____

_____

_____

_____

_____

_____

_____

_____

_____

IT TAKES THE TIME THAT IT TAKES

MANAGE YOUR EXPECTATIONS

STEP 1: DO A "THOUGHT/EMOTION" SURVEY

Survey your thoughts for the day to see what you're thinking and how you're feeling and calculate your positivity ratio.

THOUGHT	EMOTION	POSITIVE?	NEGATIVE?
Ex. I didn't get enough done today. I don't have enough time for my reinvention.	Sad, angry		X
Ex. I had a great meeting with a Native today who gave me three more leads.	Excited	X	
TOTAL:			

My Positivity Ratio: _____

STEP 2: CREATE A REINVENTION TACTICAL PLAN

Set a monthly Reinvention Goal; e.g., have meetings with three Natives, send Reinvention Bio and pitch to four client prospects.

Monthly Goal: _____
Break down your monthly goal into the weekly action steps you'll take to accomplish it.

Examples: *e-mail six Natives, send out four LinkedIn networking requests, send one client pitch letter.*

Weekly Action Steps:

Week 1: _____

Week 2: _____

Week 3: _____

Week 4: _____

List the tasks you'll do on a daily basis to accomplish your weekly action step.

Examples: *draft client pitch letter; update LinkedIn profile and send out a networking request; e-mail a Native; spend fifteen minutes researching industry news.*

Task List:

1. _____

2. _____

3. _____

4. _____

5. _____

6. _____

7. _____

8. _____

9. _____

10. _____

STEP 3: CREATE A REWARD AND ACCOUNTABILITY PLAN

Brainstorm ideas about how you plan to reward yourself during your reinvention launch and what milestones you must hit to earn the rewards:

MILESTONE	REWARD
Ex. Score a meeting with a native	Take myself to a movie
Ex. Send out three Reinvention Résumés	Buy that new novel I want to read

Brainstorm ideas about how you plan to hold yourself accountable during your reinvention launch, and how often you'll do it:

ACCOUNTABILITY TACTIC	FREQUENCY
Ex. Ask a friend to check on my progress	Daily call
Ex. Give status reports to my Reinvention Team	Weekly

THE WORLD BUYS INTO
AN AURA OF SUCCESS

STAY IN TOUCH WITH YOUR VALUES

Take a moment and write about your higher purpose in life. What are the most important things to you? What impact do you want to make on the world? What legacy do you want to leave? What things do you want to accomplish in life? Why do you think you are alive on this planet?

_____

_____

_____

_____

_____

_____

_____

Opportunity Analysis: Take a moment to analyze the opportunities that have been presented to you and how well they would have delivered your vision:

OPPORTUNITY	WHAT DID I SAY I WANTED IN MY VISION?	DID THE OPPORTUNITY DELIVER IT? YES OR NO?
Ex. Strategic planning job at large paper company	Work at small company in a loft-style office	No
Ex. Consult for a local graphic design firm	The ability to make my own schedule	Yes

ACKNOWLEDGMENTS

O ne of the lessons of this book is that you can't reinvent yourself by yourself—you need the help of others. So I take a moment to offer my heartfelt thanks and gratitude to the people who have been kind enough to include me in their "circle of giving":

To the subjects who bring the book to life:

Alton, Bruce, Christina, Felina, Jeanette, Jeffery, Julie-Anne, Marianne, Reggie, Terrie: Thank you all for so generously sharing your stories. You are an inspiration.

To the clients and students of The Reinvention Institute: It is a privilege to serve you as you build a pathway to your new career. Thanks for the honor of being your Reinvention Coach®.

To the advisors who made the book happen:

Amy Hertz at Dutton: You believed in this book and gave incredibly smart feedback on how to make it better. Thanks for trusting my vision and for giving me a shot to pull it off in the end. A special shout-out to Melissa Miller—I am impressed by your air-traffic-controller–like skills.

Kate Lee at ICM: You sold this book by a first-time author in the middle of a down market and helped steer the project back into calmer waters—'nuff said. You rock. Thanks also to Larissa Silva for keeping the trains running.

Meredith Maran and Jane Cavolina: Fabulous writer and editor respectively, you stepped in at the eleventh hour and delivered with professionalism and grace. Thank you both for helping me to deliver my book serenely and on time.

Joyce Maynard: Writing mentor and great friend, whose Guatemala writing retreat gave birth to the closing story of this book. Thank you for encouraging me to tell my story, too!

James Mauch and Jody Sherman: Clients, friends, and the smartest of readers—thanks for your wise comments on early drafts of the manuscript.

Bruce Seidel: Friend first and foremost, you deserve a special thank-you for (1) putting me in touch with Alton, and (2) helping me come up with a blockbuster title for the book.

Dr. Gregory Berns at Emory University: Thanks for taking the time to explain the science behind the emotional challenges experienced by aspiring Reinventors.

Diane Stefani, Francine Foerster, Larry Lux, Karen Berend, Jim Farrand: Wonderful friends and colleagues, and the first advisory board for The Reinvention Institute (before it was even called that!), I am deeply appreciative for all the counsel you've offered and the friends you've been to me over the years. You are some talented people!

Kyra Bruning at Oi Offices: You believed in my business and my book. Thank you for your patience as I went through the wild time of writing it.

To the friends who make my life happen:

Norm and Elaine Brodsky: Dear friends and entrepreneurial mentors, thanks for being role models for how to build a business aligned with my values, and for showing me the rewards, lifestyle-wise, of doing so. Norm, thanks for the sometimes pointed yet always smart advice about the business of my business. Elaine, thanks for the emotional support and reminding me that taking care of myself comes first.

Joy Harris: Loyal sister-girlfriend who stands by me through thick and thin *and* keeps me looking good. Thank you, my friend.

Diane, Mary Ellen, Rose, Sylvie, aka the "Mitchell Mavens": Ladies, thanks for keeping me connected to my fun, high-powered, New-York-woman self and for celebrating my every accomplishment. A girl couldn't ask for a more fabulous crew.

Allene, Bill, Karen, Kendall Lee, Alex, Veronique, Denise, Corry, Holly aka Niña, Jill, Jane, CB, Rosa, Lea and Catherine, Lyn, Markus, Sandy, Teryl, plus many, many more: Thank you all for being such good friends and sticking by me through my various reinventions! You all have opened doors and enriched my life in countless ways.

To the family who stands by me as life happens:

Marcia and Fernando Sanchez: Lucky me to have a second set of parents as warm and generous as you. *Muchas gracias* for welcoming me into the family, for your love and support in times good and not-so-good, and for the food when I was too busy writing a book to cook!

Barbara Holt, Allen Reed, Robert L. Reed, Jr., Qurone Williams, and Terrence Reed: My aunts and uncles who have taken care of me and watched over me since the day I entered this world. Thank you for being there, without fail, at every important moment of my life. Special thanks to Allen for the plane tickets when I needed to get to New York for meetings and to Terry for sharing his story in the book!

Yvette Mitchell and Yvonne Guerin: My sisters, who despite being twins have each been completely unique in their support of me. You're the best.

To the two individuals who make me happen:

Jeanette Mitchell: You gave me life, and you continue to give me life every day. You are a wonderful mother, a great friend, a constant support, and a wise advisor. I've said it thousands of times before, and I say it again: "Thanks, Ma."

Paco Zayas: You are there for me, always, and I am the luckiest girl in the world to have you. I could not do what I do, or be all that I could be without you. You are essential to my life, my business, me. Thank you for being an amazing husband and for being the one who gives me the strength and the space to soar.

And last, but most certainly not least:

To God, without whose call that day in Sainte-Maxime, none of this would have happened. Thank you for showing me the way I'm meant to give back to the world.

WORKS CITED

Berns, G. S. (2009, April 14). Telephone interview with the author (P. Mitchell, Interviewer).

Boehm, J. K., & Lyubomirsky, S. (2008). "Does Happiness Promote Career Success?" *Journal of Career Assessment, 16* (1), 101–116.

Bureau of Labor Statistics (2008). *Number of Jobs Held, Labor Market Activity, and Earnings Growth Among the Youngest Baby Boomers: Results from a Longitudinal Study.* Washington, D.C.: Bureau of Labor Statistics.

Chandler Jr., A. D. (1977). *The Visible Hand: The Managerial Revolution in American Business.* Cambridge: Harvard University Press (later printing).

Csikszentmihalyi, M. (1990). *Flow: The Psychology of Optimal Experience.* New York: HarperCollins.

Diener, E., & Seligman, M. E. P. (2004). "Beyond Money: Toward an Economy of Well-being." *Psychological Science in the Public Interest, 5,* 1–31.

Ferrazzi, K. (2005). *Never Eat Alone: And Other Secrets to Success, One Relationship at a Time.* New York: Broadway Business.

Fowler, J. H., & Christakis, N. A. (2008). "Dynamic Spread of Happiness in a Large Social Network: Longitudinal Analysis Over 20 Years in the Framingham Heart Study." Retrieved May 10, 2009, from BMJ: BMJ 2008;337:a2338doi:10.1136/bmj.a2338; http://www.bmj.com.

Fredrickson, B. (2009). *Positivity: Groundbreaking Research Reveals How to Embrace the Hidden Strength of Positive Emotions, Overcome Negativity, and Thrive.* New York: Crown.

Gladwell, M. (2005). *Blink: The Power of Thinking Without Thinking.* New York: Little, Brown and Company.

Gladwell, M. (2000). *The Tipping Point: How Little Things Can Make a Big Difference.* New York: Little, Brown and Company.

Iyengar, S. S., Wells, R. E., & Schwartz, B. (2006). "Doing Better but Feeling Worse: Looking for the "Best" Job Undermines Satisfaction." *Psychological Science, 17* (2), 143–150.

King, L. A. (2001). "The Health Benefits of Writing About Life Goals." *Personality and Social Psychology Bulletin, 27* (7), 798–807.

Koyama, T., McHaffie, J. G., Laurienti, P. J., & Coghill, R. C. (2005, September 6). *"The Subjective Experience of Pain: Where Expectations Become Reality."* Retrieved April 28, 2009, from *Proceedings of the National Academy of Science of the United States of America*: www.pnas.org/cgi/doi/10.1073/pnas.0408576102.

Lehrer, J. (2009). *How We Decide.* New York: Houghton Mifflin Harcourt.

Luna, D., Ringberg, T., & Peracchio, L. A. (2008, August). "One Individual, Two Identitites: Frame Switching Among Biculturals." *Journal of Consumer Research,* 279–293.

Lyubomirsky, S., Kasri, F., & Zehm, K. (2003). "Dysphoric Rumination Impairs Concentration on Academic Tasks." *Cognitive Theraphy and Research, 27* (3), 309–330.

Most, S. B., Scholl, B. J., Clifford, E. R., & Simons, D. J. (2005, January). "What You See Is What You Set: Sustained Inattentional Blindness and the Capture of Awareness." *Psychological Review,* 217–242.

Pink, D. H. (2001). *Free Agent Nation: How America's New Independent Workers Are Transforming the Way We Live.* New York: Warner Books.

Rock, D., & Schwartz, J. (2006, Summer). "The Neuroscience of Leadership." *Strategy+Business (reprint),* 3–4.

Sheldon, K. M., & Schachtman, T. R. (2007, April). "Obligations, Internalization, and Excuse Making: Integrating the Triangle Model and Self-determination Theory." *Journal of Personality,* 359–382.

The Reinvention Institute. (2006, October). *What Works—and Doesn't—In Career Reinvention.*

Whyte Jr., W. H. (1956). *The Organization Man.* New York: Simon and Schuster.

A

Accomplishments, relevant,
102–104
Accountability measures, 184
Actions, matching to words, 66
Adrenaline, 38, 39, 48
Allen, Barry, 111
Ambiguity
ambivalent words, 201
aversion, 75–76, 175
examples of, 76–77
American Golf Corporation,
147–148, 150, 154

Ameritech, 109–112
Anderson, George W., 131
Anxiety, 157
Atlantic Wine & Spirit, 165,
169–170
Automotive industry, 10

B

Bader, Dan, 112, 124
Baker, Anita, 193
Banks, Tyra, 171
Baruch, Bernard M., 87

Basal ganglia, 27, 28
Beatles, the, 107
Believing words, 201
Benefits, 8
Berns, Gregory S., 76
Berra, Yogi, 74
Biculturalism, 153–154
Black Filmmaker Foundation, 191
Black Pain: It Just Looks Like We're Not Hurting (Williams), 194
Blair, Nancy, 112
Blink: The Power of Thinking Without Thinking (Gladwell), 43
Body (Law 2), 37–51, 75, 105, 121, 180
    Hidden Conflict analysis, 46–48
    lesson behind, 41–46
    Living the Law, 48–50
    reinvention story, 37–41
    workbook, 225–227
Bojar, Tia, 112, 124
Boll, Judy, 111
Bragging, 158–159
Brainstorming, 32–34, 121, 222–224
Brennan, Robert, 167, 169, 170
British Medical Journal, 127
Brodsky, Norm, 120
Brown, Alton, 3, 69–74, 82, 85
Brown, Alton Crawford, 71
Brown, DeAnna, 72–73
Brown, Sandye, 123
Bureau of Labor Statistics, 3
Burke, Edmund, 7
Burnouts, 137–139, 145

Business cards, 95–96
Business cycles, length of, 8, 10, 11
Buyer's remorse, 45

C

Career identity, 93–96
Career reinvention
    fantasies, 25–26, 31–32
    flexibility and, 26
    honesty and, 27–28
    Law 1 (*see* Vision)
    Law 2 (*see* Body)
    Law 3 (*see* Excuses)
    Law 4 (*see* Road less traveled)
    Law 5 (*see* Tools)
    Law 6 (*see* Reinvention Board)
    Law 7 (*see* Natives)
    Law 8 (*see* Language)
    Law 9 (*see* Timeline)
    Law 10 (*see* Success)
    myths, 23–25, 30–31, 217–219
    visualization and, 25, 31
Career Reinvention BootCamps, 6, 47, 136
Carroll, Lewis, 17
Chandler, Alfred Dupont, Jr., 7–8
Chatfield-Taylor, Adele, 55
Child, Julia, 19, 69
China, 10
Christakis, Nicholas, 127
Citibank, 4
Clayton, Bill, 113

Clued-In Colleague board
member, 122, 125
Collins, Marva, 129
Columbia University, 205
Comfort zone, living outside,
27, 185
Commitment, making a, 66
Company Man, 8–9
Complaining, giving up, 65
Confidence, 195–196
Conscience, 61
Corporate structure,
beginnings of, 7–8
Cover letters, 162–163
Creative thinking, 2
Credit cards, 118
Csikszentmihalyi,
Mihaly, 32
Cultural elitism, 158–159
Cultural immersion, 154
Culture shock, 3

D

Daily Success List, 200
Davis, Miles, 187, 188, 190–
192, 194, 200
Diener, Ed, 115
Downsizings, 9
Drill Sergeant board member,
123, 124

E

Edison, Thomas, 25
Energy, 48
Epictetus, 175

Excuses (Law 3), 53–67, 80,
105, 180
categories of, 58–59
Hidden Conflict analysis,
63–64
lesson behind, 58–63
Living the Law, 65–67
as manifestation of fear,
60–61
reinvention story, 53–58
workbook, 229–230
Expectations
changing, 177–178
unrealistic, 175–176

F

Facebook, 135
Faith, crises of, 204
"Fake it till you make it"
strategy, 80–81, 195
False fear, 61
Fantasies, 25–26, 30–31, 217–
219
Fear, 84, 207
excuses as manifestation of,
60–61
functional and false, 61
moving through,
62–63, 80
Federal Express, 3, 89–92,
102
Ferrazzi, Keith, 142
Flexibility, 26, 114
Food Network, 3, 69, 73–74
Frame-shifting, 94
Fredrickson, Barbara L.,
179

Free Agent Nation: How America's New Independent Workers Are Transforming the Way We Live (Pink), 9
Free agent philosophy, 9–10
Fuller, Howard, 112, 113, 122, 124
Functional fear, 61

Honesty, 27
Hopelessness, 157
Horton, Julie-Anne (*see* Selvey, Julie-Anne Horton)
Horton, William L., 148–149, 151
How We Decide (Lehrer), 83
Hudlin, Warrington, 191

G

Gallagher, Steve, 131–132
Garza, Christina, 37–40, 42, 47–49
Garza, Juanita, 38
Gates, Bill, 62
George, Nelson, 193
Gide, André, 69
Gladwell, Malcolm, 43, 44, 122
Globalization, 9
Goals, 182–183
Good Eats (television show), 69, 73, 74
Graham, Martha, 41
Great Depression, 9
Greater Houston Partnership, 40, 49
Gut instinct, 41–42, 50, 226–227

I

IAC/InterActiveCorp, 151
Iconoclast (Berns), 76
Identity, letting go of old, 93–96
"I'll be happy when . . ." syndrome, 25
Inattentional blindness, 78
Incentive system, 183–184
India, 10
Industry trade publications, 152
Inner knowing, 197–198, 203
Instinct vs. intellect, 41, 45–47, 50, 82, 83, 225–226
Irving, Bruce, 17–21, 26, 32–34
Irving, Debby, 19, 20

H

Happiness, 22, 115, 127, 204
Hee, Marianne, 165–170, 175
Helen Bader Foundation, 112
Hoffman Process, The, 20, 21

J

Job-matching, 11
Job security, 8–11
Jobs versus skills, 97–98, 102, 160

K

Kehm, Ray, 111
Kissinger, Henry, 187
Knack, The (Brodsky), 120
Knight-Ridder Financial, 4–5
Know-it-all-ism, 158–159

L

Labor unions, 8–10
Language (Law 8), 103, 124,
    147–164, 182
  Hidden Conflict analysis,
    156–159
  lesson behind, 151–156
  Living the Law, 159–164
  reinvention story,
    147–151
  workbook, 243–244
Law 1 (*see* Vision)
Law 2 (*see* Body)
Law 3 (*see* Excuses)
Law 4 (*see* Road less traveled)
Law 5 (*see* Tools)
Law 6 (*see* Reinvention Board)
Law 7 (*see* Natives)
Law 8 (*see* Language)
Law 9 (*see* Timeline)
Law 10 (*see* Success)
Layoffs, 9, 11
Learning curve, 105
Legitimacy points, 99–103,
    162
Lehrer, Jonah, 83
LinkedIn, 135
Loyalty, 8, 9, 12

M

Madonna, 3
Magical thinking, 177, 207
Master Connector board
    member, 121–122, 125
Maximizers, 205
McGoohan, Patrick, 1
Mebane, LaRhonda, 89–90
Mebane, Reggie, 3, 87–92, 95,
    98, 102
Media industry, 59
Mental frames, 94
Mitchell, Jeanette Reed, 107–
    113, 117, 120–124, 127
Momentum, 178–185
Money, 115–118, 207–208
Morash, Marian, 19
Morash, Russ, 19
Murphy, Eddie, 187, 191–192,
    200
Myths, 23–25, 30–31, 217–219

N

Native board member, 123–
    125
Natives (Law 7), 104, 129–145,
    181
  Hidden Conflict analysis,
    139–141
  lesson behind, 134–139
  Living the Law, 141–144
  reinvention story, 129–134
  workbook, 241–242
Negativity
  myths, 23–24

Negativity (*cont.*)
   negative voices, 79–81
   thoughts and emotions,
     179–181
Networking, 142–145
*Never Eat Alone: And Other
   Secrets to Success, One
   Relationship at a Time*
   (Ferrazzi), 142
Newspaper industry, 10
New York Times, The, 153, 174
Nin, Anaïs, 53
Nostalgia, 159
Nye, Joseph, 4

O

Odds, 76
Odyssey, The (Homer), 79
Off-shoring, 10
Openness, feeling of, 48
Organization Man, The
   (Whyte), 8
Overseas labor, 9

P

"P.A.R." system, 103
Peace, sense of, 48
Pensions, 12
Perfectionism, 156–158
*Personal Touch, The: What You
   Really Need to Succeed in
   Today's Fast-Paced
   Business World* (Williams),
   193
Pietrykowski, Bob, 112

Pink, Daniel H., 9
*Plentiful Harvest, A: Creating
   Balance and Harmony
   through the Seven
   Living Virtues* (Williams),
   193
Positivity
   myths, 24
   thinking, 25
   thoughts and emotions,
     179–181
Positivity (Fredrickson), 179
Powers, Llewellyn, 37
Prefrontal cortex, 27
Prisoner, The (television series),
   1–2
Pro bono projects, 101, 206
Procrastination, 156
Profit sharing, 12
Promotion, 9

R

Raises, 8
Rakowski-Gallagher, Felina, 3,
   129–135
Rapid cognition, 43
Recession, 10
Reed, Robert Lee, 213
Reinvention Board (Law 6),
   119–128, 135, 181, 200,
   208, 239
Reinvention Institute, The, 6,
   22, 43, 57, 62, 65–67,
   115, 150, 159, 168, 170,
   212, 214
Reinvention Résumés or Bio,
   159–163

Reinvention strategy, 50, 104,
107–128, 181, 200, 208
Hidden Conflict analysis,
119–120
lesson behind, 114–119
Living the Law, 121–128
reinvention story, 107–113
workbook, 237–239
Reinvention Tactical Plan,
180–183
Reinvention Team coaching
groups, 66, 184, 200
Relaxation, feeling of, 48
Relevant accomplishments,
102–104
Research, 114–115
Résumés, 102
Reinvention Résumés or
Bio, 160–164
Retirement packages, 9
Risk, examples of, 76
Road less traveled (Law 4), 50,
69–85, 105, 175, 180,
205
Hidden Conflict analysis,
79–81
lesson behind, 75–78
Living the Law, 82–85
reinvention story, 69–74
workbook, 231–233
Role models, 63
Rudell, Jeffery, 53–59, 65–67

S

Saavedra, Miguel de
Cervantes, 165
Saboteurs, 138, 139, 144

Salary rewards, 24
Salk, Jonas, 25
Satisficers, 206
Schlenker, Barry, 58, 65
Secrecy, 157
Self-consent forms, 29–30
Self-criticism, 157, 158
Self-fulfilling prophecies, 24
excuses becoming, 63–64
Selvey, Julie-Anne Horton,
147–154, 160–162
Selvey, Kenton, 150
Skills versus jobs, 97–98, 102,
160
Smiling, 48
Snap decisions, 43
Stay Strong Foundation, The,
194
*Stay Strong! Simple Life Lessons
for Teens* (Williams), 193
Stress, symptoms of, 49–50
Success (Law 10), 187–209
Hidden Conflict analysis,
201–203
lesson behind, 195–201
Living the Law, 203–209
reinvention story, 187–194
workbook, 249–250
Swarthmore College, 205

T

Technology, 9, 10
Temporary jobs, 118–119
This Old House (television
show), 18–21, 33
Thoughts/emotions, 179–
182

Timeline (Law 9), 50, 165–185
  Hidden Conflict analysis,
    175–178
  lesson behind, 170–175
  Living the Law, 178–185
  reinvention story,
    165–170
  workbook, 245–248
Time Warner, 19, 21
*Tipping Point, The: How
  Little Things Can Make
  a Big Difference*
  (Gladwell), 122
Tools (Law 5), 83, 87–106,
    159, 160, 162, 180,
    199, 207
  Hidden Conflict analysis,
    99–101
  lesson behind, 93–98
  Living the Law, 101–105
  reinvention story,
    87–92
  workbook, 235–236
Torke, Lavetta, 113, 123
Traction, lack of, 206–207
Trade associations, 153
Triangle model, 58, 65

U

Uncertainty, 75–76, 177
Uninvited committee
    members, 79–81
U.S. Centers for Disease
    Control, 3, 91–92
University of California
    at Davis, 20

V

Visible Hand, The (Chandler),
    7–8
Visionary ideas, 25
Vision board, 219
Vision (Law 1), 17–35, 84, 105,
    139, 140, 181, 185, 205
  Hidden Conflict analysis,
    28–30
  lesson behind, 22–28
  Living the Law, 30–34
  reinvention story, 17–21
  workbook, 217–224
Visualization, 25, 31–32, 219–
    221

W

Wacker, Mary, 123
Wall Street Journal, The, 152,
    153
Warburton, Carrie, 133, 134,
    136
Warburton, Steve, 133, 134,
    136
Ward, Angie, 113, 123
Warm 'n' Fuzzy board
    member, 123, 124
Warner Music Group, 150–
    151, 161–162
Washington, Denzel, 188
Web sites, 152
Whyte, William H., Jr., 8
Williams, Charles, 188–189,
    192
Williams, Marie, 188–189, 192

Williams, Terrie, 3, 187–195,
    197, 209
Winfrey, Oprah, 171
Wittgenstein, Ludwig, 147
Women, in workforce, 10
Words
    ambivalent, 201
    believing, 201
    matching to actions, 66
Workbook exercises,
    217–250
    Body (Law 2), 225–227
    Excuses (Law 3), 229–233
    Language (Law 8),
        243–244

Natives (Law 7), 241–242
Reinvention Board (Law 6),
    237–239
Road less traveled (Law 4),
    231–233
Success (Law 10), 249–250
Timeline (Law 9),
    245–248
Tools (Law 5), 235–236
Vision (Law 1), 217–227

Z

Ziol, Jane, 113, 123

ABOUT THE AUTHOR

Former entertainment exec turned coach *Pamela Mitchell* is founder and CEO of *The Reinvention Institute*, a dynamic organization devoted to individual transformation. She is a popular and in-demand speaker who gives talks around the country to individuals, corporations, and industry groups who are interested in learning fresh strategies for navigating in the midst of change. As the nation's premier career reinvention expert, she has appeared on the *Today* show and has been profiled and quoted in top media publications, including *The Wall Street Journal*, *BusinessWeek*, *More*, *Men's Health*, *Good Housekeeping*, and *Black Enterprise*.

Prior to founding The Reinvention Institute, Mitchell spent nearly fifteen years in senior-level positions leading international business development and relationship management for high-profile media and entertainment companies. In addition to being a certified coach, Mitchell has a B.A. from Harvard University and an M.B.A. from the top international business school, Thunderbird. She lives in Miami, Florida, with her husband and rescued kitty.

ABOUT THE REINVENTION INSTITUTE

Founded in 2003, The Reinvention Institute (TRI) is a dynamic transformational seminar and coaching company devoted to providing knowledge, tools, a network, and inspiration for clients ranging from successful professionals to Fortune 500 companies to entrepreneurial firms. TRI offers corporate and public seminars, teleclasses, one-to-one and group coaching, assessments, downloadable eCourses and eKits, and an online community.

The Institute runs innovative programs such as the Career Reinvention BootCamp, an intensive course designed to fast-track your career reinvention launch, and Reinvention Team coaching groups, ongoing mastermind coaching circles for Reinventors. For more tools, tips, and resources, plus to download a free companion guide to the workbook that contains extra exercises, visit www.reinvention-institute.com.